# FORGING FAME

# FORGING FAME

## THE STRANGE CAREER OF SCHARMEL IRIS

# FAME

NORTHERN ILLINOIS UNIVERSITY PRESS

DeKalb

Craig Abbott

Library of Congress Cataloging-in-Publication Data

Abbott, Craig S., 1941–

Forging fame : the strange career of Scharmel Iris / Craig Abbott.

   p.   cm.

Includes bibliographical references and index.

ISBN-13: 978-0-87580-376-0 (clothbound : acid-free paper)

ISBN-10: 0-87580-376-8 (clothbound : acid-free paper)

1. Iris, Scharmel, b. 1889.  2. Poets, American—20th century—Biography.

3. Literary forgeries and mystifications.  4. Plagiarism.  I. Title.

PS3517.R5Z55 2007

811'.4—dc22

[B]

2007012441

# CONTENTS

# ILLUSTRATIONS

# PREFACE

"Why have I not heard of Scharmel Iris before this?"

—Oliver St. John Gogarty, Epilogue, *Bread out of Stone*

In the chapters that follow I describe the career of Scharmel Iris, a twentieth-century American poet who participated in the Chicago literary renaissance of the 1910s and continued to write and to be published until his death in 1967. That the public should not remember—and likely never have heard of—a poet, even a fairly prolific one such as Iris, is not surprising. After all, most poets are forgotten or ignored. Even those who tried to give the public what it wanted came to learn that it really didn't much want poetry, at least not on its bookshelves. Although the residual romanticism that predominated for at least the early years of Iris's career enabled poets to claim some genius or cultural authority, it also pictured them (or let them picture themselves) as alienated, marginalized, and neglected. Indeed, some argued, the greater the neglect, the greater claim to genius. That role appealed to Iris. The child of poor Italian immigrants on Chicago's West Side, he chose the life of a poet in his pursuit of the American dream.

In that pursuit, he engaged in an extended, ambitious campaign of self-promotion, which served him also as self-definition. This campaign involved him—sometimes in fact, often in fantasy—with some of the major poets of his day, including T. S. Eliot, Robert Frost, Joyce Kilmer, Ezra Pound, Dame Edith Sitwell, and W. B. Yeats; with artists, including Salvador Dali, Augustus John, Pablo Picasso, and Diego Rivera; and with such other public figures as Jane Addams, Winston Churchill, Theodore Roosevelt, Eleanor Roosevelt, Samuel Cardinal Stritch, William Wrigley, and Woodrow Wilson. If, as David Hume said, all poets are "liars by profession," then Iris was exceedingly professional. He resorted to lies, imposture, forgery, and plagiarism from the beginning to the end of his career. His lies extended from his poetry to his person. He not only made up much of what he said about himself but also got others to speak his lies for him. And when the others would not say what he wanted, he would say it for them, using their names, deploying them in forged prefaces, epilogues, forewords, afterwords, and dust jacket blurbs. Even our acquaintance with modernist allusiveness and use of personae and with postmodernist critiques of originality and textual authority does not lessen our sense of Iris's audacity in his attempts to gain patronage and publication and to write himself into literary history. Despite all these efforts, Iris did not emerge from obscurity.

I do not argue with history's verdict that Iris was a distinctly minor poet. Nevertheless, I think that he really ought to see what was going on if, in a preface to Iris's *Bread out of Stone,* a collection of his poems published in 1953, Yeats supposedly claims that "of poets writing today, there is no greater" and if, in a later volume, Eliot calls Iris's poetry "one of the most important contributions to the literature of our times," and if in yet another preface Wilson says that he would rather have written one of Iris's poems than to have been president of the United States. If we grant Iris some of the attention he haplessly courted all his life, we discover a figure, often parodic, for an art whose status had become marginal and source of value uncertain. His life provides commentary on the place of poetry during his time.

The research that led to this book began many years ago, in the 1970s, when I took an assistant professorship in the English department at Northern Illinois University. A colleague there told me of an old and largely forgotten poet that had lived on the campus of Lewis University, which in the 1950s had been

Lewis College, near Joilet, just south of Chicago. The curious thing, my colleague said, was that this poet, Scharmel Iris, had a book with a preface by the old and greatly remembered poet William Butler Yeats. The next time I went to the library I checked out that book, *Bread out of Stone,* which I saw had been published in 1953, 14 years after Yeats's death. Sure enough, though, there was a preface signed by Yeats. And what a preface it was. In it Yeats spoke of carrying the book's manuscript around with him for days and shedding tears he could not stem. It was there he said of Iris, "Of poets writing today there is no greater."

I simply could not believe that Yeats had ever written any such thing about the author of the verse contained in the volume. My suspicions about Iris grew as I continued to run across his memorable and improbable name while I undertook other research in the dusty corners of twentieth-century American poetry. Finally, in 1983, I had uncovered enough to publish a scholarly article revealing instances of Iris's literary forgery, as well as his lying and plagiarism. At the time, Iris's papers—his manuscripts and letters—were not available, but recently I was able to gain access to them. I was somewhat taken aback by what I saw. While I didn't have to retract what I'd said in my article, I did recognize that I had previously uncovered only a small portion of Iris's strange career. That career, now, is the subject of this book.

Iris had died before I knew of him, but I have been able to speak with a few people who did know him. Even they, though, probably did not know him well. Iris may have had no close friends except those he invented for himself, namely, Frederick Vincent and Vincent Holme. He never married, and at least in his later years he does not appear to have kept in touch with any family members. His pocket address book was quite full—but mostly with the names and addresses of writers, artists, publishers, philanthropists, and others he thought might be useful to him. He would write most anybody, and anybody often replied.

Printed and manuscript documents are by far, then, the predominant raw material for this book. That poses a particular difficulty, because Iris engaged in forgery of letters, prefaces, and other materials, because he frequently wrote lies about himself, and because he managed to get others to repeat his lies in what they wrote. In using these documents, I attempt to make clear what I think is authentic and truthful and what isn't. There remain, however, some items about which I am unsure, and I have not investigated every claim Iris made about his life. Perhaps someone else would like to discover whether Iris was, as he boasted, Queen Elizabeth's first dancing partner after her coronation.

For permissions and assistance, recent and old, I am very much indebted to many librarians, archivists, and manuscript specialists, including Susan Summerfield and Elizabeth Stege Teleky, at the Special Collection Research Center at the University of Chicago; Diane Haskell, Katie McMahon, and James W. Wells, at the Newberry Library, Chicago; Ellen Dunlap, at the Harry Ransom Humanities Research Center, University of Texas at Austin; Marianne Hansen, at the Bryn Mawr College Library; Julie A. Stazik, at the Archdiocese of Chicago's Joseph Cardinal Bernadin Archives and Records Center; Michelle L. Sweetser, at Maynor Memorial Libraries, Marquette University, Milwaukee; and Ngadi W. Kponou, at the Beinecke Rare Book and Manuscript Library, Yale University. I am grateful to those who shared their memories of Iris, especially Charles Ellis, Peter Pastorelle, Francis Pastorelle, and Kathryn Pastorelle, and the late Father Joseph W. Peoples, Jr. My greatest debt in this project is to Brother Bernard Rapp, archivist at Lewis University, Romeoville, Illinois, who turned me loose in the Iris papers there, found for me items I would have missed, and offered encouragement. Also at Lewis, Brother Lawrence Oelschlegel kindly endured my thinking out loud about what Iris had been up to. Two readers for Northern Illinois University Press—C. D. Blanton at the University of California, Berkeley, and William Savage at Northwestern University—deserve credit for much that is good here and blame for nothing that might not be.

FORGING

FAME

# YOUTH OF GENIUS, 1889–1913

"Flattery is the cheapest coin in circulation, yet it purchases an amazing number of folks."—Scharmel Iris, "The Garden of Life"

Gen the traditional trope of par-iver authorship, it seems appropriate that Scharmel Iris was a child of uncertain paternity. Throughout his long career as a poet, he engaged in forgery and plagiarism, producing texts under multiple names, real and invented. Indeed, even his own name was largely his own invention. He was born Federico Scaramella on 10 February 1889 in Castelcivita, 60 miles south of Naples in the Italian province of Salerno. His mother, Mariarosa Scaramella, was at the time an unmarried woman of 26. Not long after his birth, Mariarosa married Francisco Vincenzo, who had returned from the United States to his native village. In late February 1892, three-year-old Iris, with his mother and stepfather, boarded a passenger steamer for the voyage from Naples to the United States. They had third-class accommodations in steerage and suffered through a rough crossing. Reaching New York on 21 March 1892, they took a train to Chicago and arrived at the Burlington Station at Polk and Dearborn Streets. Two days later, Francisco Vincenzo, whom Iris called Father, was doing manual labor at $1.25 a day.

Along with thousands of other poor Italian immigrants, they found housing in the crowded Near West Side neighborhood of Chicago. The family continued to grow, with three daughters and three sons born over the next 13 years. They belonged to the parish of Holy Family Church at 1080 West Roosevelt Road, where at age 11 Iris, who was not yet Iris, was confirmed and given the middle name Leo, in honor of Pope Leo XIII. He attended Polk Street Public School, where he impressed his teachers with an ability to recite poetry. He also took advantage of Jane Addams's Hull-House social settlement, which had been established in 1889 in the former mansion of Charles J. Hull, just a few blocks from Holy Family. The settlement already was growing to fill a whole block, adding its gymnasium, theater, art gallery, music school, library, club rooms, and residences for men and women—mostly women—who ran its programs and engaged in social and political activism. Like the Chicago Public Library, Art Institute, University of Chicago, and other Chicago cultural institutions associated with the "upward movement," Hull-House was founded on a belief in the power of high culture to lift and refine people,[1] and it had some heavy lifting to do in Little Italy. At the settlement, Iris would have seen walls bearing fine paintings and prints. He could have joined a discussion of, for example, a George Eliot novel and attended lectures on Florentine architecture. He could have belonged to a Dante Club, Plato Club, and Shakespeare Club. Hull-House served as a place of contact not only between Iris and elite culture but also between him and the participants in and sponsors of that culture. He met artists, musicians, actors, playwrights, poets, and philanthropists. Encouraged by school and Hull-House, Iris chose the life of a poet.

All of that is true or almost certainly true, but it did not always satisfy Iris, who throughout his life continued to remake his expanding past while inventing his diminishing future. At some point, probably early in life, he wrote out a few pages, entitled "Father," where he added some false or almost certainly false flourishes to an account of his origins: his father, Federico Iris

Scaramella, was from Florence and had died shortly before his birth; his baptism was performed by Pope Leo XIII, who put him under the protection of the Blessed Virgin Mary; and his father's Florentine brother, a cardinal, arrived at the wedding of his mother and new husband, Francisco, with a velvet suit for Iris and a pair of earrings for his mother. Later, when interviewed or when writing about himself, Iris used whatever version of himself seemed right for the moment. So at times Iris claimed to have been born in Florence; at others, in Chicago. His parents were Italian, or his father was Greek and his mother Irish-Italian. His family was wealthy; his family was impoverished. Iris often said that in his infancy his parents lived in wealth on Michigan Avenue but moved after three years to the Near West Side so that his mother could engage in charitable work among the poor, assisting Jane Addams at Hull-House and becoming the first patron of Mother Francis Xavier Cabrini. But, when this version of his life didn't suit his purposes, he said he was a neglected, tubercular child who foraged in garbage cans to sustain himself.[2]

Then there is the matter of his name. Through the common practice of Americanization, his Federico Scaramella became Frederick Scharmel and sometimes, as on his Social Security card many years later, Fred Scharmell. But also, as a sort of self-fathering, he gave himself the last name Iris, which he used on most occasions as his "real" name. He would have people believe that the name came from his almost certainly invented Florentine father, who was all the more Florentine because the coat of arms of Florence bore an iris (the Florentine iris) as its fleur-de-lis. Of course, the name also recalled from Greek mythology the virgin goddess who served as a messenger of the gods, especially of Juno, and who was represented by or identified with the rainbow, a bridge between heaven and earth. Then too, Fred Scharmel was an opera fan, and at the time he was naming himself, he might have been impressed by Pietro Mascagni's opera *Iris* (1898), first performed in the United States in 1902 and dealing with estrangement between father and child. In it Iris, a poor Japanese laundry girl, is abducted by a rich libertine, who has her displayed in a whorehouse after she rejects his advances. Her father finds her and, thinking her fallen, throws filth upon her. Seeking death, she plunges into a sewer, but her body is retrieved and stirs with a little life as the rising sun warms her and as flowers bloom around her. She then ascends into the sky during a concluding "Hymn to the Sun." As a story of a heroine of humble origins who suffers neglect, mistreatment, and alienation from a father but is finally rewarded with a new and glorious birth, the opera would have appealed to Scharmel. At any rate, *Iris* would be a good name for a poet, so he took it. During his lifetime he also took *Wesley Ames, Stanley Blackpool, John Creagh, Manoel Holme, Vincent Holme, Seth James, Everett Owens,* and *Frederick Vincent.* For that matter, at times he used *T. S. Eliot, Robert Frost, Dame Edith Sitwell, William Butler Yeats,* and other very good names for a poet—not to mention some good names for a philosopher (*George Santayana*), cleric (*Samuel Cardinal Stritch*), statesman (*Woodrow Wilson*), and so on.

Iris was already Iris in 1905 when he had his debut as a poet in the *New World,* the weekly paper of the Chicago archdiocese. It was edited at the time by Charles J. O'Malley, who saw the paper as the embattled organ of an embattled church. Dipping his pen in vitriol and vinegar, O'Malley used its pages to do battle with Protestantism, modernism, socialism, secular journalism, and much else. Himself a poet, however, he had a soft spot in his ample heart for verse. He had a reputation for encouraging young writers, even if he could not pay them for contributions to his paper. As a boy of 14, Iris may have read O'Malley's telling commentary on a story he reprinted from another paper. It was the sad tale of a young woman with literary aspirations. Just after receiving a marriage proposal, she received also, from an editor to whom she had submitted a poem, an effusive letter "telling her that she was a great genius and praising her works to the skies." So encouraged, she turned down the marriage proposal and took up a literary career. It was mostly a failure. If the editor had not told her she had genius, "she might have married and lived out her life on a farm or in some country village, happy because she had never greatly hoped and greatly suffered because of failure." Not without some confusion, O'Malley then begins to question the story, which he evidently takes somewhat personally, perhaps having been accused of offering excessive encouragement. The young woman could have married anyway, he suggests. Maybe she did have genius but adopted "a wrong view of the literary life." "Self-centered people" tend to accept illogical views. "Many people of genius fail because they elect to propagate notions that are erroneous."

Charles J. O'Malley, ca. 1900, the editor of the *New World,* in which Iris had his poetic debut in 1905. Moffett photo, courtesy Lewis University.

Still, most young writers receive "small encouragement." "We do not believe in indiscriminate praise." But "our frank belief is that an editor who does not encourage deserving young writers round about him is unworthy of his position."[3]

Not long after, O'Malley was encouraging Frederick Scharmel Iris. On 22 July 1905, at the age of 16, Iris published his first poem in O'Malley's paper. "As Thou Bidst" was a pledge to serve God despite the temptations of the world, and it was not a bad performance for a 16-year-old novice. Although a bit unsteady on its metrical feet, it showed that Iris had learned what a poem might look and sound like, so much so that the poem seems more harvested than written. It is as if Iris has gathered from his reading bits and pieces of poetic phrasing and bound them together with meter and rhyme: "My all" will overcome "evil's thrall" because I "upward cast my eyes" and thus will find "grandeurs fair" and avoid "folly's cup." Despite Iris's uncertain verse, O'Malley was sufficiently impressed to offer him the continued encouragement of publication and began publishing him regularly. When for the 26 August 1905 issue Iris contributed the "The Cheerful Road," O'Malley promoted him to stardom in the "galaxy of literary stars" published in this issue celebrating the paper's move to a new building. O'Malley's brief biographical note on the contributors went on to describe Iris as "an Italian, a mere boy of seventeen." (Iris had evidently added a year to his age.) This boy, whose "poetry is genuine," O'Malley said, is "probably the first Italian poet in America who writes in English."[4]

With the 28 October 1905 issue, however, O'Malley was replaced as editor by the Reverend Thomas E. Judge, the archdiocese having become dissatisfied with O'Malley in part because of his "strident and harsh treatment of Protestants."[5] Iris found the pages of the *New World,* under Judge's less poetic editorship, closed to his work. O'Malley, though, moved on to edit another paper, the *Catholic Sun* in Syracuse, New York. There, he continued to offer Iris the support provided by publication. After Judge died in early 1908, O'Malley returned to the *New World,* where on 21 March and again the following week he devoted a whole page to praise and congratulations he had received on resuming the editorship. Iris also welcomed O'Malley's return. Until O'Malley's own death two years later, Iris's work again frequented the *New World.* Meanwhile, beginning in December 1907 and continuing through August 1913, Iris found a particularly hospitable reception at the paper of the San Francisco archdiocese, the *Monitor,* edited by Charles Phillips, another poet-editor (and, later, a professor of English at Notre Dame).

In these papers, Iris kept company with some poets now almost entirely forgotten but at the time considered of some importance, including Madison Cawein, Maurice Francis Egan, Louise Imogen Guiney, Seumas MacManus, and John B. Tabb. O'Malley and Phillips also offered generous selections from their own poetry, and they occasionally reprinted poems by more widely known figures such as Bret Harte, Francis Thompson, and Oscar Wilde. Phillips would reprint Irish poet William Butler Yeats, but O'Malley had strong reservations about Yeats and the praise Catholic Americans, including their press, had heaped upon him. O'Malley found himself growing "sick of the folly of pouring a flood of adulatory drivel upon an individual who, however great his ability may be, certainly is not of us and really is against us." Yeats, he said, belongs to pagan, not Christian, Ireland, and thus "his poetry does not uplift but degrades and hence is not true art at all."[6]

Iris's poems were not much different from those of most other contributors or, for that matter, from the dominant mode of the time favored by editors. They were earnest, sentimental, and conventional in thought and expression. Some explicitly religious, some not, they were intended to "uplift" their readers by idealizing their subjects and using stock language to evoke stock responses, as in his "To a Morning Cloud," from the 2 May 1908 *Monitor*:

> Fair cloud, enchanting heralder of day,
>> The blue-gold lake bewitching mirrors thee!
>> Where driftest thou? Is't to eternity?
> Art Eldorado bound? A lamb at play
> Within the pasture-sky, blithe, jocund, gay?
>> Or wandering minstrel troubadour? Ah, me,
>> Thou float'st thro' upper space triumphantly
> A mystery of amaranthine sway!
> O tranquil dream upon the sky's calm breast—
>> O downy orb, before the dayflush wanes
> Thou shalt have vanished in the Golden West!
>> Fair limpid cloud, bright harbinger of rains
>> Lead, lead a glad soul homeward to its rest
> Where bides perfection o'er yon fir trees' crest.

For the poet devoted to ideality, the contest between reality and imagination is no contest at all. What the poet observes in nature, a "fair cloud," becomes displaced by what he imagines—by his "dream" of it. He then asks this dream to guide him to perfection.

Iris's poem "The Lyre," in the 4 July 1908 issue of *New World*, likewise not only engages in idealization and uplift but also takes them as its theme:

> My heart is like a wind-strung lyre
> That takes the wind's joy as it sings;
> The storm's deep soul, the birds' gay choir
> Each thrill its rhythm o'er the strings.
>
> Within its soul naught it exiles—
> Nor grief no pain nor songs of May;
> The snows, the tears, the loves, the smiles,
> Each in their turns upon it play.
>
> Ah, though the winds upon it blow,
> And though the night be black with rain,
> From out my heart gay songs outgo—
> Gay songs like stars to light the plain!

The poet compares his heart to a lyre played upon by the wind. Open even to the winds of grief and strife, his heart nonetheless transforms all experience into "gay songs." Iris's work might have problems with pronoun and subject-verb agreement (as in the line "Each in their turns upon it play") and with redundancy ("From *out* my heart gay songs *outgo*"), but it was typical of most verse at the time in its embrace of gentility and ideality. After the Civil War, realism and naturalism came to dominate prose fiction, but lyric poetry in general was a refuge from those movements. Through it, Iris the uplifted (thanks in part to Hull-House) could now count himself among the uplifters.

Beginning with the 9 April 1910 issue, Iris also contributed to the *Monitor* a section entitled "The Garden of Life." In it he offered aphorisms, advice, and lofty thoughts, like these:

> An honorable failure is better than an inglorious success.

> Selfishness turns a garden into a desert, but love turns a desert into a garden.

> Stop for a moment, friend! Listen to the song-bird in your
> heart. It isn't necessary to dig into the dark places of life and bring
> out its skeletons with their horrid, grinning faces. In every little se-
> cret corner of your life isn't it true that good calls forth good? And
> what is the life of the world but a counterpart of the life of the in-
> dividual? Shall we not rather show the beauty, the grandeur, of
> life, until the good rises to meet good, and evil and wrong sink
> back ashamed? For truth begets truth, honor begets honor, and it
> is deeper than mere surface things. It's the soul of life—the real in-
> stead of the false.

"The Garden of Life" appeared from time to time as part of a col-
umn entitled "Here at Home," edited by Jennie Devlin. This col-
umn featured advice, recipes, household hints, and other items
intended primarily for women readers. They could learn here
how to cook potato fritters, remove fruit stains, and cure hic-
cough; they could find tongue twisters to amuse themselves and
their children; and they could satisfy a hunger for stirring and
lofty sentiment, some of it supplied by Iris. The *New World* had a
similar column with the evolving title "Woman's Quiet Hour,"
"The Family Circle," and "The Family Sitting Room." Here too,
readers would find pretty thoughts and practical advice. They
were, for example, instructed in politeness:

> Walk straight, with a firm light step.
> In passing a church, priest, sister or elderly person, incline the head.
> In public avoid making gestures, talking loud, or calling your
> friends by their names.
> Be careful not to make a noise when chewing your food.
> Express your regrets for anything you have broken.
> Never slam doors.[7]

Iris's poems also found a congenial place in this column.

Both O'Malley and Phillips intended their papers as civilizing
forces, and at least indirectly they encouraged Iris to view poetry
as a means, as John Keats said, "to sooth the cares and lift the
thoughts of man." When, upon returning to the *New World* in
1908, O'Malley was again the subject of complaints by, in his
words, "hundreds of chronic flawpickers, shameless egotists, sub-
servient lickspittles, unmitigated strife-stirrers, anonymous cow-
ards, and darker scoundrels," not to mention "the liar, and the
fool, and the unwhipped meddler, and the malevolent busybody

and the man-with-an-axe-to-grind, and the well meaning mili-
tant Christian, and the language purist, the race-crank and the
ineffably contemptible knocker at everything which is not under
his personal supervision," he was most angered by a letter calling
for him to "cut out all the near-poets rubbish down to the small
point of nill whittled off." O'Malley replied that "back in the
Catholic ages," the popes encouraged poets and other "men and
women of genius." He questioned whether the complainer was a
Catholic, calling him a "blithering utilitarian" who would de-
prive "Catholic young men and women of a deserved opportu-
nity to elevate themselves above muck-worms."[8]

O'Malley and Phillips were particularly interested in develop-
ing and trumpeting Catholic literature—in large part to counter
what they saw as the baleful influence of popular secular litera-
ture but also to demonstrate the artistic and intellectual re-
spectability of a church that otherwise in America was associated
with impoverished immigrants and was often charged with anti-
intellectualism.[9] Both frequently ran articles bewailing the neglect
of the Catholic press in general and Catholic literature in partic-
ular. They were, though, contradicting themselves. On the one
hand, they sought to present Catholics as enlightened. On the
other, they took Catholics to task for neglecting the Catholic
press in general and Catholic literature in particular. Catholic po-
etry, especially, was a sign of intellectual and artistic accomplish-
ment. Its neglect was an equally strong sign of Catholic benight-
edness. One thing, however, was clear: poets had a noble calling
but faced a largely unappreciative world.

If Iris needed a lesson in the neglect of poetry, he had only to
consider the case of Charles O'Malley himself. After he died in
Chicago on 26 March 1910, the *Monitor* published his obituary
on the front page, fulsomely calling him the "foremost Catholic
poet of America" and "chief of our authors." The obituary was
followed the next week by a lengthy appreciation by another
poet, Henry Coyle. A year later, Phillips's article "Some Catholic
Writers of Today" said that there was "no question" that O'Mal-
ley was one of "the big poets of the century." Indeed, "Swin-
burne has not done more exquisite work, and Poe, Shelley, and
Keats—all that rare galaxy—would be proud to own some of his
beautiful songs."[10] Yet, when the *New World, Monitor,* and other
Catholic papers sought to gain subscribers to a memorial edition
of his collected poems, their lengthy campaign could not attract

enough subscribers to pay for the venture. In an editorial Phillips explained why: "It is because our so-called Catholic 'reading public' is still asleep to the noble qualities and splendid range of O'Malley's writings," despite Egan having called him "the greatest of our American Catholic poets." Not only does his grave lie unmarked, Phillips added, so too is the "fitting monument" of his gathered poems yet to be realized. Meanwhile, his widow and nine children, though "struggling to earn their daily bread," are making sacrifices to achieve the publication that was the poet's dream. "And still the great Catholic public that O'Malley served and slaved for, yes, and died for,—for if ever Catholic Journalism claimed a martyr, he was one—the 'Catholic reading public' takes no heed. What a shameful confession for us to make."[11] Almost three years after its beginning, asking only a dollar per subscribed copy, the campaign had gathered subscribers for only 195 copies. (Iris was among the subscribers.) At least 300 subscriptions were needed to meet costs.[12]

Iris himself was presented as a neglected poet. In his papers at Lewis University is an undated clipping, probably from a 1907 issue of the *New World,* quoting from the *Catholic Bulletin* remarks by Helen Hughes Hielscher, a physician, on the neglect of Catholic writers, Iris in particular:

> In Chicago I met a young Italian boy—one of a family of seven.
> His threadbare coat was neatly brushed, and his shock of dark hair was in order, but his pale pinched face and unnaturally big black eyes showed he was far from well. Yet this boy of only eighteen years could write into his verse the very heart of the flowers, the soul of the bird's song, and the ripple of the running waters; but how ill-equipped he was to fight his way in the world.

Dr. Hielscher concluded, "What Catholic literature needs to-day is the 'Patron,' the 'Protector,' of the olden times." (Ironically, one of the neglected Catholic writers Hielscher mentioned was Thomas Chatterton, a youth who in the eighteenth century fabricated archaic texts and documents and a number of poems he presented as the work of a fifteenth-century poet he named Thomas Rowley. The fraud was not revealed until 1777, seven years after the impoverished Chatterton, at age 18, had poisoned himself with arsenic.)

When Iris, lopping off his first name and becoming simply Scharmel Iris, debuted in the *Monitor* on 14 December 1907 with "On Reading Dante's *Inferno* in Italian," he had already been imagining himself as the neglected poet. In the poem, he identified himself with the aged Dante, who has fled from his home in Florence and, after a life of miserable wandering, is living out his last days in Ravenna:

> His cloak is slung about him cold and sore
> > The Florentines have closed their scornful gate
> > The beret on his head folds desolate.
> In the Ravennan street before my door
> He passes grave and solemn as of yore;
> > His marble face is sad, mournful his gait,
> > His eyes gaze upward as he weeps with fate;
> Around his heart the bleakest tempests roar.
>
> I, too, O, Florentine, have heard the knell,
> My ears have caught the cries from sorrow's cell,
> > The blood-stained linen of the languishing
> Upon the pain-couch at the vesper bell.
> The people voice: "Lo who has been in hell?"[13]

Certainly as important to Iris as publication was the notice he received in the papers, especially in the *Monitor*. Unable to pay their contributors of literary pieces and eager to stir up public appreciation, the editors dispensed praise from a very large reservoir. Two weeks after his first appearance in the *Monitor,* an editorial there boasted that it had "'scored a hit' in securing as a regular contributor Scharmel Iris, the young Catholic poet and writer, whose work, though he is only yet a boy . . . , has already won him a place among the first poets of the land."[14] Praise for Iris continued, and since the editors relied on Iris himself for biographical information, their notices of his work also became opportunities for Iris's self-fashioning. Thus, Phillips's 10 April 1909 *Monitor* article "Scharmel Iris: A Florentine American" recalled that for the past two years readers of the paper had enjoyed the work of this "young Catholic author and poet whose name is surely destined to live in our literature." It then went on to sketch the "facts" of Iris's life. He was born 10 February 1888

Scharmel Iris in 1909, at age 20. Morrison photo, courtesy Lewis University.

[*sic*], in Florence, Italy, the son of a Florentine father who died before his birth and of a mother who was a native of Castelcivita in the province of Salerno. His mother came to America and remarried. The poetic gift may run in the family, for his aunt Antonia "has an established renown among the Italian peasantry as a poetess." From her, Phillips said, Iris doubtless got much of the material for his "Italian Fireside Tales" that were published as a series in the *Monitor* the previous year and that will soon appear in book form. Charles J. O'Malley, "himself a poet of renown, has fostered the young Florentine's muse and trained it more than anyone else." The article was accompanied by a photograph of Iris and by five of his poems.[15]

When in 1911 Iris began contributing poems and brief book reviews to the *Monitor*'s literary column taken up by the widowed Sallie Margaret O'Malley, she welcomed him and continued the "encouragement" her husband had begun. She wrote that this "young Italian who has lived a number of years in America" already "deserves high rank among our younger American poets." The remarks accompany Iris's poem "Invitation," and they indicate, as Phillips's article also did, that even at this early date Iris had ambitions beyond magazine publication: "His 'Italian Folk Tales,'" Mrs. O'Malley said, "will very likely appear in book form, and another proposed volume is 'The Garden of Life,'" a collection of epigrams and short verse.[16] In the Christmas issue that year, Mrs. O'Malley called Iris a "brilliant young Florentine," and, relying on what Iris must have told her, she assured her readers that Iris has his name "by right of family and christening."[17]

All the "boundless praise" bestowed on Iris may not have been particularly helpful for a young poet. It certainly did whet Iris's appetite for that sort of thing. He would spend the rest of his life seeking it, and when he didn't find it, he would invent it. Invention may in fact have already been well underway. In her 2 September 1911 column, Mrs. O'Malley printed Iris's poem "Sappho's Last Song" and accompanied this "remarkable utterance"—which ends "The darkness falls. I die, Beloved, I die!"—with "some critical opinions" that "show how high he really stands":

Richard Watson Gilder: "Scharmel Iris is a true poet."

Joaquin Miller: "The poems have grace, beauty and power; they fascinate; they are particularly fine."

James Whitcomb Riley: "A poet worthy of encouragement. My sincere wish is that he receives the great success that he deserves."

Robert Underwood Johnson, editor of the *Century*: "Poems that show excellent literary execution."

Charles J. O'Malley: "What a striking series of pictures are presented in the poems of Scharmel Iris! His 'Winter Sunset' is a remarkably graphic piece of work; his 'Song of the Growers' is destined to live; 'Sappho's Last Song' is worthy of Sappho herself; 'Had I Thy Love' is a perfect poem. He paints with words and his canvases are fuller of color than are those of George Innes. The poems are reproduced in many of the leading weeklies of the world and his name will go down to posterity as that of a poet who toiled not in vain."

Charles Hurd: "The poems are worthy the best poets."

Richard Le Gallienne: "A gift of melody and depth and tenderness of feeling. His nature poems are a blessing."

Madison Cawein: "Scharmel Iris is a name that will live in American literature."

Charles Phillips: "He sees the inner beauty in the things of life. He has the 'divine fire.' Although he is yet a boy, his work has already won him a place among the first poets of the land."

Some of these were persons of considerable note at the time. Cawein, after all, was the celebrated "Keats of Kentucky," and Riley, remembered nowadays, if remembered at all, for his "When the Frost Is on the Punkin," was the best-read American poet of his day. All of them except Gilder were still alive when these statements were printed.

While Iris's literary fortunes seem to have been rising, so were the Vincenzo family's financial ones. In 1911 the family had been able to buy a house at 331 South Trumbull Street, in a working-class neighborhood in the East Garfield section of Chicago. The Vincenzo family that moved into the house that year had swelled considerably in size. In addition to Fred (our Scharmel Iris, age 22) and the parents Frank and Rosie (ages 47 and 48), there were three daughters (Jennie, 18; Josephine, 14; and Mary, 6) and three other sons (James, 16; Carmel, 11; and Tony, 6).[18] Despite the move, Iris maintained contact with Jane Addams at Hull-House, and he used her in much the same way he evidently had used or attempted to use Charles O'Malley. In late 1911, while Iris was having his success in the Catholic press, he asked Addams to send selections of his work to Harriet Monroe and Edith Wyatt, two Chicago poets. He wanted their evaluations of his poetry. At first, Addams offered to give her own "expert testimony," but after Iris supplied her with some samples she was sufficiently impressed to send them along to Monroe as work of "unusual promise" written by "an Italian boy" whom she had known for some time. The "boy," she wrote, had worked as a stenographer, but now, since contracting tuberculosis, he spent his time reading and writing poetry. She asked Monroe's opinion of the poems, since she is "casting about to get them published."[19] Monroe's response is not known and thus must not have been especially positive. If it had been, Iris would have made use of it in his campaign of self-promotion. Addams nonetheless continued to help him search for a publisher of a collection of his poems. On 30 September 1912, for example, she wrote on Iris's behalf to Wallace Heckman at the University of Chicago, suggesting that the poems of "Fred Scharmel, who writes under the name of Iris," were "worthy of wider circulation." Should Heckman "find it possible to publish them," she said, he would "be advancing a piece of good literary work."

Monroe herself was well aware of, in her words, "the slight attention and meager, if any, compensation granted to poets by publishers and the public."[20] Her indignation over that fact had been fed in 1903 by her own difficulty finding a publisher for *The Passing Show,* a collection of her short plays in verse. Houghton Mifflin did finally agree to publish the volume but only after one of her friends agreed to bear the expense. Most of the edition of 500 copies went unsold. In 1892, in her mind at least, Monroe had struck a blow for poetry by finagling the planners of the World's Columbian Exposition into commissioning a dedicatory ode so that the fair would add poetry to the arts it was already supposed to celebrate alongside the latest developments in technology. Monroe herself won the commission, and she received for her poem a $1,000 payment. At the dedication of the buildings, held in October 1892, six months before the fair's opening, the six-foot-tall actress Sarah Cowell LeMoyne recited to a vast audience portions of Monroe's "Columbian Ode," and a chorus of 5,000 voices sang two of its embedded songs. Later, the public was probably even more impressed by a $5,000 settlement Monroe received after a court found the *New York World* guilty of copyright violation in printing her poem without permission. Still, after Monroe had an edition of 5,000 copies of the poem printed for sale at a quarter each, she found book dealers and the public "unresponsive." She used the pamphlet for fuel to heat her bedroom-study.[21]

In 1911, at the time when Iris was seeking her expert opinion and she had no commercial publisher for any book of her own and at a time when magazines used poetry largely to fill space left over by prose, Monroe was planning another blow against the neglect of poetry: she would create a magazine devoted entirely to poetry. It would, she hoped, help to develop a greater audience for a greater poetry. As she said in a circular advertising her venture, the magazine would be "a modest attempt to change conditions absolutely destructive to the most necessary and universal of the arts."[22] She took from Whitman the magazine's motto: "To have great poets there must be great audiences too."

On 13 November 1912, a month after the first issue of the magazine, Iris submitted some poems to Monroe. His letter enclosed a clipping of testimonials gathered by "the late Mr. Charles J. O'Malley"—evidently a clipping of the article that appeared in the *Monitor* on 2 September 1911. Iris explained, "As editor of a magazine of the nature of 'Poetry' it is well to know what others beside yourself think of the work of one of your contributors—for one can hardly judge a poet from merely a few specimens, such as Miss Addams sent you." Iris also said that Maurice Francis Egan, then American minister at Copenhagen, would be writing a preface for his forthcoming book of verse and introducing him as "the first Italian in America to write poetry in English." Despite Monroe's fondness for the work of poets residing in Chicago, her view of poetry as a melting pot, and her penchant for using her magazine as what her associate editor called a "forcing frame for young vegetables,"[23] and despite the clipping and its ample testimony of quality, Monroe rejected Iris's submission.


Perhaps to bolster his standing with a resistant Monroe and certainly to aid in securing a publisher for his book, Iris sought still more testimonials. He sent to the poet Louise Imogen Guiney (whose name he misspelled "Quiney") a batch of poems. The accompanying letter, written on Hull-House stationery and dated 16 December 1912, was a clumsy appeal to her ego, to her sympathy, to her sense of solidarity with a fellow Catholic, and finally to what Iris imagined was her sense of self interest. Iris explained that he "came to love" her poems through Charles O'Malley (who considered her "the leading poetess of the day"), that he has "been tubercular for over six years," and that his "family are very poor Italians." He was writing her, he said, at the suggestion of Jane Addams, with the request that she say what she thinks of his work, which O'Malley considered "to be that of a genius." Miss Addams, he said, will show her opinion to a publisher, who might then accept his book without demanding that he himself bear the expense of publication. Iris went on to praise Guiney's verse, offer to review one of her books, and suggest that she drop a note to W. B. Yeats and Edmund Gosse since he would be writing them too. On 4 January 1913 Guiney sent her gracious reply directly to Addams and enclosed Iris's letter. She confessed that the poems were "just good enough to be quite hopeless, from a publisher's point of view, and from posterity's point of view as well." Iris showed "real refinement of temperament, and little else." She "cannot pretend to admire merely nice verses" nor boost Iris—"the young man with that feminine-sounding name and signature"—with Yeats and Gosse without violating her honesty.[24]

Addams sent Iris's letter and Guiney's response to Monroe. By that time, Monroe probably had met Iris in person. Unsuccessful in submissions to Monroe's magazine, Iris had quickly sought the aid of Helen Hughes Hielscher, the physician from Minnesota who had written years earlier of the need for patronage to support the young boy of the threadbare coat and big eyes. Under his prompting she had sent Monroe two of his poems ("Darling Boy" and "Come Thou, My Love"). Writing to Iris on 7 December 1912 and calling the poems "uneven and not quite in shape for publication" but also discerning in them "a true poetic gift," Monroe had invited him to the *Poetry* office, where she would look at more of his work and give him "some hints." At this point, Monroe may have already been a bit wary of Iris. She would have been even more wary if she had known that, unsuccessful in finding a book publisher by means of an authentic letter from Addams, Iris had forged a letter dated 15 February 1913 from Addams to the "MacMillian [*sic*] Company." Introducing Iris as a "true poet in the full sense of the word," the letter claimed that he had been praised by Ruskin, Swinburne, and Francis Thompson and that Maurice Francis Egan was writing a preface for the collection. The letter went on to say that the "excellence of the poems" and the "critical opinions from the foremost living poets in England and America make this book an unusually good business proposition." For "advertising purposes" the letter submitted a blurb calling the book "an excellent piece of literary work," this last phrase having been taken from an earlier authentic letter of Addams.

The forged letter's reference to Ruskin, Swinburne, and Thompson anticipated Mrs. O'Malley's column for 8 March 1913, where she considerably expanded the chorus of praise offered to Iris. She reprinted the statements attributed to Cawein, Gilder, Hurd, Johnson, Le Gallienne, Miller, and Riley and added these:

> Francis Thompson: "We are indebted to Mr. O'Malley for having discovered a young poet of the first rank, Scharmel Iris. His poems are sublime in conception, rich in splendid imagery, full of remarkable metaphors and new figures, and musical in expression."

> Algernon Charles Swinburne: "He writes with imaginative ardor, and impassioned is the word which best illustrates his utterance. He is genuine and sincere, and his lovely poems display energy of emotion and a true sense of poetic restraint."

> William Butler Yeats: "Poems that are distinguished and far removed from commonplace. They are exceptionally beautiful and fascinating."

> John Ruskin: "Scharmel Iris, that rare casket of purple and golds! He is a youth of genius whose poems are marvelously beautiful. His heart has felt the pathos of life, and he has set that pathos to music. His poetry, being both human and exquisite, will enrich the treasure of Poesy."

Rudyard Kipling: "Song to him is natural, and like a bird, he sings for the very joy of singing. He has an individuality, and the depth and beauty of his songs have power to charm."

George Bernard Shaw: "His book will be received by two continents. His poems are not echoes of dead poets; they glow with the fire he has given them."

John B. Tabb: "The same blood that coursed through the veins of Sappho, Dante, Milton, and Keats flows in the veins of this poet. His poems are gems of the first water."

Edmund Gosse: "He is the first Italian in America to write poetry in English, and the whole English-speaking world will learn to love him as Rossetti was loved in England."

Mrs. O'Malley claimed that these statements about Iris, which, again, "show how high he really stands," came from letters sent by these luminaries to her husband.

Mrs. O'Malley, like her husband and like Phillips, was eager to promote Catholic literature. She was also eager to show her husband as having been in contact with major writers of his time and to claim for him the honor of discovering such a poetic genius. How else explain the credulity that allowed her to accept all of these statements as genuine evaluations or even as kind words offered as polite taffy? Not only are their evaluations so exaggerated as to be improbable, but so are the circumstances under which some would have had to be written. Although Gosse, Kipling, and Shaw, who were not likely to be readers of the *Monitor,* were quite alive in 1913, Ruskin had died in January 1900, after five or so years during which his correspondence and contacts had been much curtailed. He thus would have been praising the work of a boy who was, at most, ten at the time.[25] Further, Charles O'Malley would not have been seeking Ruskin's opinion of "a youth of genius" with whom he himself was almost certainly not acquainted. Before taking on the editorship of the *New World* in 1904, he was editing Catholic weeklies in Pittsburgh and then in Louisville and Lebanon, Kentucky. His and Iris's paths would not likely have crossed until after Ruskin's death. The appearance of Gosse and Yeats in the chorus raises another issue, one that Mrs. O'Malley would not have been aware of. Why would Iris in 1912 have asked Guiney to tell

Gosse and Yeats that he would be writing them for their opinion if Charles O'Malley had already gotten that opinion before his death in 1910?

Iris himself must have supplied Mrs. O'Malley with the quotations and the story of their source. In both of her columns there was also some indication of his motive. In the earlier column, Mrs. O'Malley commented that "want, privation, and every other conceivable obstacle" were keeping Iris from "giving to the world the real music that is in his soul." In supplying Mrs. O'Malley with the statements, Iris was hoping for support that would ease this want and privation. In supplying the later, more impressive quotations, Iris was also hoping for assistance in securing a publisher. He not only got Mrs. O'Malley to say that he had ready for the printer a collection of his poetry with a preface by Egan but also had Shaw predicting success for his book.

At any rate, Iris had pretty much everything needed to be a poet—want, privation, and genius. In her column for 30 August 1913 Mrs. O'Malley printed Iris's "The Visionary," subtitled "Against the Modern Treatment of the Poet":

> He stole the pennies on a dead man's eyes,
>> To buy him bread who spilled the gold of song,
>> He struck at error; with the right was strong.
> The future shall his dream materialize!
>
> God's golden bird, loosed from Paradise,
>> Died unbeknown, a-near a wayside inn.
>> A breast-wound showed where late a grief had been—
> I laid two pennies on the dead man's eyes.

Mrs. O'Malley found a "grim truth in these simple lines." Lacking bread, the visionary poet must steal coins. Despite his golden song, he dies without fame, and only in death is he rewarded with coins, which now cover his now visionless eyes. That was the modern treatment her husband had received, minus those postmortem pennies. The next time the poem appeared, the pronoun beginning the last line became *they*, and Iris's identification with the neglected visionary poet was complete. Aside again from those final pennies and aside from the issue of striking at error and being strong with the right, the poem foretells much of his life.

Iris's attribution of visionary power to the poet raises the issue besetting poetry at the time. The increasing dominance of science (and its genre, prose) was seen to dispel the Romantic notion of poetry as a vehicle for transcendent truth. The visionary as seer gave way to the visionary as impractical dreamer. What then could be the value of poetry? It had diminished power in the marketplace: the "gold of song" buys little bread, and poets cannot command the recognition of the public: they die "unbeknown." Although Iris's poetry would evolve over time, growing more superficially modern, he continued to justify it as visionary in the Romantic sense, sought ways to translate its gold to bread, and schemed with unflagging persistence to make a name for himself as Scharmel Iris. He became a rather feckless scoundrel as well as a figure of poetry seeking a place within a culture dominated by the concept of value as economic and truth as prose.[26]

# CHAPTER TWO

# NEW POET,
# 1913–1922

"There were strange unveilings in those days; indeed, every year of *Poetry*'s history holds the record of exaggerated egoisms, cases almost pathological of hidden or blatant self-belief in genius."—Harriet Monroe, *A Poet's Life*

From what Harriet Monroe knew of Iris, notably his letter to Louise Imogen Guiney, she might have assumed that she was dealing with no more than the normal bumptiousness of youth. Although she still had not accepted any of his work, she did not banish Iris from the *Poetry* office, or at least did not banish him for long. At that office, Iris was for a time able to supplement the education he received at Hull-House. Monroe later recalled those early years at 543 Cass Street: "Poets from far and near came as to a kind of headquarters of the art, hoping to find sympathy with their elusive moods, and readiness to discuss their problems. Youngsters would bring sheaves of manuscripts, as eager to consult the editor as if she were an oracle.

Sometimes there was promise, if not achievement in what they showed, but more often the halting and platitudinous rhymes amazed when they did not amuse." At the office Iris not only found encouragement and guidance but also met other Chicago-area poets, those whose names still ring bells, such as Edgar Lee Masters and Carl Sandburg, and many more whose names don't, such as Maxwell Bodenheim, Helen Hoyt, and Eunice Tietjens. Here, too, he could meet poets passing through Chicago, including Rupert Brooke, Robert Frost, Sara Teasdale, and the winner of the 1913 Nobel Prize for literature, Rabindranath Tagore. He would also have been aware of letters sent to *Poetry* by the likes of Ezra Pound, letters that Monroe said "sharpened the edge" of debates among poets frequenting the editorial office.[1]

It must have become clear to Iris that he had emerged as a poet at just that moment when the direction of poetry was about to make a radical change. He had pretty well mastered the mode of the 1890s, which called for a poetry of ideality rather than reality. He had learned to prettify and romanticize, to make ingenuous assaults on readers' emotions and serve up conventionally poetic thoughts and forms. The so-called poetry renaissance was now beginning to challenge that mode and in a few years would displace it. Right there in Chicago, Monroe's *Poetry* magazine was at the center of that rebirth. Further, thanks to its patrons, the magazine was able to pay contributors for their work and to grant cash prizes.

At first, news of the founding of *Poetry* was greeted enthusiastically by Iris's champion at the San Francisco *Monitor*, Mrs. O'Malley.[2] After a few issues, however, she complained that the magazine, eagerly awaited by "lovers of poetry" and now being published, had already "degenerated": "Its April [1913] issue contained some of the most degenerate stuff we have seen in print. It was from the pen of Ezra Pound, and was rank with insincerity and pose. It was neither poetry nor prose, but apparently the mad vaporing of a vacant mind. . . . it is the very thing that gives poetry a bad name, and holds the great art of Dante and Petrarch, of Poe and Francis Thompson, up to ridicule." Mrs. O'Malley expressed her hope that the magazine's "'new beauty' spasm will soon have passed," and she regretted "to see so promising a venture proving itself so utterly 'penny wise and Pound foolish' . . . as to sell itself to the cubists of verse for the sake of a little sensational notoriety."[3]

The issue in question contained Pound's group "Contemporania," which included his two-line imagist poem "In a Station of the Metro":

> The apparition    of these faces    in the crowd :
> Petals    on a wet, black    bough .

It also included "Salutation the Second," which asked its readers to observe how conventional readers would respond to his poems:

> Watch the reporters spit,
> Watch the anger of the professors,
> Watch how the pretty ladies revile them:
>
> "Is this," they say, "the nonsense
>         that we expect of poets?"
> "Where is the Picturesque?"
>         "Where is the vertigo of emotion?"

As Mrs. O'Malley's response indicates, Pound was not disappointed. "Contemporania" caused a critical hullabaloo. Although Floyd Dell, in the *Chicago Evening Post* gave Pound extravagant praise ("you are the most enchanting poet alive"), his poetry was parodied in the *Chicago Tribune*'s "Line o' Type" column and attacked by the literary establishment (notably in the conservative, Chicago-based *Dial*) for violating decency and dignity and the sacred art of poetry.[4] Still, Mrs. O'Malley recognized that the magazine had quickly become a prestigious place for contemporary poets to appear and that it had at least drawn some public attention. Thus, in her 23 August 1913 column, she congratulated Iris for achieving "admittance to the exclusive pages of 'Poetry Magazine,'" and she printed his poem "In Italy."

> In Italy, in Italy,
> The oranges hang on the tree,
> As lanterns bright, aglow with light,
> They shine for lovers thro' the night.
>
> In Italy, in Italy,
> Oh, life is one long Arcady!
> The moon grows pale; the nightingale
> Stirs every heart, with wail on wail.

> In Italy, in Italy,
> The rose exhales an ecstasy;
> Each humble heart acts well its part,
> And welcomes thee, whoe'er thou art.
>
> In Italy, in Italy,
> The sky steps down to meet the sea,
> The redbird swings, with flames he sings,
> And shakes the sunset from his wings—
> In Italy, in Italy,
> Oh, life is one long Arcady!

She took the pretty little song as reassurance that Iris was not following the example of Pound.

Despite what Iris may have told Mrs. O'Malley, he had not yet secured admittance to *Poetry*. He was still knocking at that door, yet he was in sufficiently good graces with Monroe to be invited to a banquet that she saw as early validation of her magazine's contribution to poetry and as "a milestone in literary history." Iris was one of the 100 poets, artists, patrons, and local magnates invited to a dinner sponsored for Yeats by *Poetry* and held on 1 March 1914. There, at the Cliff Dwellers Club, overlooking Lake Michigan from the top floor of Orchestra Hall, Iris heard Yeats urge poets to "to lead lives of humility and simplicity" and "to express themselves as they are," without "the sentimentality, the rhetoric, the 'moral uplift'" against which he and other members of the London Rhymers' Club had rebelled but that he still found when he opened "the ordinary American magazine." At the banquet he also heard Yeats praise Vachel Lindsay's "earnest simplicity and strange beauty" and Pound's experiments with free verse. He heard also Lindsay read—chant, really—a new poem, "The Congo," with its recurrent line "Boomlay, boomlay, boomlay, boom."[5]

Also in 1914, the exuberantly erratic Margaret Anderson founded in Chicago the *Little Review*, a magazine that competed with Monroe's *Poetry* and that would become best known for serializing James Joyce's *Ulysses* (1918–1920). In November 1914 it gave Iris his secular debut by printing five of his poems under the collective title "Lyrics of an Italian." An editorial on the discovery—"Another New Poet"—must have made use of a clipping of Mrs. O'Malley's *Monitor* column of 8 March 1913. It said that

Iris "at the tender age of ten, and later, was praised by Ruskin, Swinburne, Francis Thompson, Gosse, and other men who may be assumed to know what good poetry is," and it quoted some snippets of the praise: "He is a youth of genius and his poems are marvelously beautiful" (Ruskin); "He is genuine and sincere" (Swinburne); "I believe Scharmel Iris to be a poet of the first rank" (Thompson). The editorial announced the forthcoming publication of Iris's *Lyrics of a Lad* and confessed (in language suggesting either Anderson or Iris as the editorialist) that "personally, we love Mr. Iris's work," which "remains in your mind as part of that art treasure-house which is your religion and your life." The *New York Times Book Review* picked up on the editorial and admitted that "some of his poems . . . have an excellent lyrical quality, although scarcely reaching the superlative degree suggested by Ruskin and Swinburne." In fact, the *Times* had its doubts about the authenticity of the testimonials: "There are few, if any, credible instances of so fine a precocity as such authoritative estimates as these give us in the case of Mr. Iris."[6]

Although aware of Iris's early maneuverings to get Guiney and through her Yeats and Gosse to recognize his genius, Monroe admitted four of his poems to *Poetry* in the month following his *Little Review* appearance. At least three of the poems reflected Monroe's lessons in directness and simplicity, as in "After the Martyrdom":

> They threw a stone, you threw a stone,
>     I threw a stone that day;
> Although their sharpness bruised his flesh
>     He had no word to say.
>
> But for the moan he did not make,
>     Today I make my moan;
> And for the stone I threw at him
>     My heart must bear a stone.

In two other poems it is as if Iris felt he must resort to extremity of theme or situation to replace the poetically lush language that he had been used to. Thus in "The Mad Woman" a fallen woman succumbs to madness and complains of the world's scorn, and in "Lament" the poet has been so smitten by a woman's lament that he himself suffers a life of sorrow. In

"Early Nightfall," the fourth poem, however, Iris indulged his taste for more conventionally poetic language:

> The pale Day drowses on the western steep,
> The toiler faints along the marge of sleep,
> Within the sunset-press, incarnadine,
> The Sun, a peasant, tramples out his wine.
>
> Ah, scattered gold rests on the twilight-streams,
> The poppy opes her scarlet purse of dreams;
> Night, with the sickle-moon engarners wheat,
> And binds the sheaves of stars beneath her feet.
>
> Rest, weary heart, and every flight-worn bird;
> The brooklet of the meadow lies unstirred;
> Sleep, every soul, against a comrade breast,
> God grant you peace, and guard you in your rest!

The year 1914 was something of an annus mirabilis for Iris. In addition to appearing in *Little Review* and *Poetry,* he found at last a publisher for a volume of his poetry. He turned to artist-designer-publisher Ralph Fletcher Seymour, probably known to Iris as the publisher of *Poetry.* Seymour was, moreover, a friend of Ellen Starr, Addams's associate at Hull-House, and his office was in the Fine Arts Building, a major meeting place for Chicago literary figures at the time.[7] He did much commercial work, including bookplates, magazine covers, playbills, calendars, and the like, but he also produced small-press books. He had, in fact, published a slim volume by Monroe and another by her associate editor, Alice Corbin Henderson.[8] Although most of his work was done on commission, Seymour agreed to publish Iris's volume, *Lyrics of a Lad,* by subscription. He produced a four-page flier advertising the book, which was to be "published on receipt of the least number of orders necessary to assure the interest which should be shown in the appearance of so serious a contribution to our poetic literature." That is, it would appear when the publisher's costs had been met. Subscribers were to fill in a form on page four and return it to Seymour along with one dollar for the book and eight cents for postage. The flier claimed that Iris, a young Italian, "promises to win a similar place in the ranks of the more important American poets to that held by Rossetti, in England." It also said, "Such men as John Ruskin, Algernon

Frontispiece and title page, *Lyrics of a Lad,* 1914. Eugene Hutchinson took the frontispiece photograph in 1911, when Iris was twenty-two.

Swinburne, and Edmund Gosse have expressed their belief in the inspired nature and in the power of this young poet."

The book appeared on 2 December, just in time for Christmas gift giving. It was a handsome book, in brown paper over boards, with brown cloth around the spine and with a front cover bearing, in gold, a decoration enclosing the title and the author's name. Its title page decoration, attributed to Michele Greco and including a woman strumming a lyre, showed the influence of the arts and crafts movement that marked fine printing at the time. The book's colophon noted that the edition consisted of a thousand copies printed in November 1914.[9] The book also featured a frontispiece photograph of Iris by Eugene Hutchinson, a portrait photographer whose studio was also in the Fine Arts Building. Hutchinson had made portraits of actress Sarah Bernhardt, poet Rupert Brooke, dancer Anna Pavlova, and other notables whose celebrity Iris sought to share through association. Iris later claimed that his portrait session coincided with that of Brooke in 1914, when he was passing through Chicago.[10] There is, in fact, some resemblance in the two portraits. Both men are posed in a sort of semiprofile and have open-collared shirts. But

Iris, despite his head of luxuriant dark curls and his large eyes, cannot quite compete with Brooke, whom Hutchinson described as "an unbelievably beautiful young man" and whose portrait Monroe kept framed on the wall of the *Poetry* office.[11] There is another difference. Hutchinson took the portrait of Iris in 1911. In fact, he took several, all with the open-collar pose later used for Brooke and several with Iris clutching a book, his shoulders draped by a cloth or academic robe.

Yet Iris did have his portrait taken in 1914. The photograph bears the imprint "1914 Matzene, Chicago." In it, Iris stands regally erect, wearing a wig, floor-length dress, and large fur coat slung off the shoulders. On the reverse, Iris annotated the photograph as depicting him as Fedora in *La Fedora,* a successful turn-of-the-century opera by Umberto Giordano. In it, the title character, a wealthy widow, seeks revenge for the murder of her fiancé, discovers that the death of her unfaithful beau isn't worth avenging, falls in love with his murderer, and finally poisons herself (for earlier having set in motion events leading to the death of her new lover's brother). It was based on a play by Victorien Sardou in which Bernhardt starred in the lead role. The particular occasion for the photograph is not known, but at about the same time Iris was the subject of several snapshots in which he was wearing women's clothing and posing on what appear to be the grounds of a large estate. It was evidently not out of character. Furthermore, he was enamored of Bernhardt—or of himself as a sort of forged Bernhardt playing Fedora.

As Iris had promised, the book contained a preface signed Maurice Francis Egan.[12] The preface, relying on information supplied by Iris, introduced him as having been born 10 February 1889 in Florence and emerging as "the first of the Italians in America to write poetry in English," a phrase that already had seen some heavy use. It then recited the litany of those who had praised Iris's verse: Le Gallienne, W. D. Howells, Thompson, Swinburne, and Ruskin. In fact, Egan said, it was through Ruskin and Swinburne that he came to know that Iris was "an Italian graft on an Illinois,—peach tree is perhaps the best word," though he had to admit never having seen peach trees in Chicago. After truth broke in with all its matter of fact about peach trees, however, Egan returned to his own poetic mode:

Iris in 1914, posing as Sarah Bernhardt in the role of Fedora in the opera *La Fedora*. Matzene photo, courtesy Lewis University.

> . . . I did find in his poems the color and the freshness, the inexpress-
> ible glowing, almost lucent tints of the peach blossom, the warm lure
> of Spring and of love and of hope. The healthful cold of the winter,
> with all its frost pangs, gave beauty to the roseate blossoms, as the
> busy life of the poet has helped to make the delicate bloom of his
> Spring delightful. Life has taught him, that the gift of song is a solace,
> and he says that speechless hearts must be sadder than his own.

Drawing on a Romantic formula also dear to Iris, Egan charac-
terized Iris's verse as "the garden of a young poet, who forgets
the brevity of his life and the reality of his griefs in the joy of the
art he cultivates." And he said that because of Ruskin and Swin-
burne, two "men of mark of our age," he read Iris's poems
with "renewed interest." The assertions are improbable, un-
less Egan meant that he came to know Iris not through
Ruskin and Swinburne but through whatever clippings or let-
ters Iris may have supplied. Improbable or not, the preface
bears Egan's name. He never repudiated it; in fact, he later
wrote another. On 13 November 1917, having been sent a
manuscript by Iris, Egan thanked Iris for kind words about his
own poems, said that he had "made very frank notes" on
some of Iris's poems, and promised to send under separate
cover the preface he had written for Iris's second collection.
He also said that he would "be glad to subscribe for five
copies of the book." So Egan does seem to have been respon-
sible for the preface to *Lyrics,* even though Iris could not have
done much better himself and despite its heavy flirtation
with improbability.

Almost as impressive as Egan's preface was Iris's note acknowl-
edging previous publication of some of the poems:

> The courteous acknowledgments of the author are extended to *The
> Century Magazine, The Little Review, Atlantic Monthly, Scribner's Mag-
> azine, The Forum, Poetry* and the *Cosmopolitan,* of America; *The
> Cork Examiner, Freeman's Journal* and *Dublin Review,* of Ireland; and
> The English Review* and *Blackwood's,* of England.

That is a list any poet of the time would envy. The trouble is that Iris
had appeared or would soon appear in only 2 of the 12 magazines
listed—the *Little Review* and *Poetry*—and he failed to acknowledge
that many of the poems had appeared in the *New World* and *Monitor.*
Along with its substitution of wish for fact, the note has another fea-

ture typical of Iris's writing. He often had the words but not the tune. So his note said that "the *courteous acknowledgments* of the author are extended" to the magazines. Most authors acknowledge courtesy extended to them, not courtesy they extend to others.

As an early draft indicates, Iris had planned to dedicate the book to his mother: *"To the sacred memory of the woman that bore me* / Rosa Maria Scaramella-Di Vencenzo / mother of eight children and the first American friend of Francis [*sic*] Xavier Cabrini." In memorializing his mother, the wording implied that she was dead, when in fact she was very much alive at the time, as was Mother Frances Xavier Cabrini, who died three years later (and whom the Church would canonize in 1946 for her work among Chicago's poor). In the typescript for the dedication, Iris wrote, over the word *friend,* the word *patron.* Although his mother could not read, Iris may have been worried about implying that she was dead and concocting the story about her patronage of Mother Cabrini. More likely, though, he realized that another dedication could prove more useful in his own quest for patronage. He replaced the earlier dedication with one *"to that patron of arts and lover of Italy* / Mrs. Harold F. McCormick." That was Edith Rockefeller McCormick, daughter of John D. Rockefeller, founder of Standard Oil, and wife of International Harvester's chairman. Iris knew of her philanthropy, notably her support of the opera, and of her founding the Lovers of Italy club at the University of Chicago.[13] Iris had his eye on her.

The book contains 61 poems, almost all written in the conventional manner of what was called "magazine verse." They represented a mostly competent versifying that made no great demand on its readers but rather fed their hunger for sentiment by dishing up generous servings of stock themes, images, and diction. Here, for example, is the third and final stanza of "At Morning":

> The dawn is glad with melody
> As Spring is born;
> On rosy wings the daylight sings
> Good morn! Good morn!

Throughout the volume are roses red, sylvan sheens, tired hearts, bosoms fair, sweet perfumes, azure air, mournful nights, and golden hair. Almost one-third of the poems include at least one reference to roses, and there is plenty of room for poppies, daffodils, lilies, violets—all the poetic flowers. Readers could, however, find some diversity of subject. On facing pages, for example, Iris made an odd pairing of poems, "Her Waiting" and "Twilight Lullaby." The juxtaposition is only initially jarring. The first poem is spoken by a woman who, in the evening, breathlessly awaits her lover and his "warm kiss" and "fond embraces." The second is addressed to a child, a "sleepy curlyhead," who is told to "toddle off to dreamland." There is also some diversity of style since the book reprints Iris's early contributions to the *New World* and *Monitor* along with later work that seems to bear the influence of Monroe and the modernizing of poetry taking place in her magazine. By and large, though, the poems reflect a poet who had accepted the view that poetry was devoted to beauty, refinement, uplift, ideality, spirituality, and tradition.

In their predominant sentimentality and conventionality, the poems seem the product more of emulation than of composition. Indeed, in at least one case, emulation verges on plagiarism. Iris's "The Heart-Cry of the Celtic Maid" sounds much like its obvious model, Laurence Hope's "Love Lightly," which had appeared in *India's Love Lyrics* (1902).[14] Iris's poem began,

> There were blackbirds in the hedges and sunshine in the sky,
> Red lilies in the sedges where blue rivulets ran by;
> The spring's gay flowers and children—Oh, how jubilant they were [.]
> Veiled was the wall of heaven by blithe singing-birds astir!

Hope's had begun,

> There were Roses in the hedges, and Sunshine in the sky,
> Red lilies in the sedges, where the waters rippled by
> A thousand Bulbuls singing, oh, how jubilant they were,
> And a thousand flowers flinging their sweetness on the air.

There are further echoes. For example, Iris wrote,

> What use the heart-red roses, or the azure of the sky?
> They were fair in Love's reposes; my love shall never die!

Hope had written,

> What use the scented Roses, or the azure of the sky?
> They are sweet when Love reposes, but then he had to die.

One might argue that Iris intended a poetic reply to Hope. After all, in Hope's poem a rejecting former lover, tired of a love that lasted a season, tells the rejected lover to forget him or her. In Iris's a maid complains that she cannot forget the one who rejected her, cannot even die, though life and nature have lost their beauty. Yet why then would Iris substitute a Celtic maid for Hope's Indian one and replace her Indian bulbuls with Celtic blackbirds?

This particular instance of plagiarism—there are probably more in the volume—draws attention to an additional feature held in common by Iris's and Hope's volumes and, for that matter, those of a great many other literary figures: the extension of pretense from the literary work proper to its "packaging." Hope had given her original poems the appearance of translations of love lyrics from India, "arranged in verse by Laurence Hope." Moreover, Hope was actually Adela Nicolson. Both "deceptions" served to insulate her from the passionate themes of her poems.

In light of the derivative nature of Iris's poetry, it is curious but perhaps not coincidental that one of the reviews of the volume claimed for it great originality. In the December 1914 issue of the *Little Review*, after introducing Iris as "the first of the Italians in America to write poetry in English," Milo Winter (a Chicago book illustrator) wrote that Iris's poems "came to be respected as art through their freshness and originality." They are "direct and spontaneous." There are no "trite, worn-out . . . phrases." Because the book is Scharmel Iris, it is "distinctive" and "without sham and without affectation." Winter pointed to "The Heart-Cry of the Celtic Maid" as a particularly "graceful composition." If, in fact, Winter rather than Iris wrote the review, he must have had Iris's help. Otherwise, how would he be able to say that Iris wrote amid "the grime and barrenness of Halsted Street," and how would he know of "many years of discouragement and the hardest work"? Perhaps more tellingly, how else claim for Iris "a power far beyond that revealed by many of today's singers"? And how else admit that the book contains "more real poetry than any volume of modern verse it has been our good fortune to read"? And probably it was Iris who, even after his book had been advertised as being published by subscription, would say that his publisher bore the cost of the edition. This review reappeared as a page-one story in the Chicago archdiocese's *New*

*World,* where it was quoted in whole after a brief paragraph noting that Iris was a Catholic and had been a contributor.[15]

The issues of originality and struggle also came up in a notice published in the *Chicago Daily News.* Much of the story contrasted Iris's hardscrabble life selling newspapers and doing odd jobs and his receiving high praise from Ruskin, Gosse, and Swinburne. But it also quoted Iris's claim that he had "never read poetry until a year or so ago." The reason, he indicated, was that he didn't want "to echo the dead." "I want to be myself," he explained.[16] The reviewer for the *Chicago Herald* likewise saw Iris's sweet poetry as his "relief from strenuous bread-winning endeavor." This reviewer brought up the oddity of Iris's being praised by Ruskin and Swinburne: "Since Ruskin died fourteen and Swinburne five years ago Iris must, indeed, have been a lad when their praises moved him." Sufficiently impressed by Iris's poetry, however, the reviewer did not question the statements. She supposed that Ruskin approved of Iris's form and Swinburne of his "springing lyric impulse." She found both these qualities in "The Heart-Cry of the Celtic Maid."[17]

In the San Francisco *Monitor,* Mrs. O'Malley reviewed the book at length. She too picked up from Egan's preface the theme of song-out-of-suffering. "This poet," she said, "has suffered." What poet hasn't? she asked. Besides, Iris "has sung in his suffering, to give ease to his own heart and comfort others." Pleased with the success of a poet discovered and nurtured by her late husband, Mrs. O'Malley struggled to find superlatives. Iris was "unquestionably . . . a genius," he possessed "real greatness," he had "the passionate heart and tender eye of the true poet," he was "great and will be greater," and he would "grow to be one of our big American poets." Mrs. O'Malley also recommended "The Heart-Cry of the Celtic Maid," which she called "an Irish poem that has real Celtic fervor and the real Irish swing to it." She did think it a mistake, though, that Iris had chosen to permit his portrait to be used as a frontispiece and had titled the book as he had. The title was "just slightly an appeal to favor that jars on the sensibilities."[18]

Even the less enthusiastic reviews were nonetheless positive. The reviewer for the *Chicago Daily Tribune,* who liked his musical name, acknowledged that Iris wrote in the mode of Keats, without reaching that master's "heights," and that "almost every poem" exhibited some unevenness or fault. But she found his poems "essentially original" and "charming in spite of their faults."[19] In a brief review, Harriet Monroe regretted Iris's frequent imitation of Keats and other classics and his fondness for "stock figures and phrases." (She no doubt had read Milo Winter's praise of Iris's originality in the magazine of her rival Margaret Anderson.) Yet she also credited Iris with "a delicate fancy and a true lyric touch."[20]

Whatever misgivings Monroe had about Iris and his poetry were not sufficient to dissuade her from including him in *Poetry* again, in September 1917, and in the first edition of her and Henderson's anthology *The New Poetry* that same year. It was a hospitable gathering. Containing 431 poems by 101 poets, it printed work by poets now lost but also by those who came to epitomize modern poetry, including Eliot, Pound, Stevens, and Williams. Packaging the poetry renaissance for public consumption and taking it to schools, women's clubs, and the general public, the anthology had considerable influence. Through it, Iris reached a much larger audience than he had through *Poetry* or through his own book.[21]

Iris's appearance here resulted in his finding his way into F. Scott Fitzgerald's *This Side of Paradise*.[22] In the novel, Amory Blaine's college chum Tom D'Invilliers delivers a sweeping attack on contemporary American literature. When Amory asks, "How does little Tommy like the poets?" Tom replies that he is writing a satire on them and has finished the last few lines, which at Amory's urging he recites, "pausing at intervals so that Amory could see that it was free verse":

> So
> Walter Conrad Arensberg,
> Alfred Kreymborg,
> Carl Sandburg,
> Louis Untermeyer,
> Eunice Tietjens,
> Clara Shanafelt,
> James Oppenheim,
> Maxwell Bodenheim,
> Richard Glaenzer,
> Scharmel Iris,
> Conrad Aiken,
> I place your names here
> So that you may live
> If only as names,
> Sinuous, mauve-colored names,
> In the Juvenalia [*sic*]
> Of my collected editions.

Amory roars his approval. Tom's mauve names, intended as a sign of his (and Fitzgerald's) knowledge of contemporary poetry, came from *The New Poetry*. It was the only single source that included all 11 poets. To assemble the list would otherwise have required wide reading in the little magazines. And even in those it would be easy to miss some. Fitzgerald, like most readers, took his poetry anthologically.

Despite his appearance in *The New Poetry*, Iris so far was new more chronologically than poetically. His poetry reflected no substantial break from the Romantic mode predominant at the turn of the century. That mode itself seemed to invite, even license, the fulsome treatment accorded Iris by Egan, Mrs. O'Malley, and others. The poetry and the response to it were both exaggerations of Romanticism's fidelity to the imagined rather than the actual, to what the heart desires rather than to what the head knows.

# APPARITIONAL SCHEMER, 1923–1939

"Without a true face handy, masks were dandy."

—Scharmel Iris, "Shuttlecock"

Iris's publishing successes, his self-laureation through forged praise, and the public notice he received fed without satisfying his appetite for fame, and there were some other real appetites too. It was all very well for some modern poets, such as at times Ezra Pound, to turn the economic nonviability of their work into a point of pride and a sign of true artistry, but a poet still needed to earn a living.[1] Iris thus turned his skills from the pursuit of fame to the pursuit of fame and fortune. His efforts, though, were largely unsuccessful. In what was a major blow to his ambitions and career as a poet, Monroe discovered some of his deceptions. After his reappearance in the September 1917 issue of *Poetry* magazine, Monroe shut to him its usually open doors, and she removed him from *The New Poetry* when it went into its second edition in 1923.

On 18 April 1923, writing anonymously as "A Friend" and using the stationery of the Arts Club, Iris sent a letter to Mary Agnes Amberg, the director of the Madonna Center, a pioneer Catholic social settlement in Chicago serving primarily Italian-Americans on Chicago's West Side. Referring to Amberg as also a friend of Iris, "A Friend" proposed "creation of a thirty thousand dollar trust fund for Iris," who is "incapacitated for actual life from tuberculosis." Iris wanted Amberg herself, whose father had made a considerable fortune selling business supplies, to contribute, but he also wanted to use her as a means of access to Edith Rockefeller McCormick, whom he had earlier tried to manipulate by dedicating to her his *Lyrics of a Lad*. She in turn would be a way of getting to her father, John D. Rockefeller, and so he suggested "an audation" (an audacious audition?) with McCormick, who "might be so kind as to interest her father in KOTO PLAYER an ancient Oriental work of art which at its purchase over thirty five years ago in Europe was considered one of the choicest finds in existence." If her father would buy the art work, the proceeds would go toward the trust fund. And this "fund-sum is not too great—less than that spent on opera proteges who rarely make good." "What more is there to say?" he asked. Well, he added, he himself will contribute $1,000 as soon as Amberg acts on his suggestions, such action being "a serious Christian duty not to beignored [*sic*] as it is the means of saving a genius from further complications of pathetic physical and mental nature."

Iris concocted another scheme a few days later. He intended to extract money from William Wrigley, the chewing-gum manufacturer who in 1921 had erected in Chicago a French Renaissance–style headquarters, at the time the city's tallest structure. Evidently Iris first spoke to Amberg's friend and Madonna Center associate Marie Plamondon, suggesting that she enlist Dorothy Offield to convince Wrigley, her father, to purchase Iris's poem "The Wrigley Building." To help her make a case, he then forged over Monroe's name and on *Poetry* magazine stationery a letter to himself. The letter asserted that the editors of the *Dial* "will pay two-hundred-and-fifty dollars" for his poem and also award him its "yearly prize of two-thousand dollars." The letter advised Iris to consider the offer but noted Jane Addams's opposition to it: "She firmly believes it should become the property of Mr. Wrigley himself, because he had the foresight to erect a thing of beauty in the building." As beautiful as the building is, however, "the poem is superior to the beauty of the building and deserves to be cast into a bronze tablet where it can be worshipped [*sic*] by millions of people today and millions yet unborn." Wrigley's participation in this plan would be "a civic asset to the city" and "stamp him above the average man of business." (Monroe later received a typed copy of this 29 April 1923 letter and wrote on it "A forgery." Iris did not receive the 1923 Dial Award for the poem. That year it went to Van Wyck Brooks.)

On 9 June 1923 he sent Plamondon the forged letter, enclosing it with his own, which he signed "Fred." In his letter, Iris told her that "Monroe's testimony" would be useful in backing the poem when she approached Offield and, later, when Offield in turn approached her father. Iris also claimed that the head of a large advertising agency had told him that the poem had "great commercial value" as a business card, "as an exchange business card—a method employed by business men." He also foresaw its use as a back-page magazine advertisement and personal bookplate. Earlier, Iris had sent Plamondon a gift, a sculpture of a goddess. It was a little something to make her feel indebted. In the letter, he reminded her of it, commenting that, even with the goddess's wings missing, "the beauty of her form and drapery are deathless." "In this," he confessed, "she has the advantage over a mere mortal. It is such a struggle to keep mine."

After a day or so, declining to give his name, Iris or some other man called Offield to ask whether she had heard from Plamondon about the poem. She had not yet. Eventually, Plamondon did give her the poem and the forged letter or, if not the letter itself, the gist of it, and she in turn presented it to her father, who chose not to buy the poem.[2] Eventually, word of this affair reached Monroe, who complained to Amberg, telling her that the letter with her name had been forged. In reply, on 19 October 1923, Amberg assured Monroe that she and Plamondon "never had even the very least reason to question the integrity of Fred Scharmel's character" and that an explanation of Monroe's noninvolvement would be extended to Offield and Wrigley.

In his fixing on his goal of patronage, though not in his means to secure it, Iris may have been encouraged by the series of essays Pound wrote under the title *Patria Mia* at about the time Monroe was founding her magazine. In the essays, Pound made a case for patronage as a means by which the wealthy, in supporting young artists, might function also in an alternative economy —an aesthetic economy—where they thus could participate in the creation of an art that would redound to their "credit" and leave a lasting testament to their virtue.[3] Iris had offered Wrigley a poetic testament to his virtue and had sought in return Wrigley's lasting testament to his. Ironically, Iris's use of the Dial Award in his attempted negotiation with Wrigley recalls another attempt to turn the aesthetic into the economic, one that also involved the award and that showed modernist poetry to have commercial value of the sort Iris sought for his own. As Iris would have known, *Dial* magazine published Eliot's *Waste Land* in its November 1922 issue and announced in the following month's issue that Eliot had received the second annual Dial Award, which included a cash prize of $2,000. What he did not know about was the intense, almost year-long negotiation in which Eliot and Pound achieved an arrangement by which the editors of the *Dial* would accept, sight unseen, Eliot's poem; pay him $150 for it; agree in advance to sweeten the deal with the *Dial* Award; time its publication with that of the poem in Eliot's own magazine, the *Criterion*, and with book publication by Boni and Liveright; and commit to buying 350 copies of the book. (Boni and Liveright gave Eliot $150 against royalties of 15%.) This arrangement marked what Lawrence Rainey has called "the crucial moment in the transition of modernism from a minority culture to one supported by an important institutional and financial apparatus."[4] Eliot's success could only heighten Iris's sense of failure in translating his poetry into cash (and perhaps even more his failure to have a poem worshiped by millions). At the time his own successes were distinctly minor affairs. As Monroe complained to her attorney on 24 November 1923, for example, Iris had forged yet another letter over her name, this one introducing him to Mr. and Mrs. Adolf Bohm and "soliciting tickets for the Bohm entertainment given one Sunday in October at the Apollo Theatre." Iris received the tickets.

Getting published continued to be difficult for Iris, now even more difficult because of what Monroe knew about his propensities. Probably in early 1924, however, after the death of Maurice Francis Egan on 15 January and of Woodrow Wilson on 3 February, Iris dusted off the preface Egan had written for him in 1917 and attached it to a typescript of 70 or so poems gathered under the title "Bread and Hyacinths." The title for the collection may have had its source in Sandburg's "Tentative (First Model) Definitions of Poetry," which had first appeared in the *Atlantic Monthly* for March 1923 and which presented 38 definitions.[5] Number 36 reads,

> Poetry is the achievement of the synthesis of hyacinths and biscuits.

It was even more likely that Iris had read journalist Harry Hansen's section on Sandburg in his *Midwest Portraits*, published the year before.[6] There Hansen quoted the definition and then told of a conversation in which Sandburg recalled a Persian proverb about selling one of two loaves of bread to buy hyacinths to feed the soul. According to Hansen, Sandburg responded to the proverb by voicing a complaint: "I have two baskets of white hyacinths and I wish to God I could sell one and buy me some bread to feed myself." That would be Iris's complaint as well.

To help sell "Bread and Hyacinths," he prepared a one-page preface signed with Wilson's name and purportedly dictated by him to Egan in 1923. The invented circumstances of the preface's production are not altogether implausible. After all, Wilson had never fully recovered from the stroke he suffered in October 1919, he did rely on dictation, and Egan was in fact on good terms with Wilson. Yet the letter Iris concocted to authenticate the preface cannot stand up to scrutiny. Bearing Iris's tracing of Egan's signature from a genuine letter (of 13 November 1917), the letter says, "I am enclosing preface dictated to me and signed by Woodrow Wilson with your manuscript, Bread and Hyacinths." The main difficulty, however, is that Iris dated the letter 12 October and gave a return address in Washington, D.C. At that time, Egan was already fatally ill and had been since 9 September, when an attack of gastroenteritis exacerbated his chronic kidney failure. Suffering periods of un- and semiconsciousness, he was confined to his summer home in Beach Haven, New Jersey, and then to his daughter's house in Brooklyn until his death on 15 January 1924.[7]

The publication of the preface itself would have led to its exposure as spurious. It has Wilson recalling Swinburne's and Francis Thompson's improbable praise of Iris's "April" as "the finest poem in the entire range of English literature," noting that Iris was "the first of the Italians in America to write poetry in English," and describing *Lyrics of a Lad* as shining "above the wrangling gutter snipe poets." About half of the preface, however, was plagiarized from Monroe's introduction to her anthology *The New Poetry*, where it appeared in both the 1917 and 1923 editions. Monroe's characterizations of the new poetry thus became Wilson's of Iris's, and at one place Monroe's quotation of Yeats's characterization of modern poetry becomes Wilson's of Iris's. Here is part of the preface:

> *Bread and Hyacinths* achieves a concrete and immediate realization of life; it discards the theory, the abstraction, the remoteness, found in all works of a lower order. It has set an ideal of absolute simplicity and sincerity, and is written in the language of contemporary speech. This poetry has passion, glamour, magic, spontaneous rhythm, and glorious imaginative life. It is like a cry of the heart.

And here are its sources in Monroe's introduction:

> The new poetry strives for a concrete and immediate realization of life; it would discard the theory, the abstraction, the remoteness, found in all classics not of the first order. . . . It has set before itself and ideal of absolute simplicity and sincerity. . . .
>
> Great poetry has always been written in the language of contemporary speech. . . .
>
> Synge wrote his plays . . . in a form which, whatever one calls it, is essentially poetry, for it has passion, glamour, magic, rhythm, and glorious imaginative life.
>
> As Mr. Yeats said in Chicago: . . . . We tried to strip away everything that was artificial, to get a style like speech, as simple as the simplest prose, like a cry of the heart.

The preface ends with "Wilson's" confessing that he "would rather have written [Iris's] 'After the Martyrdom' than to have been the president of the United States."

If it is difficult to fathom why Iris would feel the need to resort to plagiarism in forging the preface, it is even more difficult to understand why he would plagiarize from a work as popular as *The New Poetry* or from an editor who would have been wary of anything bearing Iris's name. Because Iris's forgery and plagiarism would certainly have been found out if "Bread and Hyacinths" had been published, it is tempting to conclude that Iris thought that being found out was at least to be found. That, he might have supposed, would be preferable to life as a lost poet. There is, however, a more likely possibility. Although the forged letter has Egan saying that he would "place the manuscript with the publisher who can best handle it," Iris may have intended sale rather than publication of the manuscript. Evidently he did sell it, for it made its way to the Dauber & Pine Bookshops, New York, where in 1928 it was sold to a collector for $150, no doubt largely because of the "Wilson" preface. The manuscript was never published, although some of its poems would appear in periodicals and in Iris's later books.

The poems reflect notable effort on Iris's part to modernize his work. Although some are in the old-fashioned manner predominant in *Lyrics* (indeed, a few are reprinted from there), most strive for the features that Monroe's introduction to *The New Poetry* identified as characteristic of modern poetry—concreteness, simplicity, contemporaneity of speech and subject, and metrical freedom. Many, in fact, adopt traits especially associated with Monroe herself and the other Midwestern poets she tended to favor, including major ones like Masters and Sandburg and minor ones like Mary Aldis and Eunice Tietjens, both of whom had editorial positions with Monroe's magazine. Like these poets, Iris turned out poems in which he talks to or for denizens of the city, especially members of the working class, as in "Steam Shovel Man":

> Lower that shovel. Keep
> Your nerve. Scoop it down deep—
> Lift it up. Let its mouth
> Vomit the wet clay out.
> And what's a drizzling rain
> When one can run a crane
> And show his sand and feel
> A skyscraper in steel?

Like them, he also adopted the old-fashioned device of apostrophe and used it to address not Romantic subjects such as clouds or birds but new-fashioned ones, as in "The Skyscraper," which could well be the poem he wanted William Wrigley to buy.

> Like a lily straight and white
> Obelisk of steel and light,
> Stem the night
>
> Guardsman of the city's power,
> Climbing marvel from your tower,
> Strike the hour.
>
> Lake and river flow and meet
> At the bridge beside your feet
> And the street.
>
> Tower, with your jewel of light,
> Fling your challenge to the night,
> Shining, white.
>
> Bird and plane about you fly;
> Lift your arms and touch the sky!
> Flash your eye!

Unfortunately, Iris came to this Midwestern style late. Its heyday was over. Even as early as 1917, it was clear that the high point of the first phase of the modernist revolution, in which Midwestern poets had a major part, had passed. As one reviewer of Monroe's *The New Poetry* said in 1918, "For the past year or two most of our poets have been merely repeating themselves."[8] And as Ellen Williams has observed, "The work of Lindsay and of Masters in 1917 and 1918 indicates that the brief glory of the middle-western renaissance was over."[9] Monroe's characterization of the new poetry might have fit that first phase. Now, however, especially after the publication of Eliot's *Waste Land* in 1922, there was a new way of being modern. Although Monroe continued to favor a potentially popular poetry marked by an affirmative attitude and a simplicity of thought and language, she was increasingly seeing a poetry of irony, complexity, discontinuity, and doubt, the product of what Monroe called "intellectualists," who believe that poetry "must rise above all contact with the common people" and who prefer "intricacies of motive and style."[10]

The forged preface to "Bread and Hyacinths" itself sent mixed messages about Iris's sense of himself as a "new" poet. On the one hand, it adopted for Iris's poetry Monroe's old-fashioned characterization of the new. On the other, it reached even further back into the past and dusted off testimony attributed to Swinburne and Thompson. For that matter, neither Egan nor Wilson carried with him any association with modern poetry of any type. Iris was naive or desperate—or both—in identifying voices to appropriate, yet his situation mirrored that of modern poets in general. From what sources might they leverage some cultural authority for their work? The literary past (Ruskin and Swinburne)? The state (Wilson)? The Church (Egan, roughly)? Several years later, Eliot would introduce a collection of his own literary essays as expressing a point of view "classicist in literature, royalist in politics, and anglo-catholic in religion."[11]

Perhaps for "Bread and Hyacinths" Iris also sought a preface from George Bernard Shaw, likewise not associated with modern poetry but at least alive and writing. Besides, he was a great writer of prefaces to his own work. Always fond of using intercessors, real or forged, who could help him get his way, Iris hit upon a new tactic for his approach to Shaw. He would adopt another pseudonym and become his own intercessor. Or, more precisely in this case, he would be offering an intercession on behalf of another intercessor, Jane Addams. Americanizing his first name and borrowing his stepfather's last name (also Americanized), he became Frederick Vincent. Using that name, he wrote to Shaw on 5 September 1924. He told Shaw that he was writing on behalf of Addams, who would appreciate Shaw's writing a preface for Iris, a neglected poet of great quality. Shaw finally replied on 19 December. He admitted that although Addams's interest in Iris did make "a claim on his attention" and although he was "sorry for a poet of some real talent who finds the publishers obdurate," he nonetheless declined to produce the desired preface:

> Every writer must succeed on his own merits. Hardly a fortnight passes without my being informed by some author that a publisher is willing to publish his book if I will supply a preface. That means simply that the publisher is willing to publish a book by me if he can get it for nothing. That kind of operation is quite out of the question. . . . I think Mr Iris will feel, on thinking the matter over, that he must stand on his own legs. If there is no market for his work in America nobody can make one for him by any legitimate means, or indeed make one at all for more than a season.

Iris presumably resented the advice to stand on his own legs and limit himself to "legitimate means." He may have resented even more Shaw's comment and advice about his name. Shaw wondered if his name was in fact Scharmel Iris, a name that "is enough to kill ten poets." He suggested that Vincent tell Iris to present his name to some movie star and to adopt in its place the name Peter Wilkins or "something credible and sensible."


Late the following year Iris learned of the founding of the John Simon Guggenheim Memorial Foundation and its fellowships to support work in the arts and sciences. Here there was no question of standing on one's own legs. The foundation required applicants to supply letters of recommendation. Iris asked Sandburg and Addams. On 19 December 1925 Sandburg replied, "I hope that the Committee will give full consideration to all your claims. Your book, 'Lyrics of a Lad,' should convince of your exceptional ability in a work of sustained length and of genius in lyric lines. You are deserving, finely and emphatically so, of a year of the advantages and opportunities of the Fellowship." The brief and relatively restrained support for Iris's "claims" suggests that the letter, on *Chicago Daily News* stationery, is genuine. Sandburg as well as Iris was capable of the presumably inadvertent pun in the phrase "genius in lyric lines."

On 21 December, Iris received a two-sentence letter from Addams. She addressed it to the foundation's selection committee: "I have know [*sic*] Fred Scharmel Iris intermitently [*sic*] for several years, during which time he has struggled with ill health and many other disabilities. With many of his other friends, I should be glad if he could have a year of liesure [*sic*] in congenial surroundings in which to go on with his writing."[12]

Probably after sending these letters on to the foundation, Iris learned that the application process was a bit more formal than he had imagined. He needed a plan for the fellowship period. And another letter, a stronger letter, would be useful. So on 10 February 1926 he typed out copies of Sandburg's and Addams's letters, altering Addams's to correct misspellings and to say that she had known Iris for many years rather than "intermitently." He sent the copies, along with a plan of study for the grant period, an extract from Egan's preface to *Lyrics,* and sample poems from *Lyrics,* to Edgar Lee Masters. He planned to write and translate: "I wish to continue creative work already begun in the field of lyric poetry. Furthermore, I greatly desire to search the principal libraries of Italy and France in order to collect and translate into metrical English the best lyrics of the countries." In Paris, he also will consult with Ezra Pound; in London, arrange with John Lane the publication of some translations and poems. He concluded: "To enrich the art of poetry is my hope, my aim, my religion!" In his accompanying letter, Iris asked Masters, whom he addresses as "friend," to write him a recommendation, just "as Miss Addams and our good friend Sandburg has [sic] done." He asked that it be "convincing, spirited, and snappy." Perhaps to jog Masters's memory of him or even to create a memory, he then asked, "Do you remember when we used to drink Bulgarian sour milk?" In a postscript, Iris requested that the letter or a copy of it be sent to him.

On 14 February, Masters replied that he would supply the letter but that he would rather see Iris plan to "write of America—its change through absorption of other people" and to do this "through his Italian émigré eyes." Three days later, Iris thanked Masters for replying, and he explained that he would undertake some "creative work" as well as the translation and that travel to Europe would help him "do the work from the standpoint of an Italian émigré." Double underscoring the first three words, he added: "Confidentially, dear Masters, while I am in Europe both Augustus John and [illegible name, possibly "Picasso"] will do portrait heads of me which is some thing even for a poet to appreciate. These men are big and these portraits along with my work will get me a publisher. In order to get across I had to do something that would interest the professorial mind so I included the translation idea. . . . The "Lyrics of a Lad" were done before my eighteenth year." He urged Masters to say that he needed a two-year fellowship.

Masters then wrote his letter addressed to the selection committee.[13] It is longer than the Addams and Sandburg letters, but not much. Relying on the extract from Egan's preface to *Lyrics*, Masters noted that Iris is "an Italian American poet of Chicago, who has had many difficulties in the prosecution of his creative work." He said that Iris desires to visit libraries to collect and translate lyrics from Italy and France and to pursue his "creative interests . . . centered upon an interpretation of America and of this particular period of American life, which the work in the lyrics of Italy and France would help him to do." He "very heartily" recommended "him and his cause."

Meanwhile, perhaps from Sandburg or Addams, Monroe heard about Iris's application. She told Henry Allen Moe, of the Guggenheim Foundation, that Iris had forged a letter from her to boost his poem on the Wrigley Building and that the *Chicago Examiner* had revealed an instance of Iris's plagiarism.[14] Iris did not receive a Guggenheim fellowship.

Remaining in Chicago, Iris was increasingly isolated. Years earlier, Chicago's bid to become the nation's literary center flopped. The *Little Review* left Chicago for New York in 1917 and then for Paris in 1924. In 1918 the *Dial,* too, went on to New York, and there, no longer playing the role of critical old fogy as it had in Chicago, it modernized itself and stole most of the major modernists away from *Poetry*. Monroe continued to smart under the charge that the Midwestern poets, in contrast to Eliot, were "ploppeyed bungaroos."[15] Furthermore, as she made clear in an October 1930 editorial, she considered her early hopes for *Poetry* as a self-sustaining enterprise thoroughly dashed. In the editorial she recalled her dream "of winning the ten thousand subscribers whose two or three dollars a year would enable the magazine to carry on without further support from guarantors." Now, she realized, the magazine could not make even half that goal. The supply of poetry greatly exceeded the demand. The Depression was making matters worse for the magazine and for the poets, who "shouldn't have to be paid starvation wages or nothing at all." Expressing sentiments with which Iris would agree, Monroe called for "men and women of sufficient wealth and culture" to "subsidize poetry" just as they have the other arts.[15]

Iris's situation was particularly difficult. Until her death in 1936 Monroe remained a major impediment to his career. Perhaps for that reason there is little record of his activities in this decade. He did make an appearance, at least twice, in June Provines's gossip column "This Gala World," published in the *Chicago Daily News*. In each case he emerges somewhat mysteriously among a swirl of celebrity that, by implication, would be better granted to him. He steals the show.

On 9 April 1930, Provines had Sandburg, "in his own fashion," tell of seeing Iris in the company of Edith Rockefeller McCormick, Jane Addams, and Mei Lan-Fang, the star of a troupe of Chinese actors then touring the United States:

"Were you ever haunted by a face?" [Sandburg] asks. "He had been the subject of a rapid sketch by Sargent, and Boldini had painted him with the loveliest of all present-day beauties, Lina Cavalieri. It was like meeting a ghost as he emerged from the Casino flanked by Chicago's queen of society and America's dean of sociologists. With China's finest actor they stepped into a liveried vehicle and sped to a gray stone house inclosed by a huge iron fence."

"I could not forget that face, but it was the Muse who whispered: 'It is none other than the poet, Scharmel Iris.'"[17]

Sandburg's fashion here was surely Iris's. If Sandburg saw the column, he doubtless joined Monroe as someone Iris could no longer turn to for help. When another celebrity, in this case Irish poet Æ, visited Chicago in October of the same year, Iris had another opportunity to make a haunting appearance:

The tea was for George (A.E.) Russell, and the long tea table was covered with a brocade of gold and silver threads woven in a classical oriental pattern. The glistening gold service had graced the palace of an empress and the room was a bower of yellow chrysanthemums grown only for the empress of China by a special imperial decree.

Warm and mellow grew the room with the hum of sparkling conversation and the aroma of jasmine tea, the almond cookies and sweets colored like confetti at a carnival.

After two hours, during which dignified dowagers awaited the arrival of the Irish mystic, he was to be seen outside saying farewell to SCHARMEL IRIS, the young poet, in whose company he had nearly forgotten his tea engagement.

"More than any one else I have enjoyed your company," A.E. said, breaking a silence that had lasted over a five-mile walk.

He handed Scharmel Iris a book.

"W. B. YEATS asked me to give this to you. He had it printed by hand at the press of his sister and it consists of but one poem . . . your poem 'April' . . . one of the finest lyrics in the entire range of English literature. Good-by."

These items must have been fed to Provines by Iris himself, who at 41 was still playing the part of a "young poet" and imagining himself possessed of exceptional beauty and good connections, even if he was also something of a ghost, someone who would likely be forgotten were his face not so exceptional. There is no evidence that the press alluded to in the column, Cuala Press, ever printed Iris's poem. There is the possibility, of course, that Iris had forged the "book" to which the column refers and was here manufacturing some authentication for it. It might have fetched a tidy sum in the market for "fine editions" that burgeoned in the 1920s and 1930s.


Iris would not have been forgotten by Monroe. Iris could expect little welcome from the offices of *Poetry*, but in the 1930s, in the midst of the Depression, using pseudonyms and appealing to that part of Monroe (and it was a big part) that saw her magazine as an instrument of charity and to that part (also big) that saw it as a discoverer of primitive singers of genius, Iris hoodwinked Monroe into accepting him nonetheless. Drawing in part on poems he had collected for "Bread and Hyacinths," as Seth James he had six poems in the August 1931 issue of *Poetry*; as Wesley Ames, five poems in the September 1931 issue; as John Creagh, five in the October 1931 issue; as Stanley Blackpool, four in the May 1934 issue; and as Everett Owens, four in the August 1934 issue.

Iris submitted the poems with letters telling stories of terrible hardship and asking for advance payment (and in two cases asking, after publication, for additional payment). As Iris knew, Monroe used her associate editors to screen submissions. As Iris also knew, unusual letters would pass through the screen, taking the poems with them. Seth James, now living in Chicago, was "born in Wales and worked in its coal mines 'when but a youngster.'" "After migrating to China and much wandering, he is now hoping for a permanent job in South Chicago."[18] Wesley Ames, in La Jolla, California, has been "struck by a hit-and-run driver (my hip is in a cast)," and his funds have been depleted in caring for his sister, who has been "in poor health since infancy." He writes his letter on the back of a newspaper carrier's form for a daily cash account. John Creagh, of general delivery, Chicago, lost his wife in childbirth and his house by foreclosure after he first lost his job. He now lives "from hand to mouth" and sleeps "in flop house after flop house." Some of the payment will buy him a pair of secondhand shoes; the rest will go toward "the care and maintenance" of his "little baby." He has, he says, "accomplished little in life." Everett Owens, Chicago, lost his job of 15 years and spends his days walking six miles to visit his hospital-ized mother. Stanley Blackpool, general delivery, Chicago, lost his father, who "died in a bread-line on West Madison Street." By the time he had found the body, it "had already gone to medical students in the interest of science." Blackpool now earns ten cents a day, though he had been able to support his mother quite well before her death. Now, he needs an overcoat, since he sleeps "below the bridge with nothing between me and the river but a shabby suit and the much soiled draft of these poems."[19]

Monroe was not without curiosity. She asked Creagh to stop by the *Poetry* office, but he replied that he was about to leave to repair an abandoned farmhouse and would be out of town for a few months. Similarly, Everett Owens's six-mile walks occupied him fully. Monroe annotated Blackpool's letter: "Yes—If he comes in & I am at home, call me up. I don't want to miss him. Read the letter—I told him to come some A.M. before 12." In her letter of acceptance Monroe wished she could find him an over-coat and agreed to advance payment. She also remarked that the poems struck her as "rather mild for a man whose experience has been so severe." She suggested: "Why don't you write about the real things you have known and suffered instead of about the moon, myrrh and rue, and penny whistles, and Angelina in heaven, and other things that everybody writes about?" Just as she had for Iris more than twenty years earlier, so did she now offer to tutor Blackpool, who would not be able to accept her generous offer.[20]

Iris may have submitted work under other names, successfully and unsuccessfully, but the success of Ames, Blackpool, Creagh, James, and Owens makes for a record many poets would have been proud of. *Poetry* was using about 500 rejection slips a month, and additional rejections were made in person.[21] Not only did Iris's pseudonymous poems get accepted, but also two of the batches—those of Ames and James—received honorable mentions in the magazine's announcement of awards for 1931.[22]

# CHAPTER FOUR

# NONPUBLISHING POET, 1940–1949

"After all, what is a fine lie? Simply that which is its own evidence. If a man is sufficiently unimaginative to produce evidence in support of a lie, he might just as well speak the truth at once."—Oscar Wilde, "The Decay of Lying"

For the rest of the 1930s and on into the early 1940s, Iris's activities remain for now largely a mystery. The death of Monroe in 1936 did not bring him out into the open as one might have expected. He had not, however, given up his quest for patronage nor his penchant for scheming. He wanted for himself the kind of financial support Monroe had toiled for years to secure for her magazine. Because *Poetry* had never become self-sufficient, she had continued to rely instead on annual pledges from its "guarantors"—Chicago architects, attorneys, bankers, brokers, meatpackers, real estate developers, society matrons, and so on. A few years before Monroe's death, Pound told her that he regarded *Poetry* as a "monument" to the fact that she had "extracted from among the porkpackers a few less constipated and made them PAY money for the upkeep of poesy."[1] Iris too wanted "upkeep." Over the years, since the founding of *Poetry* in 1912, in addition to notable cases of direct patronage, such as John Quinn's of Pound himself and Lady Gregory's of Yeats, there had in fact arisen considerable institutional support for poets and poetry. There were a great many prizes and grants, such as the Dial award, the Pulitzer prize for poetry, and Guggenheim fellowship, and there were increasing numbers of college and university appointments available as enrollments soared and as American literature became a standard part of the curriculum. Also, during the Depression years, the federal government had supported writers through the Works Progress Administration's Federal Writers' Project (1935–1939), employing at one time as many as 5,000. In Chicago, continued by state sponsorship until 1943, the project had hired, among others, Nelson Algren, Saul Bellow, Jack Conroy, Willard Motley, Louis "Studs" Terkel, Richard Wright, and Frank Yerby.[2] Iris, though, seems to have been averse to employment and, perhaps because of his failed Guggenheim application, to the scrutiny that applications entailed. He may have had some jobs, perhaps clerical ones, but there is no record of them. Ideally, though, he would have the poet, not simply the poetry, exist in an autonomous aesthetic realm.

Even before the February 1940 issue of *Reader's Digest* printed an article on Louise de Koven Bowen, Iris knew of her lifelong service as a philanthropist and as "social conscience" of Chicago; indeed, he may well have met or at least seen her at Hull-House, one of the beneficiaries of her activist philanthropy and the headquarters for her Juvenile Protective Association.[3] After the article, she was flooded with mail from people asking for assistance. In October Iris added his request to the hundreds Bowen had already received. A reply came from Bowen's secretary, who said that she was obliged to deny all such pleas and that, given the many connections of which he had boasted, "there ought to be someone to whom you could turn who would have a strong enough personal interest in you to give you the assistance you need."[4]

The kinds of connections Iris was claiming at the time might be seen in another of Iris's apparitional appearances by way of a gossip column—this time Louis Sobol's "A Bit of This and That about People and Things" in the *New York Journal American* for 20 November 1940:

> A poet drifts with the rain-drenched crowd in Times Square. He is
> Scharmel Iris and of him Carl Sandburg once said: "He is a genius
> in the lyric field" and of his poem *April,* W. B. Yeats wrote: "It is
> one of the finest lyrics in the entire range of English literature."
> When he was a precocious youngster, the immortal Duse took his
> hands and sighed over them: "These are lovely hands—the most
> beautiful in the world. How can they belong to a boy!" Sarah
> Bernhardt read to sculptor Rodin his poem, *The Old Courtesan,* and
> Rodin was inspired to create the famous statue now bearing the
> poem's title. And on a day last week amid the afternoon's down-
> pour he drifted with the Times Square crowd.[5]

Of the figures mentioned, only Iris and Sandburg were living.
Sandburg's heyday as a poet was over, and Iris could no longer
trade on his being but a lad, a "precocious youngster."

In 1943 Iris made a more substantial appearance. He went to
Mexico to play the part of *el famoso poeta norteamericano* and to
get his portrait painted by Diego Rivera. Just who gave him the
wherewithal to make the trip and how he got it are not entirely
apparent from the evidence available but can be inferred from
the notices Iris arranged in the Mexican press.[6] Probably as Fred-
erick Vincent, Iris wrote to Archibald MacLeish, poet and librar-
ian of Congress and assistant director of the Office of War Infor-
mation, telling him that the famed Mexican painter wanted (or
at least agreed) to undertake Iris's portrait if Iris could get to
Mexico. MacLeish got Nelson Rockefeller, who was then coordi-
nator of Inter-American Relations, to arrange for flight priority.
Needing funds for the trip, Iris approached Bernard J. Sheil, aux-
iliary bishop of Chicago and founder of the Catholic Youth Or-
ganization. Or possibly Sheil had entered the picture earlier and,
drawing on his friendship with the Roosevelt administration, ran
interference for Iris with the government. At any rate, Sheil
seems to have provided financial support. Only three years older
than Iris and having grown up on Chicago's West Side, Sheil may
have known Iris and would have seen his work in the *New World.*
Besides, Sheil was known for fiscal indifference, even profligacy,
and it was said by some that his "heart was bigger than his brain."[7]
(In the following year, Sheil helped another impoverished poet. He
hired Claude McKay, the Harlem Renaissance poet, as a consultant
at his Sheil School of Social Studies, even though McKay was so ill
that he "could do little more than occupy a desk.")[8]

Iris arrived in Mexico City in February. He told reporters that, for the Macmillan publishing house and under the auspices of a coordinating committee directed by Rockefeller, he was there in Mexico to select material for an anthology of modern Mexican poetry and to have his portrait painted by Rivera. Furthermore, he had the ear of President Roosevelt, who said that a man like him "who has fought a war of thirty years for North American poetry is a good soldier." These claims may have helped Iris in dealing with his hosts. Getting Rivera to draw him did take some work, but Iris was eventually successful. Iris later would boast that he "took the chair Rivera reserved for subjects he chose to paint, not the one for those paying fabulous fees to be painted by Rivera." His boast was probably only that. On 7 April, so that Iris could return to the States with the portrait, he and Rivera completed the U.S. Foreign Service form "Declaration in Connection with Paintings, etc., and Sculptures." On the form Rivera declared that he was the artist who painted the oil portrait of Iris, measuring 17" by 21½" and having a value of $600. Rivera also completed a drawing of Iris sitting in a chair, if the frontispiece to Iris's next book can be trusted. In his accounting of purchases made in Mexico, Iris listed two caricatures he had some unknown artist draw at a cost of one peso. He could have signed one for Rivera. On the other hand, given Iris's fondness of portraits of himself, the purchase of cheap caricatures as additions to whatever Rivera completed would not at all be out of character for him.[9] Iris meanwhile had also written a series of poems set in Mexico and toyed with various titles for the collection, including "Bouquet of Mexico," "Mexican Opal," and "Mexican Recital." No anthology of Mexican poetry emerged from Iris's trip.

Just what Iris was doing when not traveling and writing poetry and letters is not clear. Later in life he would claim that he never worked at anything other than poetry and never had a Social Security card. One incident from 1944, though, gives a bit of insight into his circumstances and perhaps even suggests that he did have to resort to taking a job of some sort. Iris continued to live at the family home on South Trumbull Street as the neighborhood gradually deteriorated through the Great Depression and during the war. Quite near the house, at 3425 Fifth Avenue, was a busy tavern. Iris lodged a complaint with the police about the tavern's noisy jukebox, unruly patrons, and underage drinkers. The investigating officers reported that they found no evidence to support his complaint. They also reported that they had failed in their efforts to talk with "Scharmel Iris, 'The Catholic Poet,' whose name was given in the complaint as being able to confirm the conditions." They had gone to his residence on the second floor of 331 South Trumbull but did not find him at home. His sister, Josephine Beckman, living on the first floor, told them that he could be seen there before 10:00 a.m.[10] A job may have taken him out of the house by that hour.

Later that same year, Iris sought another vacation from Trumbull Street and another portrait. He schemed to get free lodging for two weeks in New York, where he would attempt to have his portrait painted by Salvador Dali. So, using the name Frederick Vincent, he wrote Conrad Hilton, saying that Dali had invited Iris to New York and that the poor poet needed a place to stay. Vincent would appreciate Iris's being granted a free room at the Waldorf-Astoria. Iris probably was not successful with the hotel; he certainly was not with the portrait. He would try again, though, ten years later.[11] Iris's fascination with portraits of himself reflected, of course, his narcissism and tendency to regard himself as an aesthetic object. His narcissism seemed to demand the reassurance of identity afforded by gazing at his own image. His efforts to secure portraits also provided him with opportunities to enlist famous artists in his fantasy and self-fashioning. Further, he enjoyed manipulating people, especially the famous, so that they participated in his fantasy and self-fashioning. But portraits had practical functions too. They could, he was sure, help him secure a publisher and, when published as frontispieces or as illustrations for newspaper articles, boost his reputation. He probably had in mind a frontispiece by Dali or Rivera—or both, since a large and growing stock of poems had accumulated since the publication of *Lyrics* in 1914.

In 1943, with a book manuscript in mind, Iris sought and received permission from *Poetry* magazine to reprint the poems he had published pseudonymously there in the 1930s.[12] At about the same time, he settled on the title for a collection and wrote a preface that he attributed to William Butler Yeats, who had died in 1939. He dated the preface 1934 and concocted a story explaining the delay between its composition and publication, a delay that eventually grew to almost 20 years.

For the book's title Iris chose *Bread out of Stone*. The preface begins by explaining the allusion. Robert Burns's mother, it says, was reputed to have exclaimed after a stone was placed on her son's grave, "He asked for bread and ye gave him a stone!" Iris probably was also familiar with a poem by Robert Buchanan, the nineteenth-century English poet and novelist now best known as the author of "The Fleshly School of Poetry" (1871), an attack on the Pre-Raphaelites, including Rossetti and Swinburne, that prompted a controversy that was still alive to Ezra Pound in *Hugh Selwyn Mauberley* (1920), where he refers to "Fœtid Buchanan." The third section of Buchanan's "Dedication: Ad Matrem" of his poem *The Earthquake* (1885) begins:

I asked for bread—a stone was given;
   I asked for Fame—men mock'd at me;
I asked for Love—my heart was riven
   By man's worst cruelty.[13]

Iris would have appreciated the sentiment. Also, both sources themselves allude to the conclusion to the Sermon on the Mount, where Christ asks, "What man is there of you, whom if his son ask bread, will he give him a stone?" (Matthew 7: 9). The allusion also figures in one of the poems Iris was including in the book manuscript:

**I Wander and Wonder**

I wander and wonder and walk all alone
Who ask for some bread and am given a stone.
I wonder how Christ felt when He walked like me
And wandered and wondered and saw what I see.

He wandered and wondered and He a great king.
I wander and wonder on how he could bring
To have Himself crucified high on the tree,
And all for the love of a poor one like me.

The preface claims for Iris just that kind of neglect: "For four decades Scharmel Iris sought bread in return for his poems but instead of bread the world cast him a stone." Nevertheless, Iris's false Yeats says, Iris has made "bread out of stone," a bread that can "appease our spiritual hunger." Actually, there is some complicated shifting of terms here. Initially bread refers to the means of sustenance, as it did in the earlier title "Bread and Hyacinths"; then it becomes, like "hyacinths," a term for poetry. At the same time, the allusion implies a comparison to Christ: Iris's poetry, like the bread that is the body of Christ, feeds our spiritual hunger. But there is a counter allusion too: in making bread out of stone Iris is performing a miracle that Christ refused to perform when tempted to do so by the devil (Matthew 4: 1–11; Luke 4: 1–13). Making bread out of stone is precisely what Christ would not do.

It is not surprising that the preface offers high praise for Iris. In it, a weepy version of Yeats admits, "I have carried the manuscript about with me for days, and I have often had to close it for the tears I could not stem." This Yeats says that "of poets writing today there are no greater" than Iris, whose voice is like that of St. Francis—"simple, orderly, burning with beauty and with a passion for perfection." "All is near and dear to him." The preface calls the poem "Pause during Rhythm" a "dark fire-filled gem, a gem of the first water":

> On a grape-colored hill
> Against a greying sky
> Blue-flame,
> Florescent,
> Your heels have cooled on fandangos.
> Let fall your shawl.
> Your rose-fuchsia, wine-petunia shawl.
> Let your hair fall
> Over the feet of Christ.
> You have no need of lilies, virgin.
> And do your eyes, luminous with tears,
> Search still for the last, lost glint of grace?

The preface finds "April" to be "one of the finest lyrics in the entire range of English literature":

> I loved her more than moon or sun—
>     There is no moon or sun for me;
> Of lovely things to look upon,
>     The loveliest was she.

> She does not hear me, though I sing—
>     And, oh, my heart is like to break!
> The world awakens with the Spring,
>     But she, she does not wake!

If Yeats were in fact to have written the preface, he would have had to rely on references supplied by Iris. It quotes Sandburg's Guggenheim letter, changing "genius in lyric lines" to "a genius in the lyric field." Reaching back in time, it says that Francis Thompson had judged Iris's poems "worthy of the best poets." It also tells us, again as we have been told before, that Sarah Bernhardt's reading of a French version of the poem "Old Courtezan" (spelled thus in the preface but not in the text) had "inspired the chisel of the immortal Rodin" to create his "statue" *The Old Courtesan*. (More properly known as *The Helmet-Maker's Wife* the sculpture has also been said to have been inspired by François Villon. It was completed sometime before 1885, that is, before Iris's birth.)[14] More peculiar is the fact that the preface repeats verbatim a passage from a letter Yeats wrote Monroe in January 1916, when he declined to appear in the first edition of *The New Poetry*. (At some point Iris had copied the letter, probably when he still had access to Monroe's *Poetry* office.) He detested anthologies, he said:

> It means being paraded before the public with a lot of people to whom one hasn't been introduced. Browning said of his wife, "She likes being with the others," and added that he didn't.[15]

Still smarting from his removal from the second edition of Monroe's anthology and from his sparse appearance in anthologies generally, Iris could here link himself with Yeats as one who detests this mode of publication. Yeats, however, agreed to be admitted to the second edition. Further, in 1934, when he was supposedly recalling words he wrote 28 years earlier and continuing to detest anthologies, Yeats was himself compiling *The Oxford Book of Modern Verse, 1892–1935*. He did not choose to include Iris.

The two poems praised in the preface give some idea of the range of work Iris was selecting for the volume. "April," reminiscent of Wordsworth's "A Slumber Did My Spirit Seal," had appeared in *Lyrics*; "Pause during Rhythm" was more recent work, reflecting Iris's efforts in free verse. In fact, there would be great variety in the volume and no sense of a single persona, voice, or even poet. That is not surprising, since it would include work that Iris published in *Poetry* under six different names. Although the volume's contents would change over the years as it wound its uncertain way toward eventual publication, for some reason Iris always planned for a fairly slim collection. He had the preface explain why this "sheaf of poems" should be "slender as a woman's hand." One of the many blows life had struck, according to the preface, was the theft of Iris's "poetical labours of some twenty years." That explanation excuses the slimness and simultaneously gives a sort of self-authentication for the date given the preface, 1934. It would have been 20 years since *Lyrics* appeared.

By 1945, in his search for a publisher, Iris had somehow enlisted the aid of Marshall Field III.[16] Four years earlier, the department store heir, philanthropist, and businessman had entered publishing by founding the *Chicago Sun,* as a competitor with the only other morning paper in Chicago at the time, Colonel Robert McCormick's *Chicago Tribune.* And then, in 1944, he acquired Pocket Books and Simon and Schuster. Although he was not known for meddling in editorial policy, he could prove an influential conduit to those who made editorial decisions. It may well have been through Bishop Sheil that Iris got Field's attention. Field and Bishop Sheil were friends. They served together on an American committee providing asylum for and immigration of European children during World War II, and both were mavericks in their areas—strong liberals who fought alongside one another in defense of civil liberties, in promoting child welfare, and in pursuing other social causes. Field had lapsed from faith, but evidently Sheil and he did not discuss it or it was not an issue between them. At any rate, Iris got the manuscript to Field.

Field asked his employee A. C. Spectorsky to handle the matter by submitting the manuscript to Simon and Schuster. With the manuscript, Iris had sent an unsigned one-page note entitled "Plans to Further the Interests of the Publishers and the Author." Iris wrote these plans as if everything mentioned in them had already been arranged. They called for the release of photographs of Iris with Diego Rivera and with Ezequiel Padilla, Mexico's foreign minister. The pictures would appear in *Life* magazine upon publication of the book, while at the same time the *Chicago Tri-*

*bune* would print a color photograph of the Diego portrait and the *American Weekly* would "reproduce photographs of the poet among the 300 year-old mummies of nuns and priests of the 400 year-old Mexican convent of the Carmelites." Never before, Iris added, had such photographs been allowed to leave Mexico, but he "was granted diplomatic immunity."

Simon and Schuster may not have been impressed by these plans, but they did have some interest in the poems and in the preface bearing Yeats's name. On 2 May 1945, however, Max Schuster wrote Spectorsky to say that they would decline to publish the poems. He himself said that although he "liked some of the poems immensely," he "had negative feelings about quite a few others." Because of the "extraordinary tribute from W. B. Yeats," he had asked several colleagues and editors to read the manuscript and finally sought a judgment from Louis Untermeyer, the minor poet, indefatigable anthologist, glib reviewer, and influential adviser to several publishers.

Schuster forwarded to Spectorsky a copy of Untermeyer's report. It called the collection remarkably uneven, with a few impressive poems, "pointed with sharp images and enriched with long implications." The rest are "weak" or "merely adequate." Furthermore, many of the poems were derivative, and the whole collection, then, "a jumble of influences, a bundle of broken mirrors." Untermeyer heard echoes of Hodgson, Housman, Pound, Sandburg, and the early Yeats. He could not believe that Yeats meant the preface, supposing he might have been "drunk" or influenced by Iris's plight. His "darkest suspicion," though, was that Yeats was not its author. Untermeyer, however, did leave an opening. He said that if the book were to be published, it would need another foreword or an epilogue to explain the dramatic story of Iris's resurrection and clarify the mysteries of Sarah Bernhardt's reading one of the poems to Rodin, of Sandburg's calling him genius, and of praise by Thompson (dead now for 40 years). Perhaps, Untermeyer suggested, Sandburg would "write a page or two clearing up these mysteries." On 15 May 1945 Spectorsky sent Schuster's letter and Untermeyer's report on to Field, asking what he should do next. Field asked him to send the poems to another publisher, Farrar and Rinehart, which rejected them on 25 June 1945.[17]

Meanwhile, having gotten a copy of Untermeyer's report, Iris went about gathering or manufacturing testimony to authenticate the Yeats preface and vouch for his own character and worth as a poet. He sent a letter from the Reverend Vincent E. Scheltinga, pastor of Our Lady of Sorrows Church, to Field (17 July 1945) in which Scheltinga explained that he had known Iris for 25 years and considered him "a man of unquestionable integrity." Scheltinga went on to say that Iris had shown him in late 1939 the preface by Yeats, which was dated 1934 and came in an envelope that "bore Irish stamps of a new and unusual issue" and thus caught his eye. Shortly thereafter, Iris had told him that his nephew, Robert Lee Vincenzo, who was then beginning a descent into dementia praecox and was now in the state hospital at Elgin, probably had destroyed both preface and poetry manuscript. (How the preface re-emerged to explain its own loss is not told.) Then, from a Frank Wolcott he secured a notarized letter (21 July 1945) stating that he had known Iris since 1914 and that Iris had intervened with Yeats to get a picture for Wolcott's "collection of famous sitters."

In addition, Iris possessed two notarized affidavits. One, by James B. Shanahan, of Beverley Shores, Indiana, dated 27 July 1945, affirmed that in 1928 he had seen a three-page letter in which Shaw said he liked Iris's poems but would not write a preface for free. (Recall that Shaw did write on 19 December 1924 a one-page letter refusing to write a preface.) Shanahan then provided his Social Security number in case he "should fall under the suspicion of being another pseudonym of Scharmel Iris." The other affidavit, dated 17 July 1945, came from Frank J. Corleto, 3616 West Polk Street, Chicago:

> On March 1st, 1914 while I was visiting with Miss Jane Addams at Hull-House Mr. Charles L. Hutchinson, president of the Corn Exchange Bank, telephoned Miss Addams saying that he and the Irish poet, Yeats, would like to have as their guest my neighbor Mr. Scharmel Iris at POETRY'S first dinner party that evening but that he could not find Mr. Iris listed in the telephone directory. Miss Addams informed him that Mr. Iris had suffered severe hemorrhages of the lungs but would see what she could do and so sent me to fetch him to her.
>
> When Mr. Hutchinson came in his car to take Mr. Iris to the Cliff Dwellers Club she urge [*sic*] me to go along so that he would have help in case of need and company for his trip back home. After the banquet and in the presence of B.L.T. [Bert Leston Taylor, *Chicago Tribune* columnist and writer of light verse], Wallace

> Rice (Encyclopedia Britannica's authority on English usage) and myself he called Mr. Iris's "April"—"one of the finest lyrics in the entire range of English literature" and had agreed to do a preface for the poems.
>
> I wish also to testify that years earlier when but a boy I heard Mr. Charles O'Malley twice editor of the *New World* and *Ave Maria* read a passage from a letter he had from Francis Thompson which said that the poems of Mr. Iris were "worthy of the best poets". After his death I tried to purchase the letter from his wife, S. M. O'Malley but she turned down the offer though badly in need of money. Until asked if I remembered these two incidents, not having seen Mr. Iris in twenty years, I was under the impression that Mr. Iris had died.

All of these pieces of evidence, along with copies of Addams's, Masters's, and Sandburg's letters of reference for his Guggenheim application, Iris mailed to Field on 29 September 1945. His letter accompanying the materials had gone through at least two drafts. The earlier (30 July 1945) is primarily an angry diatribe against Untermeyer, "Manhattan's poetry pope sadistically wielding the czaristic ax, but only under the cowardly cover of darkness." With a fine sense of irony (one hopes), Iris said that Untermeyer's report should be "accepted with a grain of salt" because it was "so curiously mixed with fact and fiction as to create a grave doubt as to its forthrightness." He prayed that Field would "have the fortitude" to stand against Untermeyer's judgment. The second draft, probably the final one, emphasized more the point that some 38 of the poems had been accepted for publication by Monroe, "the severest of critics." It also allowed the possibility of substituting some poems for those Untermeyer objected to. Furthermore, Iris said, he might be able to get a foreword or epilogue by Archibald MacLeish or some other poet or critic. Despite Iris's documents and pleas, Eddie Doherty of the *Chicago Sun* wrote Iris on 10 October 1945 to say that Marshall Field had done what he could to help Iris with his publishing firm Simon and Schuster. Field, Doherty said, would not interfere with the publisher's decision to reject the book, "Untermeyer or no Untermeyer."

Also in 1945, still smarting from this rejection and now writing as Frederick Vincent, Iris sent Robert Morss Lovett a whole package of material to help him in writing a foreword or introduction. At the time, hounded in the United States for his pacifist and liberal activism, Lovett was serving as a visiting professor of English at the University of Puerto Rico. But he had been a professor at the University of Chicago and a resident of Hull-House in the 1920s and 1930s.[18] He and Iris probably had met. In the package Iris put his transcriptions of the Spanish-language articles on his trip to Mexico. He also transcribed for Lovett the "Line o' Type or Two" column from the 2 April 1938 *Chicago Daily Tribune* telling a story about Our Lady of Sorrows Church, where Iris suggested that "neutral blue velvet" rather than purple velvet be used for the background of the church's replica of Michelangelo's Pieta. In gratitude, the church would send Iris a single orchid each year on the anniversary of the event. (Actually, Iris fudged this transcription. The columnist June Provines had written that she had been told Iris was sent an orchid every year but that in fact a church newsletter had simply said by way of thanks, "an orchid to Scharmel Iris for the suggestion.")

Iris also transcribed, in these instances accurately, Provines's column about his haunting face accompanying Edith Rockefeller McCormick, Jane Addams, and the Chinese actor Mei Lan-fang and her column on his largely silent talk with Æ. Finally, Vincent (Iris, remember) provided a two-page, single-spaced account of Iris's career as a poet, which Lovett was invited to use whole or in part in writing a preface to *Bread*. Lovett did write a preface, and it did in fact incorporate substantial chunks of the account, but he also found some of the account and some of the other items sent him offensive. He warned Vincent that he had left out "all references to the somewhat silly patronage of Bernhardt, Duse, Pavlova, and Lina Cavalieri." He also omitted other names dropped heavily in Iris's account, including Æ, Rupert Brooke, Mother Cabrina, Enrico Caruso, James Joyce, Joyce Kilmer, Waslaw Nijinsky, Diego Rivera, Theodore Roosevelt, and Rabindranath Tagore. Lovett avoided "the insufferably vulgar stuff of June Provines." And while he made some use of the theme of beauty-born-of-suffering, he did not, as Iris had done, draw constant parallels between Iris and Christ. Iris had seen himself in a "crown of thorns" grown from privation; he had conversed with Bernhardt in the theater as Christ had with the wise men in the temple; he had found himself "on the road to Calvary"; he had foreseen "the Golgotha which was to come"; and finally, through his art, he foresaw that he would "survive his crucifixion," and "no one will ever remember who it was that drove the nails." For a time, Iris did attach Lovett's introduction to the manuscript of *Bread out of Stone*. He later removed it so that it did not appear until 1963, when it was grafted to Iris's *A Singing Reed*, seven years after Lovett's death.

While Lovett was writing his introduction, Oliver St. John Gogarty was writing an epilogue that would be used for *Bread*. A poet, physician, and Irish political figure, Gogarty now is best remembered as Joyce's model for Buck Mulligan in *Ulysses*. He had been a friend of Yeats, who had praised his poetry even though it was out of step with the times. If Iris were lucky, Gogarty would lend the forged preface some authenticity and offer some praise himself. Iris was lucky. Gogarty sent Vincent an epilogue on 26 December 1945, and it did pretty much what Iris wanted. He had provided Gogarty with some version of the forged preface and probably the usual blurblike quotations, real and manufactured. In the epilogue, noting Yeats's appreciation of Iris and perhaps thinking of some critical response to his own work, Gogarty blamed critics for his not having heard of Iris before. But, of course, he said, critics are "like eunuchs posing as authorities on procreation." Poets alone can appreciate poetry: "That is why Yeats, the greatest poet of his period, gives this poet the greatest praise." Still, the praise Gogarty offered fell a bit short of that. Dismissing the importance of critical recognition, he complimented Iris for working well within the limitations of ballad meters. He valued Iris's formal achievement over that of Gerard Manley Hopkins, "who introduced the hiccough into English prosody." Resorting to what may be high praise or low, he found that one of Iris's poems, "Scarlet Cloak," ascended "beyond anything that can be described as verse to that which is limitless and incomprehensible as the wandering notes of a lost kingdom":

> My grief now wears a scarlet cloak
>    For love is dead—
> Love that was sturdy as the oak;
>    My brow goes gaily garlanded,
>    No ashes on my head.
> Come any day, come any morrow,
> My scarlet cloak will baffle sorrow.

Now, with a preface attributed to Yeats, an introduction by Lovett, and an epilogue by Gogarty, the manuscript of *Bread* was offered to the literary agency of Ann Watkins. (There was some audacity here on Iris's part, since Watkins had represented Yeats.) On 4 June 1946, Watkins wrote Iris, at his Trumbull Street address, to say that she was willing to take on *Bread*. But Watkins seemed not to have had much success. One definite expression of interest came to nothing.[19] On 19 May 1949, writing now to Vincent, the agency returned the manuscript, saying that there was "no chance of finding a publisher for it at present."

Iris was not relying solely on the agency. There was always the Church. In the Iris papers at Lewis University is a curious one-page typescript that seems to be both a draft of a letter and a record of letters sent. This is what appears to have taken place: On 16 September 1947, posing as Frederick Vincent, who was supposedly writing on behalf of Bishop Sheil, Iris expressed interest in the publication of *Bread*, the manuscript of which he pretended to think Duel, Sloan, and Pearce currently had under consideration. The publisher then replied to Vincent, asking to see the manuscript. Iris thus had the publisher committed to seeing the manuscript before it was sent. Iris also used the letter to authenticate the preface by Yeats and at that time was still planning to use Lovett's introduction in addition to Gogarty's epilogue. The letter also mentioned the Rivera portrait that Vincent claimed would be released by *Life* and asserted that Time-Life and the *Chicago Tribune* were attempting to have Iris visit Picasso for a portrait. On this draft Iris annotated the letter as having been typed on the "DEIR typewriter," as opposed to his own typewriter that he presumably used for the manuscript and, according to a further annotation, used for a subsequent letter to another publisher, Farrar, Straus, Inc. Although the meaning of "DEIR" is not known, it is obvious Iris's felt his duplicity was complicated enough to require records.


The mention of Picasso in his draft letter referred to another scheme, another attempt to have his portrait made. In late 1945, with the war finally over, Iris was determined to travel to Paris and meet with Picasso, so he established for himself the "Scharmel Iris Poetry Fund" and opened an account at Chicago's

National Bank of Commerce in the fund's name and with his Trumbull Street address. Signing himself "Dr. Frederick Vincent," he sent out letters seeking contributions from companies and individuals. He even gave the William Wrigley Jr. Co. another try, with no success.[20] For some contributions, he had or pretended to have the cooperation of Father Lawrence Quigley at Our Lady of Sorrows Church. Thus, for example, on 27 February 1946, one donor sent a $25 donation to Quigley and expressed the hope that Iris would "soon have sufficient funds to make his trip to Paris."[21] A surviving bank statement for the fund shows a balance of $300 as of 1 November 1946. That was about a year's work. On 27 October 1946, Iris's mother, Rose Vincenzo, 82 and a widow, tumbled to her death down the concrete steps from the first floor to the basement of the family's home.[22] If Iris received any of her estate—and there could not be much—it too may have gone to support his travel.

For his passport application Iris wrote a letter to the U.S. secretary of state—or at least there is, in his papers, the draft of one dated 17 March 1947. In it, he explained that prior to sailing to France, 24 April, on the *Queen Elizabeth,* he wanted it known that his name was Fred Leo Scharmel, that he resided at 331 South Trumbull in Chicago, and that he had registered for the draft on 27 April 1942. He explained that, born in Italy, he entered the country in 1892 with his mother "Maria Rosa Scaramella (Mary Rose Scharmel) after her marriage to Francesco (Frank) Vincenzo." His father, deceased, was Frederick Iris Scaramella. Explaining the purpose of his trip, Iris then spins a story beyond any required by the passport office. He was going to France, he said, to examine documents needed to complete a book on the spread of democracy and on the life of his late friend Jane Addams. For the book "both Mrs. Woodrow Wilson and ex-president Herbert Hoover have given [him] permission to use private material." Staying in the home of the Vandenbrieles in Creil, he will venture to the studio of Pablo Picasso in Paris only to keep his appointments for a commissioned portrait. He vowed to defend his country and assured the secretary of state that he had sufficient funds to live in France for three months. His passport was issued on 21 March 1947—to Fred Leo Scharmel, 5' 10", grey hair, hazel eyes, born in Italy on 10 February 1889, occupation writer, address 331 South Trumbull. He received a French visa a few days later.

Iris probably did not have an appointment with Picasso. In part for whatever use it might be in his hoped-for dealings with Picasso, though, he began a collection of poems entitled "Pardon, Picasso." Surely, he thought, Picasso would want to advance this work. Then, learning that the Chicago Art Institute had scheduled a Picasso exhibit, he also attempted to get the institute to commit to including a Picasso portrait of him. If the institute would show it, then perhaps Picasso would make it. But on 7 April 1947, Daniel Catton Rich, the institute's director, told Frederick Vincent that the institute could not commit to showing the portrait of Iris "without at least seeing a photograph in advance."

Iris did make his way to France but evidently never met with Picasso. There is a letter, dated 27 June 1947, purporting to be from Henry Wales, of the European bureau of the *Chicago Tribune*, to Iris, at 21 rue Pasteur, Creil, Oise (just north of Paris). Because it rehearses so much of a letter to which it is supposed to be a reply, it is suspicious. It acknowledges that a railroad strike had prevented Iris's keeping an appointment with Picasso, who had "cooled off on the matter" when Iris attempted to reschedule the meeting. Wales, if the letter is in fact his, says that he has written to Jaimie Sabartes, Picasso's friend, secretary, and exhibition organizer, "urging him to schedule another meeting." Iris may have written the letter himself to show supporters back in the States who had expected him to return with a portrait by Picasso. Aside from this letter, there is little evidence of Iris's activity in France during 1947. He eventually moved on to Spain and there completed poems that he would later publish in *Spanish Earth*.

During his time in France, however, Iris had continued to work on "Pardon, Picasso," so that by the time he returned to Chicago the collection had grown to about 80 poems. The collection also had become less favorably disposed to Picasso. It opens with a lengthy poem entitled with Picasso's address, "7, Rue des Grands Augustus," which features an introductory admonition in which Iris instructs Picasso to free himself of imitation:

> Too long have you squeezed the tube of the past, Picasso!
> Just as birds acquire the notes of other birds which may be near them
> Have you given yourself over to imitation.
> Too freely have you borrowed.

The poem continues with a description of a saintly person (presumably Iris) whom Picasso had turned away from his door:

> He had come from afar
> Like some strange star.
> Hollow his steps resound.
>
> He will not seek you now—
> Too drunk with sin
> Were you to let him in.

The rest of the poem presents a reporter's interviews with a wide variety of people who are asked what they think about Picasso, like these two:

> And what do you think about Picasso, Betty Brown?
>     "I wouldn't touch the stuff no more than a Dubonnet.
>     I'd rather a whiskey sour or a cherry lemonade.
>     I'll take my Scotch straight just like I take my tea."
>
> Has the bishop received my query, Annette Smith?
>     "The bishop wants you to know he is busy with diocesan matters.
>     Trouble him not about Picasso. Go away!"
> Christ was not unavailable. Give him that message, please.

Other poems in the collection are based on or are about pictures by Picasso, or they are Iris's impressions of people and places in France, as in "Visit to an Aging Dame Called Dutton in Rue Seine":

> Chic on her white chaise lounge
> Katherine hung between the floor and ceiling
> "Wasn't Pound the odd one: All head and no feeling.
> And you, it was my sister Dorothy
> You knew, not me."
> Like a thing by Braque
> She jelled and was made rock.
>
> Two wars have spawned a race of Duttons
> Minus their buttons.

Iris began submitting this new manuscript to publishers. He had a kind rejection from Robert N. Linscott, at Random House, who wrote Frederick Vincent on 4 August 1949, saying the poems had "real power and distinction" but were being rejected because Random House was seldom publishing poetry and was restricting itself to works by its own authors. He suggested that Vincent try Knopf or Scribner's. That phrase "real power and distinction" meant, as far as Iris was concerned, that the rejection might be overcome. So, on 13 August 1949, still as Frederick Vincent, he sought Archibald MacLeish's help in bringing Random House around. Enclosing Linscott's letter, he asked MacLeish to write a brief foreword that would reopen his case. He also asked whether MacLeish would see if ex-ambassador Joseph Kennedy might be willing to meet the publishing costs if the book carried a dedication to his son "whose memory is honored by various grants made in his name." At any rate, he said, "follow the best course open to you, but not the course of embarrassment."

At the time, MacLeish was still trying to be of help with the publication of *Bread*. But on 10 November 1949, MacLeish wrote Vincent that he had "run into a complete stone wall" in his efforts to find a publisher. There was, he said, but one ray of hope: a new publishing house was interested but was troubled by the Yeats preface because of its departure from the style and opinion of Yeats's work at the time. If Iris has the original manuscript, MacLeish said, he might send it to the publisher to reassure them of its authenticity. If MacLeish had any such reservations about the preface—and it is difficult to imagine that he did not— he did not express them to Iris, not even to Iris disguised as Vincent. On 30 November, however, he let Vincent know that he had "come to the end of [his] possibilities in the matter." He returned a manuscript (possibly "Bread," possibly "Pardon, Picasso") and some documents (perhaps the affidavits and such produced in response to Untermeyer's report) that Vincent had sent him on Thanksgiving Day. MacLeish seems to have given up helping Vincent help Iris. In a few years, however, Iris would enlist him again.

During the 1940s, then, Iris's schemes grew in ambition and complexity. Indeed, dedicated to the grandiose, Iris was not doing what most poets were. His eye on major publishing houses, he was not submitting work to the little magazines (such as *Accent,*

*Decision, Furioso,* or even *Poetry*) nor to the increasingly important quarterly reviews (such as *Kenyon Review, Partisan Review, Sewanee Review,* and *Yale Review*). In those, he could have appeared alongside poets both established and struggling for recognition and could have developed a record of publication that might interest a publisher. Aside from his assault on the charity of figures such as MacLeish, he was not developing productive relationships with editors and other poets. Not since his early years with O'Malley and Monroe had he received much in the way of encouragement or advice.

# CHAPTER FIVE

# RESURRECTED GENIUS, 1950–1953

"Immature poets imitate; mature poets steal; bad poets deface what they take, and good poets make it into something better, or at least something different. "—T. S. Eliot, "Philip Massinger"

Despite the mixed results of the preceding decade, in the late 1940s and early 1950s Iris continued to turn out poetry, becoming even more prolific and exercising his talent in a variety of modes. Indeed, in the early 1950s he had in hand, in addition to *Bread* and "Pardon, Picasso," several other book-length manuscripts. From these, he submitted to Macmillan "Twelve Pins for Fairyland," a collection of children's poems, all in the manner of "The Easter Rabbit," which began,

> Come see the Easter rabbit
>> Walk proudly on two legs.
> He plays a tune upon his flute
>> And juggles colored eggs.[1]

He also may have submitted "As the Wheel Turns," a typescript of 43 poems credited to Frederick Vincent; "Meet the Mockingbird," 135 or so poems of light verse credited to another pseudonym, Vincent Holme; and "Eagle and Serpent," a collection of about 30 poems inspired by Iris's trip to Mexico. He submitted, to Dodd, Mead, "A Singer in the Sun," about 130 poems pretty much in the subliterary mode suggested by the beginning of its "Prelude":

> Accept these songs of mine
>    I fashioned one by one.
> Think of me only as
>    A singer in the sun.[2]

Iris also had gathered little instances of his verbal wit, putting them into a book-length typescript entitled "Barbs of a Barbarian," which he divided into several sections. In one, "People and Places," he listed hundreds of people and places along with an epithet or brief description for each. So Shakespeare became "the great plagiarist who took the human heart and made it his own"; Franklin D. Roosevelt, "the old matriarch"; Los Angeles, "America's port of fantasy." His section "The Chestnut Roast" added new twists to old sayings, as in "The race is to the swift yet the fastest colors are those that won't run." In "Monkeys and Men," drawing on his experience writing for the San Francisco *Monitor,* he presented his own (or perhaps *as* his own) hundreds of aphorisms and other sorts of pithy sayings, such as "Men and pins are no good when they lose their heads." Like the poetry manuscripts, "Barbs" did not find a publisher.

While looking for publishers, Iris continued to seek patronage or similar assistance. In October 1940 he had sought the charity or patronage of Louise de Koven Bowen and had been refused. Nearly a decade later, on 18 March 1950, he forged a letter purporting to be to him from Bowen's secretary, a Miss Jackson. Iris's intention was to take the letter to a Monsignor Long, who might serve as a conduit to Samuel Cardinal Stritch, archbishop of Chicago since 1940. Stritch was the ultimate audience for the letter and, in Iris's mind, a possible source of assistance. Iris had used this technique before, despite the awkwardness it created, as when he had "Miss Jackson" telling him what he, not she, would already know. The letter also was typical in attempting to validate other bogus documents and in assuming that other people's desires and motives, in this case the cardinal's, would be the same as Iris's own:

Dear Mr. Iris:

Mrs. Bowen, financial backer of Miss Jane Addams' projects for fifty years, now in her ninetieth year, was grieved to learn of your distress. She urges you to again attempt to contact Monsignor Long, who has the ear of the cardinal and to whom Miss Garvey of St. Ita's gave you the letter dictated by the late Monsignor Quille.

It is generous indeed of you to donate the painting of 1777 of the Virgin and Child to the cardinal. Your mother, the first to make Mother Cabrini a substantial offering, refused eight-thousand-dollars for it offered by Mrs. Rockefeller McCormick.

Tell the cardinal of your willingness to write HOLY YEAR book of poems and of your desire to dedicate the work by honoring his name. Read him the preface that Yeats, an Irishman and Nobel prize winner, wrote for your poems and for no other American, wherein you were given the highest rank. The dedication would have great value. Whatever he may choose to do to advance your cause will be greatly appreciated. His protestant neighbors would subscribe one million dollars towards the building fund for a new cathedral were he to build one.

Sincerely yours,<br>[signed] Miss Jackson

It is not known whether the letter ever got to Monsignor Long and eventually to Cardinal Stritch. Iris himself didn't wait to see what might come of his effort. A few days later, on 25 March 1950, he forged another letter to himself, this one purporting to be from Paul Engle, poet and director of the Iowa Writers' Workshop. Another of those third-party letter, it was intended for the eyes of the Reverend Dr. Walter S. Pond at St. Barnabas's Episcopal Church. The letter first asked whether Iris still had a letter in which Marshall Field's "star reporter," Ed Doherty, repeated "Field's willingness of financial aid." Because Doherty was hospitalized in Canada, the letter said, Iris should see Pond "so that he can take a deep enough personal interest to get you the assistance you need and deserve." Pond was supposed to speak with Field, who would not "welch on his word." The letter then rehearsed Iris's refusal to accept Edith Rockefeller McCormick's "life grant" and all other offers of aid: "By not accepting you deprived the would-be donors of the pleasure that comes from willing giving." The letter went on to note that Bowen failed Iris too but that he forgave her because of her age, ninety. He was sorry that MacLeish's efforts to find a publisher for him came to nothing. In this letter Iris introduced for the first time another instrument of reward and punishment to use in manipulating people, an autobiography-in-progress. Still pretending to be Engle, he said, "I'm glad to learn you have reserved a warm space in your heart and space in your autobiography. Please be as generous with Dr. Pond." The letter ended: "Be careful. Don't risk the loss of your things: such as your books and mss. Look to you health. Yeats took your measure—and you are too valuable not to continue your work. God and Dr. Pond befriend you!"

On the same day that he forged this letter from Engle, Iris had received a genuine one. He, as Frederick Vincent, had written Engle for help in finding a publisher for *Bread*. Engle, busy teaching and writing during the spring semester at Louisiana State University, was not sure he would be of any help to Iris, since he had not seen any of Iris's work and since his own publisher, Harper and Brothers, had rejected the manuscript. He suggested instead that Vincent find for Iris a small press that specialized in poetry, such as Decker Press and Alan Swallow. At any rate, he said, he would not be able to read any manuscript until June. When the time came, Iris sent along the manuscript. On 13 July Engle gave Vincent the bad news. His friend at Harper and Brothers had rejected the manuscript. Further, Engle himself was not especially impressed by the poems, which "have a limited quality, being fluent and lyrical but lacking essentially deep imagination or real poetic energy." He also advised Vincent that "three forewords" (by Yeats, Gogarty, and probably Lovett) made it appear "that the poems *need* preliminary apology." Iris should stick only with Yeats.


At about this time Iris adopted the pseudonym "Vincent Holme," which came to displace "Frederick Vincent" as the primary name to use when asking favors for himself. Sometimes he substituted "Manoel" for "Vincent," and sometimes he attached a title, especially "Dr." and "Rev." These seemed appropriate, since he now began using Lewis College as his return address. The college, in the Joliet area southwest of Chicago, had been founded by the Chicago archdiocese as a technical school for boys, in large part through the efforts of Bishop Sheil. It became a college after World War II and took its name from its primary benefactor, Chicagoan Frank J. Lewis. Like Iris, Lewis had been a child in a large family of immigrants, in his case Irish. After that, his story took a trajectory much different from Iris's. By age 20, after completing an apprenticeship, he had his own roofing-tar company that eventually made him rich, so much so that he could retire and devote his full time to a philanthropic foundation he had founded. He was an especially strong supporter of the Church.[3] With the aid of Bishop Sheil, Iris made some connection there at the college and at some point was granted a residence on campus, at first a room in the "barracks," one-story frame buildings built during the war and later used to house the college's first coeds and some of its faculty members. He began using the college as his address as early as 1950 but seems not to have taken up full-time residence there until 1953. He later moved to a small cottage on campus. He never taught at the college nor had any official duties.

Vincent Holme turned out to be more than an intercessor; he was something of a poet too. In 1950, from 24 February through 5 October, Iris used that name for 15 poems contributed to the *Chicago Tribune*.[4] The poems are what one expects of newspaper verse. Many celebrate holidays—St. Patrick's Day, Good Friday, Mother's Day, and Memorial Day. One, "Nijinsky's Elegy," on the death that year of the famous Russian dancer, works somewhat uncertainly toward a fine last line in which the dancer's death is figured as an artful leap that "made eternity," the word *made* nicely suggesting performance, attainment, and creation:

> Since every star must wane,
> Ringed in solemnity we stand
> Here in the darkened land.
> Petals of roses, like bright rain,
> Shall wash away the sting of pain.
>
> Cry out his name!
> Bury him in the earth from which he came;
> Think of him only as a quenchless flame.
> Weep for Nijinsky; never for me,
> Who saw his leap that made eternity.

Holme took the opportunity of the poem's publication to place Iris's name before the public. He annotated the poem by claiming to quote a "press report" that put Iris in the company of Serge Lifor and Romola Nijinsky as one of three who "stood by the grave of Nijinsky."[5]

While newspaper publication earned him some spending money, Iris remained intent on securing book publication, seemingly convinced that, if he could only find the right person to put in the right word, he would succeed. For the next few years, then, he continued to seek prefaces from an odd assortment of figures—mostly Catholics—and to resort to forgery and plagiarism when he imagined they would advance his cause.

In 1951, from Lewis College and as Holme, Iris sought help from Padraic Colum, a Catholic Irish-American poet-playwright who, before coming to the States in 1914, had helped found the Abbey Theatre in Dublin and there became associated with Yeats and others participating in the Irish Renaissance. Iris sent him a book manuscript that Colum, in reply on 3 March 1951, called as voluminous as Tennyson's collected poems. The manuscript, perhaps a heavily augmented version of *Bread*, was simply too long, according to Colum. Besides, he added, "only a very small proportion of the poems are real achievements." Colum also had trouble with "the note" signed by Yeats, which "is altogether away from his manner." Nonetheless, Colum agreed that, if the manuscript were reduced to 40 poems, he would write a preface.

Holme must have argued a bit with Colum's comment on the remarks attributed to Yeats, because in his next letter, on 24 May 1951, Colum took a much stronger position: "I no more believe he wrote them than I believe I wrote them myself. They are nonsense, and when it comes to literature, Yeats never wrote nonsense. . . . 'All is near and dear to him!' Yeats would have blown his brains out rather than write that sentence." Colum exclaimed that he could not appear in a volume that attributed to Yeats such foolishness as the statement that "April" is "one of the finest lyrics in the entire range of English literature." Oddly, though, Colum did not wash his hands of the whole business. He selected about 40 poems from those sent him and agreed to write a short introduction or preface. He warned Holme, though, not to "expect any superlatives."[6] The resulting preface may have been used as a testimonial when Iris sought publishers; it would not appear in *Bread* but in a later volume, *Seven Hills of the Dove* (1957).


Iris decided that he could use Vincent Holme to revisit a publisher that had already rejected him. So on 24 June 1951, as Dr. Vincent Holme at Lewis College, he wrote Cass Canfield at Harper and Brothers. He referred to their earlier rejection of

*Bread,* which Paul Engle had sent them, and he said that Iris was told, back in 1940, when sent to Harper by Nelson Rockefeller's office, that this "was not the year for poetry." Holme would have bygones be bygones: "So much for past history! He buried his hurt and gave himself over to poetry writing." Now, Holme wrote, Iris wanted to submit another manuscript, one certain to be a success. One wonders what Canfield would have decided if Holme had had stopped at this point. But inept in imagining the kind of impression he was making on others, he continued by saying that, after all, Bishop Sheil, who sent Iris to Rivera in 1943 and to Picasso in 1947, will "wield his influence," as will Samuel Cardinal Stritch, Marshall Field, and Colonel Robert McCormick. Further, he knows some reviewers who will help: Mitchell Dawson, Paul Engle, Francis Hackett, and Archibald MacLeish. Canfield soon replied, telling Holme that Iris's poetry had been given "very careful consideration" about a year earlier and was not considered "as being outstanding." He asked that Holme not send another manuscript.[7]

In October 1951, as Holme, Iris sent a batch of poems with Spanish subjects and settings to George Santayana, the Spanish-born poet and philosopher who many years earlier, at Harvard, had taught poets Conrad Aiken, T. S. Eliot, Robert Frost, and Wallace Stevens, as well as other influential figures. He asked Santayana, who was then eighty-seven, for a foreword. Santayana replied on 3 November. He had read the poems on Spain, he said, and "felt they have much feeling and strength."

> But what is Spanish in them is only the *mise en scène* and external. The poor in Spain are particularly appealing, and misfortune, political and private, has always seemed to be present there, as tragedy is in Spanish popular music, beneath the frankly comic or frivolous surface. But poverty and suffering are found everywhere, and the mere expression of them in terse language does not represent the special temper of Spain. I have never come upon any English-speaking person who understood this temper. Spain is a Christian country with a tincture of Islam in it. It is unworldly. Its religion and philosophy (when it has a native philosophy) expresses a *second birth,* a revulsion from ordinary life. Foreigners in Spain are not likely to catch that aspect of feeling. Americans least of all. Iris does not catch it.

Santayana gave the example of Iris's poem entitled "A los pies del gran poder," in which bullfighters pray for a "happy death" at the feet of Jesus, "the Great Power." If the bullfighters were praying for safety or victory, Santayana said, they should be praying to the Virgin Mary or to St. Expeditus, not to Christ on the cross. Their praying to Christ "indicates that they are praying for a tragic death." "If this element of self-surrender (not for any earthly benefit, even for others) but for salvation, is wanting, the soul of Spain is wanting," he said. He told Holme that he would not write a foreword to the poems because to do so would "amount to an acceptance of them as a true appreciation of Spain" when they seemed to him "the opposite: a *foreign* appreciation of Spain."[8]

On 12 November 1951, hoping for better luck than he had had with Santayana, Iris sat down at his typewriter and began composing a letter to Salvador de Madariaga, the writer and diplomat who had left his home in Spain and taken up residence in London when the Spanish Civil War broke out in 1936. Iris was going to send Madariaga the collection of poems on Spanish subjects that Santayana had returned. The letter, a rough draft, did little more than string together Iris's publishing accomplishments and the praise earned or invented along the way. Iris then broke off the letter and used the rest of the page for a series of notes for a preface that he could write himself and attribute to someone named Del Vayo, perhaps Julio Alvarez del Vayo, who had been the foreign minister of Republican Spain and since then a leftist journalist. The notes then recorded Iris's thought that he should have this Del Vayo incorporate material from writings by Santayana and possibly Madariaga. Finally, Iris noted his plan to have Del Vayo end with these words: "To those of your [sic] these poems have distracted from your distractions, may God deny you peace, but give your [sic] glory! SALAMANCA In the year of grace 1951." Iris derived that closing from the closing of Miguel de Unamuno's *Tragic Sense of Life* (1912):

> . . . forgive me if I have troubled you more than was needful and inevitable, more than I intended to do when I took up my pen proposing to distract you for a while from your distractions. And may God deny you peace, but give you glory!

> SALAMANCA,
> *In the year of grace* 1912

If Iris read Unamuno's book, not simply plundered it, he came across this: "The man of letters who shall tell you that he despises fame is a lying rascal."[9] He would have agreed.

Iris did write an "epilogue" under the name Del Vayo, but the full name he used was Blasco Maria Del Vayo. Since Alvarez del Vayo was generally known simply as Vayo, Iris may have been confused by the name or may have been referring to someone else entirely. More likely, he was inventing someone. Whoever's epilogue it is, it has little that would link it with any particular collection of poems. Iris could have written it just for the personal satisfaction of having his work called, as his Del Vayo writes, "maddeningly and tormentingly beautiful." The epilogue does bear typical features. It begins by authenticating Yeats's appreciation of Iris. At Majorca in 1936, Del Vayo says, Yeats read to him a dozen poems by Iris. It also attempts a little self-authentication by having Del Vayo quote a letter from Yeats to Lady Gregory. In the letter Yeats tells her of his returning to *Poetry* the major part of a prize it awarded him and his suggesting to Monroe that the money go to Pound. (Iris would have known about the prize episode by reading of it in *Poetry* magazine in 1913 or in Harriet Monroe's autobiography.)[10] The epilogue offers the letter as a lesson in "the necessity of discovery": critics should treat Iris as Yeats treated Pound. In doing so, they will demonstrate that, like Yeats, they can "recognize the true from the false."

The epilogue is also typical in presenting incredible praise of Iris, including the common comparison of Iris to God. In this case, as Yeats read Iris's verse to him, Del Vayo saw the heavens open wide and Iris "seemed a deity." So Del Vayo castigates "somnolent critics" who "in their self-assured, small world of debonaire malice" have overlooked Iris just as Roman historians "missed the news of Christ." The epilogue gets Iris into a muddle of metaphors, as when it says that readers "crying for humanness and those who would feed upon the bread of beauty will find in him a candle in the wind." So they ask for humanness or bread and they get a candle—and the candle is not one in the dark but one in the wind. The epilogue never saw use. Perhaps even Iris recognized its excesses.

Iris had not forgotten Madariaga. He asked him to write a preface for the Spanish poems, which he had titled *Spanish Earth*, no doubt thinking of the 1937 documentary film of that title written by John Dos Passos, Ernest Hemingway, Lilian Hellman, and Archibald MacLeish. Madariaga agreed, and Iris had his preface.[11] Aside from its relatively mild praise of Iris and its neglecting to mention Yeats, the preface's chief peculiarity is its revision of Iris's biography: it refers to him as "a Hispano-American poet" with "a suggestion of Irishness." Iris's name or perhaps the clippings and prompts he routinely sent when asking for aid may have misled Madariaga. In fact, because of Santayana's criticism that the poems were "a *foreign* appreciation of Spain," Iris would have been tempted to claim some Spanish blood. If so, it worked. Unlike Santayana, Madariaga calls the poems "Spanish poetry written in English"; they have the "springy, essential, unadorned and spontaneous spirit" that is characteristic of Spanish life. In Iris's poem about Spanish poet Federico García Lorca, Madariaga says, "subject and poet fit each other so naturally that one might be tempted to credit the vigour and spirit of the poem to the event" rather than to the poet. But in other poems the credit clearly belongs to "a true poet" who is also "a poet Spanish in his spirit."

At about the same time, in spring 1952, Iris received an epilogue for *Spanish Earth* from Roy Campbell, the South African poet, convert to Catholicism (in 1935), and supporter of the Spanish fascists under Francisco Franco (though a leftist earlier in life and a volunteer in the British army during World War II). Thus, Iris would manage to unite in love for his poetry two well-known figures—at one extreme the liberal Madariaga, outspoken critic of Franco, and at the other, the conservative Campbell.[12] The epilogue Iris finally attached to the *Spanish Earth* manuscript was actually a joint production between Campbell and Iris, though Campbell was never aware of Iris's hand in it. Most of what Campbell wrote was political tirade, especially against English leftists during the 1930s and later for accepting the antifascist versions of events in the Spanish civil war, notably those at Guernica. But Campbell also characterized Iris's poems as historically inaccurate, especially his poems on the civil war massacres at Guernica and Badajoz: "Historically, therefore, Mr. Iris's book is rubbish, to be ruthlessly condemned by anyone with Spanish blood other than Marrano in his veins." (So much for Madariaga.) Still, he said, ambiguously, "Artistically, it is beyond praise." About one-fourth of what Campbell actually wrote found its way into Iris's revision (and eventually into the published book in 1964). Unlike Iris's version, Campbell's did not single out any poem for praise, did not call Iris a "leonine poet" or "splendid poet," and did not call his artistically imagined Spain an "aurora borealis" outshining the "mere-tallow candle" of the actual Spain. Whereas Campbell's original actually pardoned the murder of Lorca as the act of "an outraged parent who had his little son corrupted by Lorca's sodomy and money," Iris fixed that to have Campbell speaking of "the unpardonable murder of Lorca." Of course, Iris decided to omit Campbell's characterization of Lorca as "a rich Kulak, *flameur,* and landowner, with the more expensive bourgeois vices, who derived his verse from *listening-in* to us cattlemen and chalanes [horse traders, bronco-busters], though he couldn't even get on a horse and screamed with fright when they tried to teach him to swim." Campbell's version did not mention Santayana; Iris's claimed that Santayana had been sent half the manuscript by Yeats in 1935 and that Santayana had then commented on the poems. Iris went to Santayana's letter of 3 November 1951 and took from it the passage in which Santayana had said that Iris "does *not* catch" the feeling or temper of Spain. Iris has his version of Campbell quote the passage, minus the offending *not.*

Iris, as Holme, submitted *Spanish Earth* to Simon and Schuster, probably in late September to early October 1952. To urge things along, he asked Marshall Field III to put in a good word, telling him that Iris was dedicating the book to him. Field forwarded the letter to the publisher with instructions that the book not be dedicated to him if it were accepted. On 20 October 1952 Max Schuster wrote Holme that there were conflicting opinions about the manuscript. Nonetheless, because of his own interest and the close vote when Iris's work had been considered previously, he was "keeping the jury out." When the jury came in is not known, but Simon and Schuster refused the book. Iris would try other publishers later.

For another collection of his verse, this one entitled "The Fountaining Years" (or perhaps the title came later and the manuscript was that for *Bread*), Iris requested a preface from T. S. Eliot.[13] Eliot replied to Holme, the pseudonym Iris was still using, on 24 June 1952. In his letter he implied his skepticism about Holmes's citations of praise for Iris. He said that, although he had read the poems sympathetically, he could not "feel the same degree of enthusiasm as appears to have been expressed by the distinguished writers mentioned in your letter." He asked whether he was wrong to think that the name of one of the distinguished writers, Carl Sandburg, "alone is so eminent in America as to command the attention of all critics?" Eliot was likely being arch. After the 1930s, Sandburg was more public figure than poet, and in critical if not quite in public esteem the popular modernism he represented had been overtaken by Eliotic high modernism. In a canon shaped by the New Criticism, which favored an anti-Romantic poetry of complexity and irony, there was little room for Sandburg.

Undaunted by Eliot's refusal, Iris wrote a brief preface himself and signed Eliot's name to it. Iris's Eliot dropped names as heavily as Iris himself. Iris's poems, "Eliot" wrote, were "so moving, so beautiful, so forceful, as to silence an audience that included Lord Dunsany, Baroness Germaine de Rothschild, Dame Edith Sitwell, Sir Winston Churchill, Lady Guiness, Augustus John, Jacob Epstein and that militant parliamentarian brought close to tears by the consciousness of living in a privileged moment of illumination, Lady Astor." Somehow this Eliot can say that Churchill raided one of Iris's early poems for the title of one of his books. What Iris and thus his Eliot evidently did not know was that the phrase "their finest hour," which Churchill had used in 1949 as the title of the second volume of his *The Second World War,* first appeared in Churchill's speech to the House of Commons during the Battle of Britain, on 18 June 1940: "Let us therefore brace ourselves to our duties and so bear ourselves that, if the British Empire and its Commonwealth last for a thousand years, men will still say, 'This was their finest hour.'"[14] It is true that the phrase occurred in a poem by Iris. The poem, "In This Hour," would not be published until four years after Churchill's book—and 13 years after Churchill's speech.

> It will be said of them:
>     They died in their finest hour—
> The youths who gave their blood
>     To hold one flower.
>
> Selfless they gave their all
>     The root to fructify.
> Blessed be they and the earth
>     Wherever they lie.
>
> The lame, the halt, and the blind
>     Have need of Thy pity, Lord
> But not the eager of limb
>     Broken upon the sword.

> Praised be youth forever,
> >   Lay wreaths where they lie—
> They died in their finest hour
> >   Who chose this hour to die.

Despite the availability of names to drop, the preface pictured Iris as "not of the establishment" and did so in a flurry of metaphors: "Long 'before the peacock screamed' . . . he drew himself up like a cock preparing to strike, chose the rock of conviction, took the hard road, and, when approached by anthologists, announced, 'If I must hang, I prefer to hang whole and not in segments.' And he said it with the slightly episcopal air of a cardinal who expected you to kiss his ring." And there was much else in the preface that its readers would have had difficulty imagining as Eliot's. In fact, some of it wasn't even Iris's. The preface had Eliot plagiarize verbatim the final sentence of Arthur Quiller-Couch's 1914 essay *Poetry* and in so doing managed to make the obligatory comparison of Iris to God:

> *"Non c'e' in mondo,"* said Torquato Tasso proudly, *"chi merita nome di creatore, se non Iddio ed il Poeta"*—"Two beings only deserve the name of Creator: God and the Poet."[15]

There are additional traces of Quiller-Couch's essay. Both Quiller-Couch and the preface said they would refrain "from technical talk." And in Quiller-Couch's beginning was the preface's ending. Quiller-Couch began by referring to Plato's story of Er, whose body "shows no taint of corruption" ten days after his death. The preface ended by assuring us that because Iris has not sold out like other poets, his work, like Er's body, "shows no taint of corruption."[16] The preface was never published.

Iris's work on prefaces and the like did not mean that he had abandoned hope for publication of *Bread*. He looked for and found another intercessor. After Eleanor Roosevelt had attended a dinner for Roosevelt College in Chicago, Iris wrote her on 8 April 1952 to say that he (as Vincent Holme) and others at the dinner were won over by her "eclat and aplomb." He wanted now to bring to her attention "the plight of the poet Scharmel Iris, author of LYRICS OF A LAD, 1914, available at 42-Fifth, N.Y.C."

(The address is that of the New York Public Library.) In the course of 38 years, he said, Iris had spent more than $800 in mailing manuscripts—"and to no avail!" He went on to tell Roosevelt this sad story of his quest to have *Bread* published: Wishing to help, Marshall Field sent *Bread out of Stone* to Simon and Schuster. Untermeyer liked the poems but advised against publication on the grounds the book might not sell. It previously had been rejected by Macmillan, the publisher of Yeats, who wrote the introduction, "an honor extended to no other American poet." Because Untermeyer suggested an explanation of the life of the poet, Iris got Lovett, "then in faraway Puerto Rico," to vouch for him. Gogarty, "astonished that the word of Yeats meant nothing to the Macmillan firm," wrote the epilogue. Paul Engle sent the manuscript to Cass Canfield at Harper without success, just as "Archie MacLeish" did to Random House. Meanwhile he was also receiving rejections of two other manuscripts, "Pardon, Picasso" and "Seven Hills of the Dove." It seems, Holme complained to Roosevelt, that "Mr. Iris, 63 and an Episcopalian and tubercular, can do nothing to change the picture"—despite the fact that Eliot, writing to Madariaga, has expressed the opinion "that the obligation rests upon New York publishers to keep his work in print" and despite the fact that Santayana has read every one of his poems and feels "that they have both feeling and strength." Holme asked Roosevelt to find a publisher for Iris. He enclosed the Yeats preface, Gogarty epilogue, and Lovett introduction.

Roosevelt sent Holme's letter and all its accompaniments to Canfield at Harper and Brothers. On 30 April 1952 Canfield assured Roosevelt that he had looked into the matters raised by Holme's letter and that Harper had rejected "Bread" as "not particularly distinguished." He promised to relieve her of more correspondence with Holme by agreeing to look at another manuscript. As promised, he wrote to Holme that same day and advised him that, having rejected *Bread* in July 1951, they were not likely to publish anything else but that they were willing to consider another batch of poems. Delighted with the news, Holme then proposed a selection from Iris's 40 years of literary labor, the book to be titled simply "30 Poems." He asked Canfield who might write the preface for it and hoped that Roosevelt would "give her column to the Iris story." Canfield agreed to consider the selection proposed by Holme but deferred comment on the preface.[17]

Holme sent along the manuscript on 9 July 1952. The letter he sent with it was heavy handed and crudely manipulative. The letter pretended to speak for a committee: "We do hope that the evaluation arrived at by your editors may coincide with our committee of selection chosen from experienced editors of *Poetry: A Magazine of Verse,* headed by its present editor, Mr. Shapiro, who hopes to print a new group by Mr. Iris." Holme added that Monroe had published 38 of his poems, two groups getting prizes. He pointed out Iris's name in *This Side of Paradise.* He claimed that Iris had met Picasso in 1947 through Colonel McCormick and that Marshall Field had financed his stay of four months in Paris. Both McCormick and Field, Holme assured Canfield, "have promised favorable reviews in their organs." "I wish to avoid superlatives," Holme said, "yet all in all, I believe a favorable climate for the work can be obtained." He asked whether he might supply critical comments for dust jacket blurbs.

On 8 August, Canfield wrote Holme to say that Harper was rejecting "30 Poems." Softening the rejection, he did say that they believed Iris "a distinguished poet" but probably what they would call "a poet's poet, without much appeal to the general public." Iris was not crushed. A month later, as Holme again, he submitted to Canfield another manuscript, "Christ," a collection of 43 poems. In his letter Holme thanked Canfield for the serious consideration given the earlier manuscript and hoped he would appreciate "the human touch" evident in the new manuscript.[18] Holme provided the names of people who, he said, had offered to advance the book: L. F. Wood, of the Associated Press, Chicago, who had covered the Roosevelt College banquet attended by Eleanor Roosevelt; also Dr. Walter S. Pond, "leading Chicago Episcopalian clergyman"; a Mr. Fleming, who "will see that the 60 branches of the public library has each a copy"; and Marshall Field, who also awaits confirmation of publication. Holme asked, "Won't you risk your money on this MS?" It was as if Iris was putting Harper to the test. Would the publisher reject Christ? The answer was yes, and Canfield returned the manuscript to Holme on 27 October 1952.

The "30 Poems" earlier rejected by Canfield may have become the "Core of Fire" manuscript sent to poet Mark Van Doren for an introduction. On 26 September 1952, Van Doren returned it to Holme, saying that he liked the poems but not in such a manner as to give him "enough to say for an introduction." Having been told a sad story by Holme, Van Doren expressed "the greatest personal sympathy for Scharmel Iris" and wished him "better health and better luck with his manuscript elsewhere." Elsewhere was Simon and Schuster, and by now Iris had added a page-and-a-half foreword he himself concocted and then attributed to George Santayana. Here, referring to a previous manuscript supposedly sent him by Yeats and writing as a self-plagiarizing Santayana, Iris incorporated from Santayana's letter of 3 November 1951, the passage explaining that Iris does *not* catch the temper of Spain, except of course that the passage was revised to say that Iris does catch it. Iris then had Santayana admitting to having memorized Iris's "After the Martyrdom," a poem that "has circled the English-speaking world" and "achieved the status of a classic among anthologists." The present manuscript, then, strikes him as "an old friend." It is not the product of mere "poetic zeal" or "religious exercise" but the "immortal wheat clean and whole from purifying fires." Iris did not allow Santayana to declare him the greatest poet, but he did have him admit that aside from the work of Iris and Robert Lowell (who are "worth more than five American cardinals") "almost all contemporary poetry leaves [him] empty." Much of the rest of the foreword was plagiarized from Santayana's *The Sense of Beauty* (1896).[19] At times there has been some revision of Santayana's wording. Thus, speaking of tragedy, Santayana originally wrote this:

> . . . first we suffer, afterwards we sing. An interval is necessary to make feeling presentable, and subjugate it to that form in which alone it is beautiful.

The foreword says this:

> First we love, then suffer, afterwards we sing. An interval is necessary to make feeling presentable, and subjugate it to that form which alone is beautiful.

Six or so such passages, culled more or less higgledy-piggledy from Santayana's book, appear in the foreword. The foreword may also contain a smattering of Benedetto Croce's *Aesthetic as Science of Expression and General Linguistic* (1909) when it says

that the "intuitions from which [images] spring are not intu-
itions of reality or unreality, not perceptions but pure intu-
itions." Croce, as translated at the time, had written:

> . . . if the knowledge of reality be based upon the distinction be-
> tween real images and unreal images, and if this distinction does
> not originally exist, these intuitions would in truth not be intu-
> itions either of the real or of the unreal, but pure intuitions.[20]

The connection there is more tenuous, and the preface's roman-
tic assertion that the poets "live in a translunary realm" seems
unlikely to square with Santayana or with Croce. Simon and
Schuster returned "The Core of Fire," along with the foreword,
on 18 November 1952.

While he was submitting manuscripts to publishers, Iris also
explored other approaches to getting published or at least to
making some money. After he had submitted "Christ" to Harper
and even before receiving a response, Iris had planned for the
eventual rejection. He figured out how he could use the rejection
in a ploy that would enable him to approach a potential donor.
As Vincent Holme, on 3 October 1952, he wrote a letter to him-
self saying that the manuscript had been rejected by Harper and
Brothers. Holme told Iris that, although the publisher said his
poems were "greatly appreciated," difficulties in marketing stood
in the way of publication. Holme said, however, that Harper and
Brothers had explained that it would take about $1,000 to pro-
duce and market a book and that if Iris could get someone to
give him that amount as a gift, the publisher would have a "Mrs.
Cooper at the Concord Book Shop, take over" and publish the
book. If Iris raised any money with this approach, it did not go
toward publication of "Christ" or any other manuscript.

One potential donor Iris had often in mind was Marshall
Field. If Field would not use his influence to have Simon and
Schuster publish a book of his, then perhaps he would supply
Iris with a "pension." Again Iris forged a letter. This one, dated
28 October 1952, pretended to be from an Ellen Van Doren-
Wells to Holme. It quoted another fake letter, one supposedly by
T. S. Eliot: "The obligation to keep Mr. Iris in print rests upon
American publishers or the poet's friends rather than upon any-

one in London." Iris's Van Doren-Wells observed, "This 'obligation,' which none can escape, rests particularly upon Catholics." The letter told Holme that Field was a Catholic, that Cardinal Stritch could approach Field on Iris's behalf, and that, if he did, Field would "gladly grant this great but unfortunate poet a pension sufficient to meet his needs so that he could go on writing as Jane Addams had hoped he might." The letter suggested $75 a week or not less than $50. Matters are urgent: "Another Illinois winter may kill him—a man not in normal health for forty years," so he needs to go somewhere with "a more clement climate." The letter writer regretted that Iris did not accept the $300 a month Edith Rockefeller-McCormick offered him when he was but a boy. Iris's plan was to have Holme approach Cardinal Stritch with the letter and thereby to prompt Stritch to approach Field.

The letter may or may not have been used. If it was, it got Iris no patronage from Field. But the letter may have played some role in Bishop Sheil's formally arranging for Iris to take up full-time residence on the campus of Lewis College in 1953. Later, in 1954, Iris took another crack at Field. As Holme he wrote to Illinois Senator Paul H. Douglas, telling him Iris's sad story and asking him to take up the poor poet's case with Field. Senator Douglas wrote to Field on 6 December 1954. Not realizing that Iris must already have been known to Field, he wrote a letter of introduction: "This note is to introduce Scharmel Iris, a poet who has had a tragic and cumulative strain of hard luck." Observing that "poetry is a profession that has no social security," Douglas asked whether Field would talk with Iris or his friend Vincent Holme, a friend of Bishop Sheil, to see if it would be desirable to help him.[21] The letter seems not to have been successful.

In early 1953, Iris finally found a publisher for *Bread,* right there in Chicago. Henry Regnery had established in 1947 a publishing house that came to be known for titles on Roman Catholic theology and conservative politics. It had especial success with William F. Buckley's *God and Man at Yale* (1951) and Russell Kirk's *The Conservative Mind* (1953). It also published important titles in American literature, including Louise Bogan's *Achievement in American Poetry, 1900–1950* (1951) and Allen Tate's essays collected as *The Forlorn Demon* (1953).[22] One day, as Regnery recalled years later, Iris appeared with the *Bread* manuscript and

Yeats preface. Regnery was not especially impressed by the poetry or by Iris, whom he recalled as a strange but convincing man who could have gotten the preface by force of personality or by skill in arousing sympathy. Regnery's editor at the time, Fred Wieck, believed the preface genuine and was sufficiently impressed by the poetry to accept the manuscript.[23]

Regnery and Iris began to publicize the forthcoming book. Iris enjoyed the attention and the opportunities to try out material he was getting into shape for his autobiography. Hearing of the book-to-be, Harvey Breit, assistant editor of the *New York Times Book Review,* wrote Iris on 3 June 1953 to ask for the story behind the book, especially its preface by Yeats. What he learned appeared in his column "In and Out of Books" in the 16 August 1953 issue of the paper, under the heading "Resurrection." By then he also had an advance review copy of the book. In his column Breit reproduced the drawing of Iris by Diego Rivera and noted how strange it was that "a book of poems by a poet we had never heard of" should appear with a preface by Yeats. And, he said, it was "still more strange" when he read the preface, along with dust jacket blurbs by Carl Sandburg, George Santayana, and George Bernard Shaw. Breit then quoted from Iris's letter of explanation, in which Iris claimed Chicago as his birthplace ("I have been reported born in three places at one time [but] I was born in prosaic Chicago") and in which he said he met Yeats "several times in Chicago." Yeats, Iris falsely claimed, read his poem "April" at the *Poetry* Banquet on 1 March 1914 at the Cliff Dwellers Club: "Because of that poem he offered to do a preface for my poems." Looking ahead and aware that his claims might seem suspicious, Iris took the opportunity to prepare the way for *Spanish Earth*—which wouldn't appear until 1964—by saying that he sent Yeats some poems on Spain and that Yeats in turn sent them to Santayana. Meanwhile, Salvador de Madariaga had written the preface: "And what a preface it is. He is available at Oxford for confirmation, He calls me the 'Hispanic American poet' and adopts me for the Spanish race." Iris also noted that Shaw read his poems, said no publisher would risk money on them, and sent him "$75 for the pleasure he derived from them." Breit concluded, "'Behold,' as it is said in Corinthians, 'I shew you a mystery.'"

In the *Chicago Daily News* for 22 August, Van Allen Bradley showed himself more gullible, perhaps because he had met in person with the resurrected Iris rather than relying on a letter. Under the headline "The Fantastic Story of a Lost and Now Found Chicago Genius" and the teaser "What's Stranger Than Fiction?" Bradley presented a photograph bearing this caption: "White-thatched Scharmel Iris, the finally discovered Chicago Genius, chats with his friend Bishop Bernard J. Sheil after a 16-year wait for his manuscript." On the right is another photograph, this one of a younger, thinner Iris and a bemused Rivera flanking his painting of Iris. Between the two photographs are two more from Iris's ample supply, one of Iris and one of Rupert Brooke, both said to have been made "on the same day in 1914 by Eugene Hutchinson." Uncritical in his eagerness for a good story, Bradley began by calling his account of Iris's life, an account he took from Iris's mouth, "strange but true." This "shy little man of 64 whom time almost passed by," Bradley said, was "buried in obscurity in Chicago" but was undergoing "the most remarkable literary resurrection of modern times" through the publication of a "precious manuscript of poems" introduced by Yeats. (All this talk of resurrection, congenial to a poet who fashioned himself in the image of Christ, itself enjoyed a second life, being quoted by Regnery when he advertised the book.)[24]

In his article, Bradley explained the loss and recovery of the manuscript. In the mid-1930s, he wrote, Yeats read the manuscript and wrote the introduction, and then Gogarty wrote the epilogue. Iris showed the result in 1937 to his friend Father Vincent Scheltinga, who in turn showed it to Bishop Sheil. Somehow the manuscript became lost in Sheil's office. Over the next 16 years Iris made occasional calls to Sheil's secretary. Unwilling to "press a prelate," Iris did not ask Sheil to search. Finally, during the remodeling of the office of the Catholic Youth Organization, "the manuscript fell out of its hiding place in the files." Overjoyed, Sheil contacted Iris and sent the manuscript to Vincent Holme, urging him to find a publisher. He found Regnery, which accepted the manuscript after Gogarty confirmed the authenticity of his epilogue and Yeats's introduction and after "Sheil himself confirmed the rest of the story." Interviewing Iris over lunch and chilled martinis in the Empire Room of the Palmer House hotel, Bradley gathered more of Iris's story. Iris told him (and he repeated) that he was born on Michigan Avenue, "the son of a Greek father 'who was in the diplomatic service' and an Irish mother." He grew up on the West Side, where he sold the *Daily News* (Bradley's paper) on street corners. He was educated by tutors and spent a year at St. Viator's College, though he isn't sure which year. He now is living at 7932 South Ellis. Dedicated to the vocation of poet, he "has no visible means of support" and no Social Security card, which Iris calls "one of those little cards you have to have to work with." Over the last 50 years, he spent $840 on postage for his poems, which earned him little money. During the interview, Bradley himself got into the act of imagining Iris, whose isolation from the world of economic realities the reporter finds particularly charming. He assumed that Iris "exists on an inheritance from his mother, who died a few years ago." Iris, Bradley explained, "said it was all right" if he made that assumption. Bradley told also the story of Iris's 1943 trip to Mexico to be painted by Rivera, and he accepted Iris's claim to have been painted by Picasso while in Paris during 1947. He was pleased to say that Iris took to Paris for distribution to the poor "a trunkful of Palmolive Soap, each bar wrapped in face cloths." Iris, "a kind and gentle little man," spent much of his time in France "picking berries and giving them away to the poor." Bradley ended his article by noting that Iris had seven additional poetry manuscripts, along with "pretty good critical backing for them" from Santayana, Madariaga, and Colum.

It couldn't get much better than that for Iris, but it did. His prepublication celebrity continued. On 10 September 1953, six days before the book's official publication date, the newspaper of Iris's old neighborhood, the *Garfieldian,* printed a large photograph of a smiling bespectacled Iris in an open-necked polka dot shirt. Beneath the headline "Poet Gets Recognition Due Him after Waiting 39 Years," the paper devoted 45 column-inches to the impending publication of *Bread* and to Iris's career as a poet. Based on an interview with Iris, with extensive quotation, the article seems written by a publicist rather than by the unnamed reporter. It got off to a somewhat confusing start by saying, "After waiting 39 years West Sider Scharmel Iris is finally getting the recognition that has been his due since the Irish Nobel prize poet, William Butler Yeats, in 1934, said of him, 'Of the poets writing today there is no greater.'" (Subtracting 39 years from 1953 puts us, of course, back in 1914, the year of *Lyrics,* not in 1934, the year Iris gave to the forged preface.) Iris recalled for the reporter some early memories, such as the many times he, Carl Sandburg, Edgar Lee Masters, and Jane Addams "would drink yogurt together on Michigan Ave." And then there was the time Iris recommended Sandburg's work to the editors of *Poetry:* "I told them it was a little rough around the edges but to go ahead and publish it for it was good stuff." He also got Joyce Kilmer's famous poem "Trees" into *Poetry,* after he revised it: "The poem struck me to be freighted with honey. I altered the last two lines to read 'Poems are made by fools like me but only God can make a tree.' Joyce was happy about the change and thought it was just the punch the poem needed." Another Joyce, James Joyce, was helped by Iris. Mrs. Nelson Rockefeller McCormick, who "had become a very good friend of Iris'," wrote him after Joyce appealed to her for assistance. Iris told her "to back him all the way." She left money in Joyce's account. For the *Garfieldian* Iris worked some variations on his education. He attended Catholic schools (no tutor is mentioned) and never attended college (not even St. Viator's College, as he had told Bradley). A dominant theme of this article is Iris's concern with integrity of being. Poetically and personally he is "against all fakery." He feels "a poet should stand on his own integrity." He finds West Siders to be "real people" and considers himself a West Sider (living at 331 South Trumbull, not on Ellis Avenue, as he told Bradley). When Rivera sketched and painted him, he discovered that the artist "was a real Christian gentleman," and reciprocally, Rivera treated him "like a real human being."

The book went on sale, at $3.50 a copy, on 16 September 1953.[25] It was a slim volume of 53 poems in 60 pages, with the forged Yeats preface in front and the genuine Gogarty epilogue in the back. A note by Iris acknowledged previous publication of 30 poems under four pseudonyms in *Poetry,* omitting mention of the pseudonym Seth James, inflating the number of poems by ten, and failing to acknowledge reprinting some poems from *Lyrics.*

The book's dust jacket gave Iris a whole new canvas for the art of puffery. On its front, boldly, is the high, obliquely self-deprecating praise attributed to Yeats: "Of poets writing today there is no greater." The front and back flaps sport blurbs attributed falsely to Shaw ("His book will be received by two continents. His poems are not echoes of dead poets; they glow with the fire he has given them"), not really accurately to Sandburg ("Scharmel Iris is a genius in the lyric field"), probably falsely to William Carlos Williams

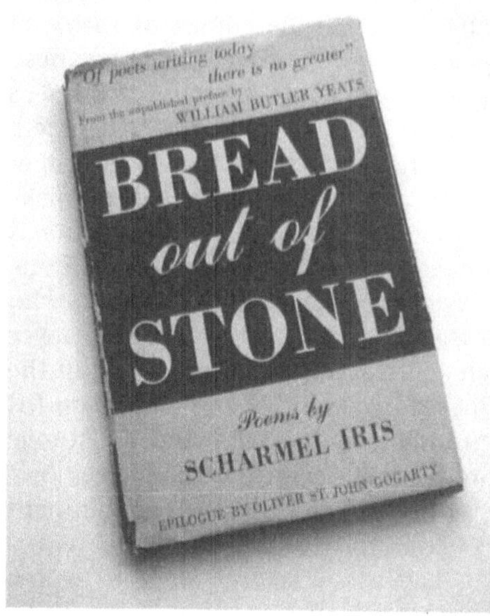

*(left)* The front of the dust jacket from *Bread out of Stone,* 1953, with a quotation from the preface Iris forged using W. B. Yeats's name.

*(below)* Frontispiece and title page, *Bread out of Stone,* 1953. The frontispiece drawing is attributed to Diego Rivera and dated March 1943.

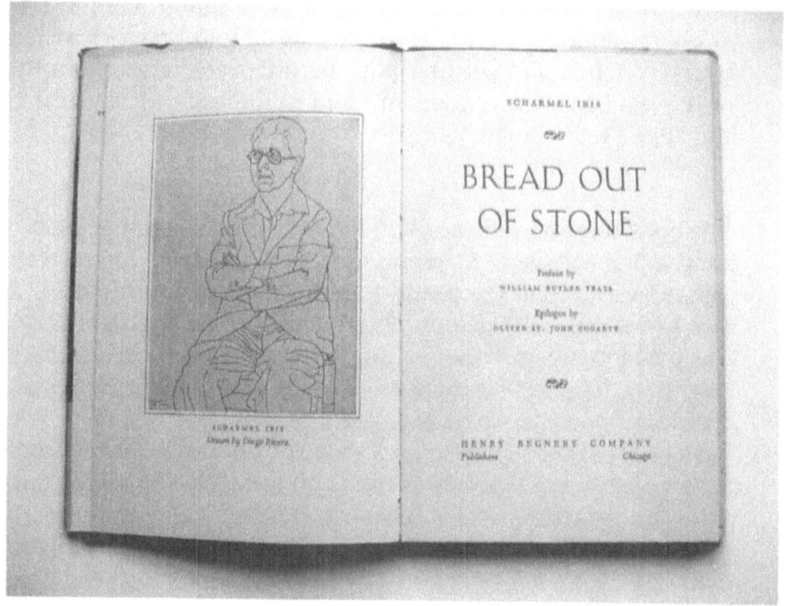

("His poems are top rank. There are not many pieces of writing you can say that about today"), only half accurately to George Santayana ("His poems have much feeling and strength, but above all, the authority we call beauty"), and possibly accurately to Robert Morss Lovett ("One of that brotherhood of genius, at war with poverty and wrong, which includes Villon, Marlowe, and Verlaine"). Gogarty (d. 1957), Lovett (d. 1956), Sandburg (d. 1967), and Williams (d. 1963) were alive on the date of publication.

On the back of the jacket, beneath a dazed-looking Iris exchanging some papers with a smiling Bishop Sheil, is the explanation of the delay between the purported date of the forged preface attributed to Yeats and the date of the book's publication. Almost 20 years earlier, the manuscript, including preface and epilogue, had been lost in the bishop's office and not found until 1953. Finally, the jacket presents a brief biographical note that has Iris born in Chicago, traveling through Europe with his parents for much of his childhood, and inspiring Rodin's "The Old Courtesan."

The book was not widely reviewed. Some potential reviewers probably had qualms because they were suspicious of all or some of the paratextual puffery accompanying the poems yet hesitant to say so in print. Further, the volume looked more like a literary curiosity than a major collection of poetry. Iris had gathered poems written in various styles and under various names over a long period of time. None of it seemed much related to the late Modernist mode dominant in 1953. It lacked the wit, irony, formal dexterity, and linguistic density of poets then making names for themselves, including Elizabeth Bishop, Robert Lowell, Richard Wilbur, and, closer to home, Gwendolyn Brooks, recipient of a 1950 Pulitizer Prize for her *Annie Allen,* which took its subjects from life in Chicago's South Side. Iris was offering stale bread. When he sent a review copy to the *Chicago Tribune*'s literary columnist Frederic Babcock, he sounded like neither an early nor late modernist but rather like Charles O'Malley, one of his earliest mentors. Iris inscribed the copy: "In appreciation of your stand against obscurantism in the divine art of poetry."[26] Still, the preface attributed to Yeats really ought to have attracted more attention. Yeats's name—that is to say, his influence and critical reputation—had survived the years much better than Iris's poetry had. Just three years earlier there had appeared a volume significantly entitled *The Permanence of Yeats* and containing 25 essays by an impressive roster of critics and poet-critics, among them W. H. Auden, R. P. Blackmur, Cleanth Brooks, T. S. Eliot, John Crowe Ransom, and Allen Tate.[27]

When Russell MacFall reviewed the book for the *Tribune*, he recognized that the poems were of a previous era. Indeed, finding in Iris similarities to A. E. Housman, Edna St. Vincent Millay, and the imagists, MacFall said the poems "seem the echoes of poems familiar now with the years." Because the poems "evidently were written in the decade after World War I," McFall did not find the story of the poems' 20-year disappearance "difficult to believe." Moreover, his own taste ran to the old fashioned, so he found some good "Sundae reading" in the book—"some solid ice cream" under the cherry preface, whipped cream epilogue, and pecan portrait.[28]

In the *Library Journal,* Gerald D. McDonald began and ended his brief review by raising the issue of credibility. He would find the history of the poems—their loss and recovery, the preface by Yeats and epilogue by Gogarty, and the earlier publication under pseudonyms—"quite incredible" except for his familiarity with "the strange ways in which the poems of Edward Taylor, Dolber, Traherne, and Emily Dickinson reached us." Further, McDonald considered Yeats's praise "well deserved." He admitted that "credulity may be strained" by the account of the book's history, but he is certain that "the poetry, written in ballad meters, has its own truth and perfection."[29]

Bernard Theall, in *Books on Trial* (published by the Thomas More Association in Chicago), noted the prepublication publicity, and he registered postpublication disappointment. The collection, on the whole, he thought, was "competent, workmanlike poetry, sometimes rewarding, sometimes on the level of the sort of thing that appears in newspaper columns in which inglorious, but not mute, Miltons work off their excess." Theall discerned in the poems pathos, bad theology, and failures in imagery (as when a fawn has "flashing horns" and is made to "thunder assault"). Bad theology and pathos combine in "Paganini," where the violinist is addressed:

> You pizzicato tease!
> Grandmothers call you *diavolo*—
> The devil is the other face of God.

But Theall liked "The Old Courtesan," which he judged better and "more economically done than Villon's famous poem on the same theme." "April" is "a lovely lyric" but cannot compete with

Wordsworth's "Lucy," which has already expressed the same theme. So he found a handful of good poems and "perhaps twoscore" good lines, not "a collection of great verse." He did not question the authenticity of the preface.[30]

The publication of *Bread* did not suggest to Iris that he should take a break from his tireless efforts to gather accolades from the famous and to present his poetry to the public. Even in the interval between *Bread*'s acceptance and publication, Iris continued to solicit introductions and the like. He asked Sandburg, for example, to supply an introduction to a manuscript entitled "24 Poems." Sandburg refused. "The influence of introductions is over-rated," he said.[31] During this time Iris did have some other successes in publishing. He had a poem in a children's anthology. Its odd landscape and curious action do not recommend it as bedtime reading, but it does have the sound of children's verse:

> The sun is like a ball of brass,
> > The sky is like a bowl of blue.
> > Your father on his flute for you
> Music is making.
> The rabbit in the desert grass
> His ear is shaking.
> > Run, little baby, run,
> > Dance with the rabbit here in the sun![32]

And also under the name Scharmel Iris, he had occasional poems in the *New York Times,* for which he received $8 each.[33]

The year 1953 thus stands as Iris's second annus mirabilis. If he was disappointed that his volume had not really resounded across the world of poetry, he never said so. Besides, his personal circumstances had been much improved. By midcentury, across the United States, colleges and universities had become the primary institutional support for poets and poetry. Whereas Wallace Stevens earned a living as an insurance executive, William Carlos Williams as a physician, Marianne Moore as an editor, T. S. Eliot as a banker and then publisher, the new generation of poets (and some of the old) were teaching and giving readings and being published by university-subsidized quarterlies. At Lewis, Iris may not have had an appointment, but he did have meals and housing and a useful address—and a great deal of time in which to do his work. He had something very like the patronage he had sought for years.

# CHAPTER SIX

# INTERNATIONAL POET IN RESIDENCE, 1954–1959

"Wheresoe'er thou art in the world's globe

I'll have an Iris that shall find thee out."

—Shakespeare, *Henry VI, Part 2*

For a time, the publication of *Bread out of Stone* emboldened Iris in his dealings with publishers. Still intent on having Harper and Brothers publish him, he sent them on 11 January 1954 a manuscript entitled "A Singing Reed." After Elizabeth Lawrence, at Harper, rejected it, Iris appealed to Cass Canfield's son Michael, now an editor with the house. Writing as Holme, on 24 February, Iris offered the instructive story of *Bread:* Sent to Harper by Paul Engle but rejected, *Bread* was published last September by Regnery. The edition of 1,500 copies is nearly exhausted, its sales having been boosted by Harvey Breit's 16 August 1953 column in the *New York Times* and by Van Allen Bradley's three-quarter-page picture story on Iris. That amount of space in the *Chicago Daily News* would be valued at $4,000. Finally, there was Eleanor Roosevelt's column. "Surely," he

said, summing up the achievement, "not a bad thing for a poet."
Holme then, while he had Canfield's attention, asked him to
serve as a go-between by introducing Iris to Salvador Dali, who
was supposed to do a sketch of him. Canfield wrote Holme,
however, to say that he stood by Lawrence's decision to reject
the manuscript and that he did not know Dali. Evidently, Can-
field was not impressed by the statement that Dali was to
sketch Iris.

Actually, the arrangements for the portrait were not yet made,
but Holme was working on them, well aware of the opportunity
afforded by Gala and Salvador Dali's presence in New York, at
the St. Regis Hotel. Answering Holme's request on 12 April, how-
ever, Gala Dali said that there was no time for a sketch. Salvador
had many engagements and would have to leave New York for
Europe on 17 April. He had hoped to be able to draw Iris, she
said. Perhaps, when they return for the Dali exposition, toward
the middle of December, he might be able to do so.

In 1954 Iris also continued work on finding "Spanish Earth" a
publisher. Again he sought the help of MacLeish, and again
MacLeish had sympathy for Iris, even though he had no enthusi-
asm for Iris's poetry. After seeing the manuscript, he told Holme,
"Poetry no better than this . . . gets published every year." He ad-
mitted that Iris's ear and his own didn't "hear the same music"
and that he did not particularly like the poetry. Still, it was "a
bloody shame he can't get his work into print." MacLeish won-
dered if the "curious political diatribe" by Campbell might not
be "throwing the publishers off."[1] On 1 November of that year,
at Holme's request, MacLeish wrote the publisher Alfred Knopf
on Iris's behalf. As Iris knew, Knopf was an eminent publisher
with books by a great many major authors to his credit, includ-
ing volumes of poetry by Willa Cather, T. S. Eliot, A. E. Hous-
man, Langston Hughes, John Crowe Ransom, Edith Sitwell, Wal-
lace Stevens, and Elinor Wylie. His own letter to Knopf, written
under the name Holme and offering the manuscript of "Spanish
Earth," did not make a good impression. Knopf wrote back on 3
November: "If you really want to interest me in SPANISH EARTH
by Scharmel Iris I must tell you that you are going about it the
wrong way. Why address me at my home on a business matter,
and by Registered Mail 'Return Receipt Requested'? Did you
think I would otherwise deny ever having received your letter?"
Furthermore, he said, "I find the whole tone of your comments

either naive or, as when you write 'then why all this editorial nonsense?' impudent." Knopf did agree to look at the manuscript but warned Holme that he was not impressed by Iris's poems that Holme had quoted from the *New York Times*. After he received the manuscript, Knopf did not delay in rejecting it. On 6 December he wrote, "We simply cannot share the enthusiasm of better men than us for Scharmel Iris and we cannot publish SPANISH EARTH."

Shortly after that, before the year was out, Iris may have finally gotten his free two-week stay at the Waldorf-Astoria, the one he had first angled for back in 1944. At least he was using the hotel as his address while following up on Gala Dali's probably casual statement that Salvador might be able to sketch Iris when he returned to New York in mid-December. Again, though, he was put off by Dali. He was also put off by Random House, to which he had submitted "Spanish Earth." Its editor Saxe Commins believed that readers "would have to be as Spanish as Senor Madariaga, or as Spanish by adoption as Roy Campbell, in order to feel the full import" of the poems. Besides, he explained on 6 January 1955, the schedule of verse publication at Random House was "over-burdened."

Iris was simultaneously seeking publication of the group of poems that Padraic Colum, back in 1951, had culled from a voluminous manuscript and for which he had written a foreword. At the time Iris had sought to involve Samuel Cardinal Stritch in the book, which he was calling "The Seven Hills of the Dove" and which may have included all or some of the poems in the manuscript "Christ." With the hope that Stritch might come to earn the favor, Iris let Stritch know that he wanted to dedicate the book to him. The chancellor of the archdiocese, the Right Reverend Monsignor Edward M. Burke, replied that Stritch had read the book with much interest, especially in light of his proposal to dedicate the book to him. They felt, however, that the book did "not come under the provisions of Canon Law on censorship and for that reason would not with propriety bear a dedication to His Eminence."[2] On 24 September 1952 Iris had renewed his effort to involve Stritch. He wrote to say that "Seven Hills" had been rejected by several publishers, although the letter from one had acknowledged that "the office girls enjoyed the quality of these poems." Out of desperation he had sought the aid of Winston Churchill and received, through the British Embassy, a refusal, which he quoted for Stritch: "I have been asked to thank you for your letter of the 12th of August to the Prime Minister with which you sent him this fine collection of poems. . . . I am sorry to say that Mr. Churchill would not feel able to try and secure their publication in England. I am sure you will understand his time is fully taken up by his official duties." So, Iris said, his efforts and genius had come to nothing. He wanted Stritch to contact a publisher, John Delaney, who had asked for a subsidy. Stritch then met with Iris and suggested that he himself get the particulars from Delaney.[3] Posing as Holme, Iris learned from Delaney that his Declan X. McMullen Co. would publish 1,000 copies for $1,500 or 1,500 copies for $1,800. If the book were priced at $2.50 and all 1,000 copies were sold, the author would break even. Iris typed a copy of that 5 November 1952 letter and sent it to Stritch, along with a copy of another, dated 14 November, purportedly from Delaney—but actually from Iris—to Holme:

> If you could get England's foremost artist Augustus John to make a portrait of Scharmel Iris in pencil we would use it as a frontispiece and that would advance sales as well as add prestige to the volume fortunate enough to have a foreword by Padraic Colum. No other Catholic poet was so honored and we will do all we can to make the fact known.

Iris thus had Delaney suggesting a portrait that Iris had already gotten John to agree to. As Holme, Iris had written John back in October 1952, telling him his sad story and asking him to help by drawing his portrait. John had found Holme's account of Iris's career "fantastic," confessed that he had neither heard of Iris nor heard Yeats or Gogarty speak of him, and agreed to do a portrait.[4] In forging Delaney's letter, Iris was attempting to get Stritch to support another of his European trips in quest of images of himself.

To show the quality of the poems, Iris also sent Stritch a letter purportedly written by Cass Canfield to Holme back on 4 January 1952. Aside from incorporating from another, later letter Canfield's reference to Iris as "a poet's poet," the letter is Iris's invention, especially so in its final paragraph:

> There is no question in our minds that Scharmel Iris is a distinguished poet; that there are many passages in this manuscript which make the reader feel he is in the presence of something rare. On the other hand, we are inclined to appraise Mr. Iris as a poet's poet. In these circumstances we see no alternative but to decline with regret. We realize the importance of the manuscript and the endorsements this author has had from those best qualified to make them such as Yeats who said of him, "of poets writing today there is no greater," yet we must make our own evaluations and if these evaluations do not coincide with promt [sic] sales there is nothing more to be done except to abandon the project of publication. The manuscript is returned herewith.

Stritch linked Iris up with the Reverend John P. O'Connell. Before he went any further with Iris, he wanted assurance that his poems reflected good Catholic thought. O'Connell examined the manuscript and must have seen need for revision. So on 24 January 1953, Iris thanked Stritch for permitting him to meet O'Connell ("I am happy to know a theologian") and falsely claimed that, to make revisions, he had recalled the manuscript over the protest of a publisher. Iris thus figured he had Stritch thinking himself responsible for the lack of a publisher. Iris also used this opportunity to ask for additional aid, which must have been financial but about which Iris would not be explicit:

> This is not to remind you that you mentioned you would send me something. What I wish to make clear is that a friend has sent me a letter; enclosed in that letter was one he had originally sent me during the Christmas post office rush which had [been] stamped "undeliverable." I trust it has not happened in your case for I should feel very bad if any thing has gone wrong. And pardon me for bringing my anxiety to your attention.

"Seven Hills," theologically improved, found its way to a publisher, Bruce Humphries, Inc., that was teetering on the brink of insolvency and doing a fair amount of publishing in which someone other than the publisher bore the costs. On 18 October 1954, the publisher expressed interest in "Seven Hills" but said publication would have to take place on "a cooperative basis." There would have to be a subsidy at least equal to the manufacturing cost of the book. It was time to involve Cardinal Stritch again. Writing as Frederick Scharmel Iris, he rehearsed for Stritch his difficulties getting published and reminded him that, at some point, the cardinal had written him on his "personal stationary [*sic*]" and thus made him his "brother." He told Stritch that Bruce Humphries looked like the best they could do. "Father O'Connell," he said, "is a fine man and has done what he could." That included, he said, getting the manuscript to Regnery, "a firm which sold 679 copies of BREAD OUT OF STONE." But that had done no good, for Iris had received a note from Regnery saying that there was an unsolicited manuscript in their office and asking him to pick it up. "Regnery," Iris explained, "is of Quaker stock" and could not be expected to appreciate "my gift as a Catholic to the Church." Certain that he had the cardinal's financial support for publication, Iris added some new business. He said that if Humphries were to send to Harvey Breit of the *New York Times* a drawing of him "by a world-famous artist," Breit would use it to accompany a notice of Iris and his book. Well, Iris told Stritch, Augustus John, "England's most famous artist," had offered to sketch him, gratis. But Iris "cannot swim." Comparing himself to the cardinal—explicitly in vocation and implicitly in sexuality—he assured Stritch: "This is not just another woman's whim. I have given 45 years of my life to the divine art of poetry, my apostolate." The letter was disjointed, as if Iris's various motives were stumbling over one another. What emerged, though, was Iris's desire for patronage. That would include support for his "mission" to England and for publication of "Seven Hills." "Bronchial asthma has consumed my earnings," Iris complained.[5]

It worked. Stritch replied on 20 November with an expression of sympathy for Iris in his time of difficulty. "It is," he said, "a sad commentary on our day that publishers hold the poet in such low esteem." He told Iris to call the chancery office and arrange to see him to work out a way to make his trip. Then, on 8 December 1954, O'Connell summarized for Stritch his and Iris's efforts with the publishers. The manuscript had gone to Devin-Adair, Harper, Bruce Humphries, Kennedy, Macmillan, Newman Press, Regnery, Scribners, and Sheed & Ward. None of these would publish at its own expense. The least expensive arrangement was offered by Humphries, which would publish the volume for $750. "Mr. Iris," O'Connell wrote, "is under the impression that Your Eminence may be able to find a patron who will help him get the book published." Both Iris and Stritch knew that to be the case. Stritch would subsidize publication of the book and a spring 1955 trip to Europe.

Meanwhile, Iris received a letter from a law firm serving as general counsel for the *New York Times*. The letter asked Iris to explain why a poem of his published in the *Times* was strikingly similar to another poem, one by Marion Edey, who had written to complain.[6] Iris's poem, "The Unicorn," had appeared in the *Times* on 22 February 1955:

> Aureoled under the moon I saw him stand—
> The unicorn who watched night take the land.
> With lifted horn, on wary hoof,
> He shone above the sand.
>
> Remote, aloof, he trod the forest rim.
> Out of the circle of my eye
> I stared at him,
> And he at me, as he went lightly by.
>
> Starring the wrinkled sand he stood upon,
> He bloomed and paled for me and now is gone.

Edey's poem had been published in a collection of her poetry four years earlier:

> **The Unicorn**
> *(Who, according to legend, would never*
> *take a path that had been used before.)*
>
> Now he is gone.
> No footprint stars the sand
> of that forgotten land he walked upon.
>
> Lightly he trod; remote, aloof,
> with lifted horn and a wary hoof.
> No other eye to stare at him
> as he stepped along to the forest rim.
> Under a deeply-breathing sky
> no other foot went by.
>
> But one summer morning he stood in his door
> and a curious feeling pricked his skin,
> the silver circle he was in

> seemed different from before.
> The sun felt warm and the wind felt cool,
> just as they should,
> but something had touched his glass-green pool,
> someone had crossed his wood.[7]

Iris borrowed some of Edey's wording, notably the phrases "remote, aloof," "with lifted horn . . . a wary hoof," and "now . . . is gone." The borrowing was not simply linguistic. He also made use, as she did, of the opposition between the miraculously elusive unicorn and the observing eye, between myth and empiricism. Iris's poem, like his much earlier but also indebted "The Heart-Cry of the Celtic Maid," suggests one of Iris's methods of composition. He sometimes wrote by rewriting. That is one reason his poetry struck readers as derivative. When the rewriting was incomplete, the result was plagiarism. A later version of Iris's "The Unicorn" continued the rewriting with an interlinear revision, perhaps because of Edey's complaint. Iris changed the third line, "With lifted horn, on wary hoof," to read, "With milk-white horn, on wary hoof." Whether Iris responded to the law firm's letter is not known. He must have thought the poem sufficiently his, though. He later included it, in its slightly revised state, in the manuscript of one of his collections, "London Poems."

On 6 April 1955, on the Italian Line ship *Vulcania*, Iris sailed from New York to Naples, reversing the voyage he had made as a child 63 years earlier. In preparation for the trip he had acquired, through the Italian Consulate General in Chicago, a birth certificate. The certificate, from Castelcivita, Salerno, listed his birth date as 10 February 1889, his name as Federico Scaramella, and his mother's as Mariarosa Scaramella. Probably not a surprise to Iris was the unfilled blank where a father was supposed to appear. It was a blank his imagination had filled years earlier. Still, it may have given Iris added incentive to go to Augustus John by way of Italy—to see as fact his place of origin. Then, too, he really needed to see Rome. After all, the seven hills in the title of his manuscript referred to the hills on which, in the traditional account, the city had been built. It was a pilgrimage and professional visit. He paid $195 for the one-way ticket and still had $750 in travelers checks.

On 29 April, shortly after arriving in Rome, Iris brought Stritch up to date. Acknowledging Stritch's kindness in subsidizing both the trip and the eventual publication of "Seven Hills," Iris had another favor to ask. He had called upon the artist Giorgio de Chirico to see about a portrait to be used in the book. What was needed, he said, was a letter of introduction "saying I am whom [*sic*] I am," since "I have no social security card saying I'm a poet." Stritch replied on 5 May: "I am much pleased that you are having a nice stay in Rome. You may show this letter to the artist as evidence that you are a poet who has done some beautiful verses expressing the mind and heart of the devout Catholic."

Iris would have found De Chirico in his home and studio in the Piazza di Spagna, what De Chirico called "the center of the center of the world." The forger Iris made an oddly appropriate subject for De Chirico, who claimed, evidently with some justification, that there were "large quantities of false paintings attributed to him."[8] By 1972, when he was 83, he maintained that the forgeries numbered at least 3,000. According to one estimate, he himself may have produced during his long career, from 1910 to his death in 1978, 3,000 to 4,000 easel paintings, along with many drawings, book illustrations, and so on. But some of these were themselves forgeries. They were self-forgeries, copies he made or works he dated as much earlier than their actual date of production.[9] At any rate, a pencil drawing of Iris, inscribed "For Scharmel Iris. / Giorgio de Chirico / Roma 1955," and appearing eventually as a frontispiece for *Seven Hills,* may be genuine. Iris told Stritch that his letter had "opened the door to Giorgia [*sic*] de Chirico," who had produced a portrait that "could not possibly be equaled by an American artist." He supposed that the "purse put in the artist's hand" had been raised with the help of Clare Boothe Luce, the American ambassador to Italy, "although she would disclaim all credit for the friendly act."[10] It is not beyond possibility that Iris pocketed the money and had the drawing made by one of Rome's sidewalk or café sketch artists.

When he reached London in June 1955, Iris had a difficult time finding John. Several times, in a state of distress, he appeared at St. Anne's House, originally the clergy house associated with St. Thomas's Church, but by then known as a meeting place for lectures and discussions, sometimes with Dorothy Sayers and T. S. Eliot in attendance. There he claimed to have come to England at John's invitation after having met him in the United States. At the time, he said, John had asked him to come so that he could paint his portrait. But now he couldn't seem to get in touch with John. Because his resources were limited, he added, he might have to go to the American embassy for aid. The assistant director of St. Anne's conveyed this story of "Mr. Iris' very difficult position" to John.[11] Almost two weeks later, on 6 July, John finally contacted Iris. He had received a message, he wrote, that he had missed an appointment, but he had made no such appointment, having merely said that he hoped to fit Iris in "among several other commissions" in which he was interested. He would be in London the following week and would let him know then if he were free. He wished he "had a copy of those two poems" Iris had shown him and looked forward to seeing all the others when they appeared.

John had not been in London but at his house, Fryern Court, in Fordingbridge, where he had taken up residence in 1927. It had a small studio. But in the 1950s John had also a studio in London, at the home of his daughter Gwyneth (on Charlotte St). His comings and goings between Fryern Court and London were unpredictable. He was at the time dealing with diminished sight and hearing, and with what he called the "potholes" on the road to the grave.[12] He also was still, at age 77, a prodigious drinker. Nonetheless, Iris did finally get to sit for him, at his London studio. John completed two drawings and afterward, on 28 July, wrote Iris that he had been "a prize model." Iris arranged with John's daughter to have one of them photographed for him. Evidently lacking sufficient funds to pay the commission, Iris got the original of neither drawing.

Nonetheless, Iris was pleased to have been one of John's subjects. He knew that he was in good company. Among John's other subjects in the postwar years were orchestral conductor Sir Thomas Beecham, poet and novelist Walter de la Mare, novelist and drama critic Charles Morgan, classical scholar Gilbert Murray, writer and lecturer John Cowper Powys, and clergyman-philosopher-physician Albert Schweitzer. John had drawn several portraits of Yeats, the first in 1907, and during his career he also completed portraits of Elizabeth, Queen of George VI and Queen Mother of Elizabeth II, Thomas Hardy, Tallulah Bankhead, Tom Mix, and Dylan Thomas. Among the portraits he drew in old age, according to his biographer, "his studies of old men are probably the best": "Of the original talent nothing remains: yet a certain ingenuity has developed, the skill of using a very limited vocabulary. The trembling contours, the blurred and fading lines convey very poignantly the frailty of old age."[13] John was pleased enough with his sanguine and black chalk portrait of Iris to reproduce it in a published collection of his drawings. Introducing the collection, Lord David Cecil commented that Iris, like other sitters, startles "the beholder by strength of personality." "Their own personality, but also Mr. John's: a portrait is always partly a portrait of the artist who paints it."[14]

John was sufficiently taken by Iris to serve as a conduit for him to Lord Dunsany, or Edward John Moreton Drax Plunkett, eighteenth Baron Dunsany, a 77-year-old poet and dramatist and, more successfully, writer of fiction with a strong element of fantasy. He sent Dunsany some poems by Iris and let him know that Iris was seeking a preface (probably for a new group, "London Poems," he had been working on). Dunsany replied to both John and Iris. Decidedly premodernist in his taste, he had some difficulty with Iris's work. He wrote John on 19 July that Iris had "a fine sense of poetry" but was "being corrupted by Eliot." He thought Iris's "The Mystic Hour" was "full of beauty" and with great effort "might even understand his dreaming still of the sun overhead while it was actually twilight." Poetry, he said, must contain two ingredients, truth and beauty, and poets must "see truth very clearly." So he cannot understand how in Iris's poem one sees "warm figs so late in the day." He discerned a "downward path" from "The Mystic Hour," "which is like poetry," to "The White Hawks," "which is more like 'modern verse.'" Having called for "clarity" in literature during his lectures in America, Dunsany said, he could not write a preface for anything of which he did not "understand every line." He hoped it was not too late for Iris to turn back from modernism. He said pretty much the same thing to Iris on 26 July. Although he enjoyed reading the poems, he could not write a preface because of what he had "been saying of late about clarity," which he thought, "with truth & beauty, an essential ingredient of poetry." He found in Iris's poems some "beauty, that is, a meter, lacking in modern verse," but found also lines that he could not "fully understand." Iris's loss, he said, was not his refusal to write a preface but rather the public's and thus the

Iris in London in 1955, holding a portrait of himself drawn by Augustus John that year. Courtesy Lewis University.

publishers' "turning away from all poetry in this decade to read instead the stuff they call 'modern verse.'"

Iris had not planned to be in London as long as he was. He had exhausted his funds, and his attempt to earn at least a little money by taking two poems in person to John Lehmann at the *London Magazine* office came to nothing.[15] On 3 August he showed up, broke, at the American Embassy. There he was allowed to borrow £40 6s 8d ($112.53) to get himself home.[16] When he reached the States he somehow ended up staying for a time with Julio de Diego at his house in Woodstock, New York. Iris may have known de Diego when the artist was in Chicago during the 1920s, and he certainly knew *of* him, thanks to his brief, headline-making marriage to burlesque entertainer Gypsy Rose Lee in 1948.[17] At de Diego's, Iris drafted a letter bringing Bishop Sheil up to date. He said that De Chirico's portrait of him, to be used in *Seven Hills,* had been forwarded to "Life-Time," by which he meant "Time-Life," the enterprise of Clare Boothe Luce's husband, Henry. (Iris had visions of his face on the cover of *Time* or *Life.*) He told of John's prolonged drawing of him: "John is a most lovable character. I lost him when he turned demijohn. Sir Humphrey Brooke, Royal Academy, whispered discreetly, 'John has no sense of time.'" The sketching and photographing of a sketch "took weeks to do and was very taxing." He went on: "I did not call for an aspirin. I *worked* and completed a new volume: London Poems." He then returned to New York, he said, exhausted and in debt to the U.S. government. But Julio de Diego took him in. Even better, he painted him and did not make "a kindly grandmother" of him, revealing instead "whatever force and character" he must possess. On the assumption Sheil was planning to have his own portrait made, Iris suggested de Diego for the artist.[18]

Perhaps even before leaving London, but probably after returning to Chicago, Iris had made what he thought were the finishing touches on his 71-page "London Poems" manuscript. One of those touches was a preface by Lord Dunsany, which Iris himself had to write because of Dunsany's refusal. The preface had Dunsany meeting Iris in Chicago while "in America on a mission for clarity in the field of poetry." It noted that Sir Herbert Read admired the poems' directness, that Æ was "carried away" by one of the poems, and that he himself liked Iris's "quiet power." Dunsany's reputation as a literary antimodernist and champion of "clarity" restricted Iris's hand. He worked under no such restrictions in writing a foreword that he attributed to Christian du Lac and considered using for "London Poems." There was no such person, at least not one with a reputation that mattered. The foreword praised Iris's poetry for embodying timeless beauty, reflecting the poet's integrity, and offering a kind of redemption. "Iris," it said, "belongs to that priesthood of consecrated men who renounce vanity and advantage." To repay our debt to Dante, Shakespeare, Goethe, and the other great poets of the past, we should "support the work of living poets." For a small portion of the foreword Iris's Du Lac went to T. S. Eliot's introduction to Marianne Moore's *Selected Poems* (1935). Eliot there had said, "Miss Moore's poems form part of the small body of durable poetry written in our time."[19] Du Lac lopped off "Miss Moore's poems" and substituted a pronoun referring to Iris's poems. In writing the foreword, Iris also kept in mind the report Louis Untermeyer had prepared for Max Schuster.[20] One reason Untermeyer had given for doubting the authenticity of the Yeats preface to *Bread* was that its exaltation of Iris didn't square with the fact that Yeats had become "increasingly critical" later in his career. So, in this foreword, Iris had his Du Lac say that Yeats, "after he had grown increasingly critical," nonetheless "crowned as supreme" Iris's poetry.

After returning from Europe, Iris had sent Bruce Humphries the manuscript of *Seven Hills*, including the foreword by Colum and the frontispiece drawing by De Chirico, and with it had gone a $750 check from Cardinal Stritch. Clearly, though, Iris was not sitting idly by while waiting for publication of *Seven Hills*. He was still faking prefaces, submitting manuscripts, and enduring rejections from publishers. Returned to him on 27 October 1955 was "Past Moth and Rust: The Christ-Centered Poems of Scharmel Iris." With the poems was a preface attributed to Paul Claudel, who had died earlier that year at the age of 86. Claudel was, of course, an ideal name to use introducing a collection of religious poetry by a Catholic poet. He was known as much for his advocacy of Catholicism (for which he was honored by Pius XXI in 1950) as for his poetry, plays, and other works. This one-page preface attributed to him performs the obligatory mention of Yeats's praise, it speaks of Iris's giving of "his money, mind and heart to the poor of Paris" in 1947, and it distinguishes Iris from "precious" poets who lack love: "Iris is not one of the coterie, he does not dance their cotillion." Although typed on Iris's type-writer and although at least some adulteration is signaled by in-terlinear insertions, the preface may have some genuine parts. It does seem relatively mild, speaking more about the Christ-like role of the poet in general than about Iris in particular. Still, it has some heavy touches that strongly suggest Iris's hand. In ad-dition to the biographical bits and the reference to the coterie's cotillion, the preface has a final paragraph that gets into trouble with its metaphors, as Iris often does. It says that, contemplated on the cross, "Christ *ripens* slowly." The image is troubling, and it doesn't get better when it adds, "thus is recovered the reward-ing *taste* of the Spirit."

By spring 1956 there was still no word from Humphries on the publication of *Seven Hills,* so Iris enlisted the aid of John Pas-torelle, a student at Lewis College, or perhaps he enlisted only his name. A letter signed with that name went to the Boston Chamber of Commerce on 9 May to complain about the pub-lisher's failure to produce the book after having "accepted $750 given by a patron to Cardinal Samuel Stritch of Chicago." The letter asked whether the firm had ceased to exist and, if so, whether the manuscript and check could be retrieved. At the foot of the returned letter, a representative of the chamber wrote that Humphries blamed the delay in publishing and the neglect in answering letters on the firm's moving. A letter of explanation, he added, had been sent Iris on 10 May.

In November 1956, thinking publication imminent at last, Iris sent Harvey Breit at the *New York Times* a photograph of his por-trait by De Chirico. In his column Breit printed the drawing, not-ing Iris's claim that he gave De Chirico $300 that Clare Boothe Luce had raised from the American colony in Rome. He briefly re-called Iris's *Bread* and its frontispiece portrait by Diego Rivera and, "magically, a posthumous statement by William Butler Yeats." Breit supposed Iris to be "a poet's poet, or painter's poet, or illusion after all." He announced, prematurely as it turned out, the forthcoming publication of *The Seven Hills of the Dove.*[21]


In late March 1957, with *Seven Hills* still in limbo, Iris began a brief correspondence with Ezra Pound. During World War II Pound had made profascist broadcasts over Rome radio, and at war's end he had been committed to St. Elizabeths Federal Hospital for the Insane in Washington, D.C., rather than made to stand trial for treason.[22] Even there, though, he was less isolated than Iris, attracting a steady stream of old and new poets, academics, and cranks. In his March letter, Iris sought to renew with Pound an acquaintance that never existed. He claimed to have pled, Pound-like, for Pound himself "before the court of Harriet Monroe and Alice Corbin" in the offices of *Poetry* 50 years earlier. Combining fact and fiction, the letter then briefly sketched those 50 years in which he had received almost no financial reward for his noble labors but nonetheless had seen his most recent volume favorably received, had taken a trip to Europe (subsidized by "an old family friend"), had been drawn by De Chirico and John, and had been treated cordially by T. S. Eliot, Wyndam Lewis, and Herbert Read. Probably aware of Archibald MacLeish's efforts to have Pound released from custody, Iris also mentioned how "Archie" had helped him in seeking a publisher. Perhaps with a further parallel in mind, Iris complained of his own institutionalization:

> Back in Chicago the house in which I lived for 40 years had to make way for the Congress Express Highway. Having no place to go, I was led here like a black sheep where I live in an abandoned barrack after burying my aged mother and a sister dead of cancer. This is an institution of learning and I have no status here, no job, no income.

It was, of course, like Iris to turn what really had been a stroke of good fortune into misfortune or victimization, thinking that doing so would stir sympathy and serve as a bond with another victim-poet. Interestingly, however, while MacLeish and others were working for Pound's release, Pound was not altogether certain that he should leave St. Elizabeths, to which he had made a fairly comfortable adjustment. Earlier, in 1949, he had supposed that the government should install him, at no cost to himself, in the rooms of the American Academy at Rome; now, though, St. Elizabeths seemed serviceable.

In his letter, apologizing for only now being able to afford to give him a copy of *Bread*, Iris asked that Pound allow him to send some more recent work for his appraisal. Iris's request was uncharacteristically muted. While Iris must have known that Pound was at least as self-regarding as he himself, he also knew of Pound's reputation for generously supporting and promoting fellow authors with whom he had sympathy.

Pound replied, but only with what Iris termed a note "in cordial anonymity." So on 1 May Iris wrote again, making much of his championship of Pound among the students at Lewis, a "beanery of learning where its profs and cons" begrudge him the light of day. He broadened his focus to describe Pound and himself united against a world in which there are "millions for heathens and not a copper coin for the poets whose brain, brawn, and love enrich the public domain." Iris then modeled for Pound the kind of praise that he must have wished Pound would offer in reciprocity: "No one ranks higher," and "only Dante would have attepted [*sic*] your cantos, one of the truly great projects of our time." While Iris again said he wanted to send Pound some recent work, expressed regret at not being able to travel to Washington, and implied that Pound could help him find a publisher, he also seemed genuinely pleased simply to be in correspondence with him ("Thank you for writing me").

Pound's reply, displaying his usual eccentricities of layout and language, was prompt and perhaps even mostly gratifying. Writing on 3 May, Pound complimented Iris for doing "more good with the younger generation that [*sic*] a lot of half faded wreathes from buzzards no longer in the height of fashion," and he praised him for "settin a fine eggzampl to such old frumps as Frost and Sandbag." He advised him to contact Noel Stock for help in publishing, though not for books yet: "All literary products shd / go to Stock. He will use what others dare not." What Pound had in mind was Stock's success in getting Poundian items, including pseudonymous ones by Pound himself, into Australian journals and in establishing his own magazine *Edge*. He offered no further help and expressed no desire to see any more of Iris's work. In his last sentence though, he in effect united himself with Iris by describing himself too as opposed by "buzzards" and concerned with the reception of his new work: "Buzzards who say no design in Cantos will object to the unprinted ones even more." The letter was a good one to show around campus. Iris wrote Pound again on 4 June. He pictured himself allied with a few kindred spirits at Lewis, including Vincent Holme, who were boosting Pound's poetry and stocking the library with his books. He advised Pound to "keep at the cantos"—to forget the buzzards "who see not beyond their beaks." He asked for nothing, and there the correspondence rested for a time.

The provision for Iris's residence at Lewis had been an act of charity. With the passage of time, though, he increasingly had come to regard "poet in residence" as his position, not simply his description. Regardless of whatever conflicts arose between him and the college, he had continued to live on campus. It is odd, then, that he had two letters that said otherwise. A letter from a Kay Stevenson "to whom it may concern," on 21 June 1957, said that "Frederick Iris" had had a rent-free room at the Paradise Ballroom for the past five years, during which time he had "no income and no employment, and has lived exclusively by the assistance of friends" who gave him clothes and food. Now, Stevenson said, the ballroom was about to be sold, and Iris needed funds to rent a room and cover his living expenses. On 16 August 1957, Stevenson wrote a similar letter, this one addressed to the Public Assistance Division of the Cook County Department of Welfare and adding that Iris occupied his "sleeping quarters" at the ballroom in return for serving as the night watchman. Iris presumably used the letters in applying for unemployment or welfare payments.

While still waiting for the publication of *Seven Hills*, Iris had three poems in the November 1957 issue of *Poetry* magazine.[23] It could not have escaped him that it had been almost exactly 50 years since he had last appeared there under his own name. And he was having serious doubts whether he would ever appear by way of Bruce Humphries. As 1958 began, Pastorelle wrote to the Boston Better Business Bureau, saying that his faith had been greatly shaken and asking the bureau to do what it could to investigate the failure of Humphries to publish the book.[24] The bureau sent Pastorelle a notice from its *Bulletin*. It said that Bruce Humphries, Inc., a company of Edmund R. Brown, had been the subject of complaints of delays, nonpayment of royalties, and failure to provide authors with royalty statements.[25] That was hardly reassuring, but on 14 February, an unsigned letter from the publisher told Iris that they were sending him ten copies of the book. Bearing the date of the year before, the book was finally published.

*Seven Hills* included Colum's foreword written back in 1951. In it Colum expressed surprise at finding religious poetry "in the America of today" but said that he had in Iris. With a Christianity more personal than social, he said, Iris is "absorbed" by the "word spoken on Calvary" and would have the heedless world likewise be absorbed by it. While Gogarty had compared Iris to Gerard Manley Hopkins (to Iris's advantage), Colum found him more comparable to the French poet Francis Jammes, "who was something of a vagrant." Iris had made only one substantive change to Colum's text. Given Colum's emphatic insistence that Yeats could not have written the preface to *Bread*, Iris must have derived some pleasure from making this small insertion in one of Colum's sentences: "I think of Scharmel Iris, *whom Yeats praised*, as the poet of the clay." If Colum ever saw the book (he didn't die until 1972), he could not have been pleased.

On the jacket too, Iris brought up Yeats. The usual quotation falsely attributed to him ("Of poets writing today there is no greater") gets prominent mention, this time on the inside front flap, while a statement just as falsely attributed to Eliot takes the front of the jacket but doesn't entirely eclipse Yeats:

> Scharmel Iris occupies a unique place in the literary firmament; he is the one American poet for whom Yeats wrote a preface. For the richest country on earth not to welcome "The Seven Hills of the Dove" and his "Seven Roman Sonnets" would be sign of spiritual defeat.

Beginning on the front flap and continuing onto the back is a synopsis that sees the book as more than fulfilling "the almost impossibly high expectations" aroused by *Bread*. The back flap goes on to present pretty much the same quotations from Sandburg, Shaw, and Williams as appeared on the jacket of *Bread*. The back of the jacket advertises other religious books published by Humphries.

Iris had finally included 58 poems, more than the 40 or so Colum had selected. The poems by and large are conventional religious verse. Some of them seem dragged along by little more than rhyme:

> Frankincense is He and myrrh,
>     Sweeter He than peach or berry,
>     Or a glen that holds a fairy.
> Who can match Our Comforter?

And some obviously bear Iris's debts to others, as when he begins "Pity Us, Lord" with this line: "Dry seeds in a dry pod we tick." Edgar Lee Masters, in 1915, had begun his "Petit, the Poet" by comparing poets' verse to "Seeds in a dry pod, tick, tick, tick." He also included a poem, "The Cardinal," in which Cardinal Stritch prays for God's help in shepherding his flock

The book received two positive reviews. Clifford J. Laube, in *Spirit,* published at Seton Hall University, discerned in the collection a sort of plot or narrative:

> This book is, by and large, the emotional and spiritual record of a Holy Year pilgrimage to Rome. From the seven hills beside the Tiber the author contemplates the ephemeral glory of temporal power and sees hovering over the See of Peter the white Dove of the Paracletian promise. Drawing inspiration from the wellsprings of Apostolic authority, he bears fresh witness to Christ's unshaken conquest, treads humbly in the steps of martyrs, bows in filial homage before the Holy Father, and finds all glory insipid except the glory of God.

He admitted that an appraisal of Iris and his poetry "calls for more than ordinary caution," and he recognized that some fine parts may "tempt unguarded judgment into overpraise." Yet Laube hardly slips into underpraise. His review found lyrics that have "the sort of fire and finish that mark them as little masterpieces," six poems that "are truly superb," and at least nine others that are "almost equally eloquent and satisfying." Laube's objections lay mostly in formal matters, that is, in jarring tense shifts and slipshod rhymes. Laube agreed with Iris, who in the role of Eliot had said that not to welcome these poems "would be a sign of spiritual defeat."[26]

Dom Wulstan Phillipson, in the *Downside Review* of Downside Abbey, England, was also impressed by the "formidable and versatile trio" of Colum, Eliot, and Shaw, and he too quoted the jacket blurb attributed to Eliot. He accepted as fact the assertion that Yeats once wrote a preface for Iris, and he judged that "fact" all the more telling since Iris writes religious poems, and those being "Catholic in feeling." Not sharing that feeling, Yeats must have especially appreciated "the superb technique of this original and discerning writer who always has something worthwhile to say in his poetry."[27]

Neither Iris nor the publisher made great effort to market the book. Iris did attempt to get to get a bit of publicity through Eleanor Roosevelt, but that didn't come to much. Her "My Day" column for 8 March 1958, distributed by United Features Syndicate, merely mentioned the publication of *Seven Hills* and of the book containing Augustus John's portrait of Iris the year before. She supposed, however, that "Iris's autobiography, which he has decided to call 'Shuttlecock,' would sell far more easily than the book of poems."

Not surprisingly, Iris did not send a copy of *Seven Hills* to Pound, for whom it would have been too "Catholic." But perhaps stirred by news that Pound had returned to Italy after being released from St. Elizabeths, Iris resumed his correspondence with him on 20 October 1958. Aware of MacLeish's role in securing Pound's release, Iris wrote Pound to pass on what he claimed was a suggestion from "Archie"—that Pound "read a short manuscript" of Iris's new work, write a preface for it, and send the whole on to his Italian publisher. "This would," Iris said, "introduce me to Italian eyes." Meanwhile, Iris added, he has rounded up the Dante Society at Lewis and put them to work on Pound's *Cantos,* and he has pressured local libraries to buy copies of Pound's books. Accompanying Iris's letter was another, this one written under the name Dr. Vincent Holme. Noting Iris's plea for a preface, Holme said his situation was dire: he was "unemployed because of tuberculosis" and had "no income." Still, he said, his influence on campus has been great. Holme asked Pound to do whatever he could.

A member of Pound's entourage drafted a reply, addressing it to Holme. (Whether it was ever sent is unknown, no copy of it appeared among Iris's papers at Lewis.) Saying that Pound had spoken of Iris as "a person worthy of consideration," the letter writer agreed to look at Iris's work and consider recommending it to "one of our better translators." "That would be the normal way of introducing it to Italian readers." Iris's request for a preface, however, drew a sharp rebuff:

> But for McLeish [*sic*] to suggest that Pound interrupt his own work to write ~~prefaces for less known writers~~ [*sic*] a preface for it is one of those atrocities that can occur only in an uncivilized country, and is due to flagrant lack of any sense of proportional values. Especially coming from a man of Mc Leish's position. [*sic*] who might

> be supposed to know something of polite habits. It causes one to
> doubt that there is any serious consideration of literature on your
> side of the Atlantic.

Iris gave up the attempt to enlist Pound and to get himself read
in Italy.

Although the national and international press took little notice
of Iris, he was becoming more of a celebrity locally. Thus, for ex-
ample, on 1 October 1959, in the *Joliet Herald-News* and exactly a
week later in the *Lockport Herald* appeared identical stories on
"honors" Iris had recently received. Iris must have supplied the
papers with a press release, either directly from him or indirectly
through Lewis College's public relations office. The papers noted
that he was "the guest of honor" at a banquet given by the
Friends of Literature on 24 September at the Chicago Art Insti-
tute Club Room. Iris, they said, had also been honored recently
by royalty. He had received a note from Queen Elizabeth, who
passed on to Iris the praise of "Sir Herbert Reed" (i.e., Read). She
herself, speaking for the royal family and the whole of Great
Britain, was "very proud of the portrait Augustus John drew" of
him. She thanked Iris for allowing her "to read the typescript of
'London Poems,' for which Lord Dunsany wrote the preface."
The papers went on to say that Iris had also received from the
King of Denmark a message acknowledging that a local com-
poser and musician, Jeanne Boyd, had performed before him on
his seventieth birthday Iris's poem "Adoration," for which she
had written the musical setting. (Over the years, Boyd had in fact
set several of Iris's poems to music, including "Adoration." They
also wrote the Lewis College song, he the words and she the mu-
sic, and dedicated it to Bishop Sheil.)[28]

By the end of the decade Iris could present himself as poet in
residence at Lewis. The college itself was sending out press re-
leases giving him that title even though it had never been officially
granted—and taking him at his word when he supplied "facts" for
their copy. He was also gaining a following in the Joliet area
among townspeople who felt privileged to know a poet, especially
one with marvelous stories about his adventures among the fa-
mous. Iris had begun his career as a child wonder, and he had
learned how to use his youth in self-promotion. In the 1950s he
became an old wonder, a status that conferred similar benefits.

# CHAPTER SEVEN

# AUTOBIOGRAPHER, 1950s AND 1960s

"Falstaff: Lord, Lord, how subject we old men are to this vice of lying! This same starved justice [Justice Shallow] hath done nothing but prate to me of the wildness of his youth and the feats he hath done about Trumbull Street; and every third word is a lie."—Shakespeare, *Henry IV, Part 2*

By the early 1960s Iris had what he considered a completed manuscript of his autobiography, although it was still subject to the change and growth that came with new days lived and old ones reimagined. This autobiography is a disappointment. Under the title "Shuttlecock," which allows Iris some sexual punning and reference, it brings together and elaborates some of the stories that he had been spinning in person and in print over the years, and it adds some new fabrications. It is not, however, a full or continuous narrative of his life, real or imagined, but rather a series of anecdotes and fulminations. Further, it often seems written out of a desire to engage in verbal display rather than out of any intention to tell a story. It conceals more than it reveals.

One of the early chapters, "Off to School and Back Again," is fairly typical. The verbal excess is striking. Here, for example, is how Iris describes Sunday in his parents' house: "Sunday was a day of rest with carafe, casserole and chasuble, but no carnival, caravan or carousel. Sunday was governed by carillons, not sudden caprice or horsey caprioles." When Iris quotes others, they too adopt the style and sound like him. So the Chicago businessman, civic leader, philanthropist, and champion of the Church William J. Onahan is said to have said,

> I would rather come upon an unclothed robot descending the stairs or a pair of proletarian buttocks on parade than be jolted out of grace by that precipitous fall from grace—a pious or twitching hermaphrodite entrusted with the teaching of the young. Why should we expect fertility from seedless hermaphrodites? . . . . With many of our educators a bunch of biddies in dowdy baroque, much that they teach is false.

The chapter consists of disjointed "recollections" from the late 1890s through 1905 or so (Iris provides few dates). He includes an opening description of his mother and of his grade school teacher, Miss Cahill; an account of a trip with his mother to visit with the teacher; memories of classmates after he was transferred to Holy Family School; and a confession that he stole an apple from the Jesuits' orchard after school—all of these serving as something of a framework for other "memories." Along the way, Iris invents his family of wealth and aristocratic descent and explains how he came to grow up in a slum neighborhood. He begins by saying that his mother, descended from Italian nobility, moved to the slums "because she was concerned about the problems facing the people there." The family left "the mansion means had built on the city's first boulevard" (Lake Shore Drive) to take up residence in "a harsh house among a hash of little frame houses." There, near Hull-House, she helped people find jobs, took in stray children, installed a two-person bathtub to wash dirty neighbors and transients. In grade school, he was a "cockerel" and was told by his mother to fight his own battles, "as every cockerel must." Iris here interrupts his narrative for other memories of cocks. He tells a story in which a corpulent man he refers to as Nancy Bird, known for excesses of rouge and lively parties, was found with his head stuffed into a barrel under his porch. He supposes, "Some criminal cock in search of a big fat hen, came upon a capon, must have wrung his neck." That story suggests another: confronting a woman named Mamie who had shot a dog—or, as Iris puts it, "had just inflicted capital punishment on a pooch that took a legal bite of her sniffy snooter over a snub"—and who had taken his mother to task for her charitable activities, Iris "flapped his arms like pinions and crowed like a cock." "The maleness of the drive drove Mamie wild." And another: the madam of a whorehouse at the northwest corner of State Street and Cermak Road had a cockatoo of a son who married a macaw of a wife. She took care of the "chits," the young female prostitutes; he the "dunghill cocks."

Getting back to his school days, Iris notes that he had retained his English accent acquired from his Oxford tutor and at school found himself shuttled from one teacher to another to recite poetry. He recalls the sights in public parks where mingled "children hoping about like exuberant frogs" and "much in the park of which we were not a part." "Old rogues," "a senile Irishman," "the greedy, the seedy and the cantankerous; old rogues and lechers; the duped and the debauched." The chapter goes on to tell of crime and corruption, with an emphasis on "rowdy houses with tumble-in girls." Through the narrative wander such historical figures as notorious first ward aldermen Michael "Hinky Dink" Kenna and John "Bathhouse" Coughlin, along with a crooked coroner named Tom "First Search" McNally, who "looked like a gentleman's room understudy."[1] One afternoon, Iris writes, a police detective named Dick Collins took him to a whorehouse to collect hush money. There Iris saw a 16-year-old girl who had briefly enjoyed refuge with him and his mother. The girl tossed him out of the house: "The victim of corruption was shielding me from corruption." Then the detective, who was "as hard as his face was fair," gave Iris a ride home. Iris's description suggests that Iris may have been Collins's prey:

> On my ride home with Collins I was to learn just how corrupt a *nice* man can really be. The desserts of America have their buzzards. So have the cities. Sleek city buzzards fly high and handsome on Sundays; on week days among the ruins, they hunt for youth. Collins was quietly dropped and with him went his New Testament of Darkness and its eight-page picture supplement. Bigmouths make as much noise as a military band, but a good example

may be a force for change. Early in life mother had sealed me to silence. Only Dick Collins knew why I held my nose whenever our paths crossed.

In several chapters Iris presents himself in association with the powerful, often as an emissary from the world of literature. In one, he tells of having tea in Illinois governor Frank Lowden's mansion. (Lowden's four-year term began 8 January 1917.) Iris depicts Lowden as eager for news about Æ, Lady Gregory, and Joyce. "Has Joyce done well with his obtuse novel," Lowden asks. (Joyce's *Ulysses* wasn't published in book form until 1922, but parts had appeared serially in the *Little Review* from March 1918 through December 1920.) In another chapter, Iris has lunch with Sir Winston Churchill, along with his wife, his "gape-toothed grandchild Arabella," and his family friend Sir Charles Wheeler, at his Hyde Park Gate House. Churchill also appears in a later chapter. It has Iris going to 10 Downing Street, London, to meet with Churchill, to whom he had previously been introduced by FDR, and then riding with him to Lambeth Palace. There they dine with Archbishop of Canterbury Geoffrey Francis Fisher, along with a third guest, the Duke of Norfolk. At the dinner Iris has the opportunity to say that he has enjoyed London and finished "London Poems" in eight weeks. The manuscript, he tells the guests, had been read by Sir Herbert Read and endorsed by Lord Dunsany. All in all, it was a good dinner in the company of "fine men of easy rhetoric and bonhomie."

In the chapter "Teddy and the Three Bears" Iris describes an earlier dinner—he obviously likes dinners—that brought together a towering political figure with an equally towering literary one. It is an account of William Butler Yeats's dining with Theodore Roosevelt. Such a dinner actually took place, on 28 December 1903, and its story had been told by Maurice Francis Egan, who had accompanied Yeats. Iris's account is remarkably like Egans's, except that Iris also places himself there at the table. First, though, Iris recalls being introduced to Egan by Charles O'Malley, editor of the *New World,* after Egan read one of Iris's poems in that newspaper. He pictures Egan as a Victorian gentleman, and he claims to have been Egan's houseguest when Yeats came to the States with a letter of introduction to Egan. Yeats got lost, having taken the wrong trolley, was finally found, and had dinner with Egan and Iris at the Shoreham Hotel in Washington.

Iris notes that Yeats "kept out of the headlines" and that "lesser fry don't." Then, saying these lesser fry have the nose for it, Iris goes off on one his tangents, briefly telling the story of a big-nosed Pedro Cordero: "Two holdup men forced him to open a safe, dropped his money in a black silk bag and left him tied to a chair. But he summoned police by lifting the telephone receiver with his teeth and dialing the operator with his nose." Then, for more entertainment or for padding, Iris takes another excursion. Yeats, he says, was "far from home and family, but not in a fix like the exile in Tristan Bernard's play *The Exile*[,] the shortest play ever published." Iris quotes the play:

> EXILE: Whoever you are, have pity on a hunted man. There is a price on my head.
> MOUNTAINEER: How much?

He then returns to Yeats, whom Roosevelt had invited to dinner. Because Iris had praised a manuscript Roosevelt had submitted to Richard Watson Gilder, editor of *Century,* Iris was also invited and soon found himself dining at the White House, there with Egan and "the Roosevelts—father, mother, Alice, Ethel, Ted, Kermit, Archie and Quentin." Referring to his guests, TR called out, "I am home from the hunt with three bagged bears!" In reporting the subsequent conversation, not actually having been present at the dinner, Iris relies, often word for word, on Egan's account that appeared in his own autobiography, *Recollections of a Happy Life.*[2] In his adaptation, though, Iris has missed Egan's joke. Roosevelt presented himself as a champion of what he called "the little people," and Egan has Roosevelt talking about the importance of preserving "the autonomy of the little peoples" in Europe. Well, in Egan's account that phrase, "little peoples," sets off the previously silent Yeats, who then holds forth on the little people that concerned him—Irish fairies. Iris's version, however, simply has Ethel Roosevelt asking Yeats if he had ever seen a fairy, a question that then elicits his comments on fairies. Iris ends by remarking that he met Roosevelt twice more—once at Hull-House and once at the home of industrialist Joseph Bowen. To this final meeting, Iris says, he took for Roosevelt "a bottle of bourbon wrapped in a late edition newspaper." Roosevelt said, "That's the best thing to ever come out of the *Chicago Tribune*."

Several chapters present Iris as an important behind-the-scenes figure in literary history. The chapter "Trees," for example, expands his story about helping Joyce Kilmer write and get published his famous poem of the same name. Oddly, in this chapter, Iris mostly abandons his overwrought style. Indeed, the first third or so of the chapter reads like the sort of soulless essay produced by many students in their first-year college writing class: "Besides being beautiful in themselves, trees have played an important role in the growth and development of the United States. They provided lumber for the building of homes, stores, churches, schools and factories." Iris thus wanders down to his subject, Kilmer's poem.

Iris says that Charles Phillips, editor of the *San Francisco Monitor*, sent him the poem so that he might use his influence in getting it into *Poetry*. The poem was, though, "over freighted and dripping with honey," and its final couplet was "a still birth." "It needed a climax desperately and the service of a skilled surgeon." Well, he says, he performed the surgery and provided a new concluding couplet. The operation was successful, producing the poem as it is known today:

> I think that I shall never see
> A poem lovely as a tree.
>
> A tree whose hungry mouth is prest
> Against the earth's sweet flowing breast;
>
> A tree that looks at God all day,
> And lifts its leafy arms to pray;
>
> A tree that may in summer wear
> A nest of robins in her hair;
>
> Upon whose bosom snow has lain;
> Who intimately lives with rain.
>
> Poems are made by fools like me,
> But only God can make a tree.

In fact, the poem, without Iris's help, did appear in *Poetry*, the August 1913 issue, and then in Kilmer's volume *Trees and Other*

*Poems* (Doran, 1914). It became one of the best-known poems by an American poet. In her autobiography Monroe recalled that the poem "coined money for publishers, composers, singers, radio people"—everybody except Kilmer, who died fighting in France in 1918, and Monroe, who edited the magazine that first published it. She noted that the head of a motto-card firm later told her that "for years he had paid sixteen hundred dollars or more annually in royalties to the publisher, to be shared with the poet's estate." "That," Monroe said, "is what it means to write two lines which the people take to heart and never forget."[3] The two lines she referred to just happen to be the two Iris claims to have written, the concluding couplet. So he is joining Monroe and Kilmer as one who never reaped the benefit of his act.

Iris also uses this story for a little revenge on Louis Untermeyer, the anthologist who in 1945 reported critically on Iris's poems to publisher Simon and Schuster. He says that soon after Kilmer's poem appeared, Untermeyer called it "a melange of silly metaphors." Charles Phillips wrote to Iris, Iris says, to defend Kilmer: "Joyce Kilmer is a quiet, unassuming fellow with an excellent sense of humor, which he doesn't show. No one demands that Kilmer have the magpie eye that searches for shining tins. He has no qualms about scratching his nose if it itches, nor is he overawed by false mandarins either of the spoken or written word." Actually, Untermeyer did call the poem "a mélange of silly metaphors" but not until 1942 (long after Phillip's death), when he defended omitting the poem from *A Treasury of Great Poems, English and American:* the anthology "omits Joyce Kilmer's 'Trees,' not because it is popular and sentimental, but because it is a mélange of silly metaphors."[4] Untermeyer had included the poem in the first edition of his influential anthology *Modern American Poetry* and in subsequent editions until 1942.[5] In abandoning the poem, Untermeyer was probably influenced by Cleanth Brooks and Robert Penn Warren's *Understanding Poetry: An Anthology for College Students,* which took into college classrooms all across the country the closely analytical approach to literature called the New Criticism—and with it a narrowed, revised canon. In the anthology, they called "Trees" a "bad poem." Though "greatly admired by a large number of people," the poem suffers from metaphorical inconsistency that becomes apparent if the reader attempts to visualize the images it presents: the tree is compared to a suckling babe, then to a woman lifting hairy arms in prayer, then to a promiscuous woman who lets snow lie on her bosom but who is intimate with rain.[6] It is generally agreed that "the immediate reception and the subsequent treatment of Joyce Kilmer's poem 'Trees' show to an extreme and disturbing degree the twentieth century's widening gulf between popular and academic tastes."[7] Iris did a lot of sailing in that gulf. In taking credit for the poem's concluding couplet, however, he clearly allies himself with popular taste.

Three and a half pages of the four-page chapter were typed by someone other than Iris.[8] With his own typewriter, Iris added a half page of somewhat incoherent rumination on works lost before we know them, implying his own lost works. He then concludes—or more precisely, he ends—with words probably meant to say that he relinquishes all claim to Kilmer's poem: "But a tree is something you stand under in a storm if you want to get knocked senseless. Let Kilmer keep his *Trees*. A tree is an object that will stand in one place for years, then jump in front of a lady driver."

Another chapter, "1916," also reflects some of Iris's probably genuine nostalgia for the brief literary renaissance in Chicago. It was, Iris recalls, a time when writers were "not rich of purse and not yet professionally jealous"; they were "a colony generously interested in the welfare of all." "We recognized talent in others," he says, "and passed each other around in a round-robin of introduction." Perhaps as an explanation, though, of his absence from the biographies, memoirs, and collected letters of the likes of Lindsay, Masters, Monroe, and Sandburg (not to mention smaller fry associated with the Chicago literary scene at the time, such as Margaret Anderson, Maurice Browne, Ben Hecht, and Eunice Tietjens), Iris admits—and his admissions seem always to come as boasts—that he has never been "a joiner by nature" and has "declined membership even when offered it in gratuity or by way of honor." Iris characterizes the period as an era of good feeling. He even says that Frost, now generally recognized to have been difficult, seemed to him "one of the most lovable of men." Nonetheless, he does charge Sandburg with an overblown masculinity and with theatrical use of his bangs when reciting poetry. And he accuses Frost as having had to subsidize publication of his *North of Boston* (1914) while in the same year Ralph Fletcher Seymour "dug deep in his pocket" to publish his own *Lyrics of a Lad*—which was published by subscription, only after sufficient funds had been raised to cover Seymour's costs. Having mentioned his book, Iris is compelled to point out (falsely) that Yeats read one of its poems at the banquet held in his honor in Chicago. The poem, though, has been (truthfully) "ignored by critics who preside over procreation." Aside from these bits, what Iris recalls is a sort of golden age from which he individually and Chicago writers collectively fell. At its height in 1916 the writers "sped their shuttles, were hard at work to make a city of intellectual life wherein the best in the mind of man should thrive and bear fruit." Unfortunately, he says, the hoped for audience and encouragement did not develop, and the city's "spiritual cripples" did not hold "their poets higher than their monopolies," with the result that "not all rendered the patronage due the poets."[9]

In the chapter on his 1943 trip to Mexico to be painted by Diego Rivera, Iris claims that he "took the chair Rivera reserved for subjects he chose to paint, not the one for those paying fabulous fees to be painted by Rivera." Later, in London, Iris says, he showed the portrait to some of his fellow authors: "Shaw accepted an invitation to view the canvas." "It made him think of Greek drama." "The irrepressibly brilliant Sitwells were hypnotized into silence." And "T. S. Eliot . . . shook his head *Yes* and *No* like a horse, but with no reins to guide him, could not make up his mind." He recalls, as well, Shaw's earlier advice after reading a couple of manuscripts in the rough and refusing two publishers a preface because they failed to meet his terms: "Portrait is dynamite. Blast the bastards. Change your name but not your style."

These chapters give a good sense of what Iris was up to in his autobiography. He had been telling many of the stories for years, and in the 1960s, using his completed manuscript, he took to reading them aloud to friends and others who would listen. Surely knowing that his lies, fabrications, and so on would have been exposed if the autobiography had been issued by a major publisher, he nonetheless submitted it to Henry Regnery and McGraw-Hill and probably to others.[10] It is difficult to imagine the publishers' not seeing the work as a mix of fact and fiction. It may be, though, that the style of the work was so unattractive that they never had to worry about the work's genre or Iris's veracity.

While writing his autobiography, Iris was also fabricating letters from himself to various notables with whom he pretended to have an acquaintanceship or even friendship. He completed at least twenty-seven such letters, his correspondents being Rupert Brooke, Maurice Browne, Sir Winston Churchill, Marshall Field III, Robert Frost, Archibald MacLeish, Nelson Rockefeller, Edith Rockefeller McCormick, Ezra Pound, Bishop Bernard J. Sheil, Mrs. Godfrey Trent, William Carlos Williams, Georgie (Mrs. W. B.) Yeats, and W. B. Yeats. (He also wrote a letter to himself from Yeats.) Iris never intended to send the letters, which are dated from 4 April 1907 to 3 August 1964, nor did he try to make these letters look like original documents. At the top of each he typed a heading that included the recipient's name and address and the date, as in "TO MAURICE BROWNE, CHICAGO LITTLE THEATRE, FINE ARTS Bldg., MARCH 1, 1913." What he evidently had in mind in pursuing this self-forgery was an edition of his letters, one that would establish a considerable place for him in literary history and serve as a supplement to and sometimes as authentication for "Shuttlecock." He may also have been motivated as much by his enjoyment of the exercise.

Like "Shuttlecock," the letters display Iris's stylistic excesses. A letter addressed to Sheil and dated 1 May 1960, for example, attains something like sheer prattle, as in its second paragraph:

> Jubileeve it? Not from a jug-bitten wet Quaker evasive in translating the truth, the Hooky Walker fit only for a wagger-pagger-bagger. I tell it to you under the rose so sacred to Harpocrates, the God of Silence, Excellency, spouted as from the Jovian head of Jupiter Carlyle before turning roast to rost. I'm rosin-the-bow fiddling the lively rorty and rosy.

At the same time, like many of the forged letters Iris had employed in his various schemes, this letter eagerly supplies information that the recipient would already know or not need to know. While praising the bishop for helping a particular young man through Lewis College, Iris tells the bishop what he indicates the bishop knows—that the student was the result of an extramarital affair of a prominent Chicagoan. He also tells the bishop what he probably did not care to know: the boy's mother "never hopped up in the saddle to ride St. George"; she was not one of those "upperberth performers." Thinking of himself, Iris adds, "The sperage son of a steerage mother is not a contemptible whiffmagig nor she a Tottie all-colours giving juice for the jelly of some Julius Caesar—a transmogriphy at the botchers for transmogrification." The spellings and coinages are Iris's.

Dispensing advice and wisdom in many of the letters, Iris frequently resorts to the aphoristic mode he employed years earlier in submissions to the San Francisco *Monitor* and later in "Barbs from a Barbarian":

> A man rather perfects than corrects his vices.
>
> To say the right thing once too often in our naked society is regarded an invasion of privacy.
>
> Virginity is an immaculate concept as well as the squirrel of the cranium.
>
> Proximity is the mother of marriage, guile the duenna of the bawdy romp.
>
> If you have a nail to hit, hit it on the head.

Also characteristically, Iris attempts to give the letters an air of authenticity by referring to actual events. The attempt is sometimes clumsy, as in his 1 March 1913 letter addressed to Maurice Browne, founder of the Chicago Little Theatre. After congratulating Browne for persuading Mary Aldis to support the theater, he offers some gossip about the infidelities of one of Aldis's woman friends. So far so good, but when he mentions that the woman's first husband "went down with the Titanic," he seems compelled to add, as if the reference would be lost on Browne, that the ship sunk "after striking an iceberg near Cape Rice, 14 April, 1912, with loss of 1,500." The same problem appears in a letter addressed to Edith Rockefeller McCormick and dated 1 January 1932. The letter takes as its context McCormick's quite genuine financial distress at the time. The value of her stocks had greatly declined and her real estate business continued to leak money. She had to move out of her mansion and into the Drake Hotel.[11] Yet any reader of the letter would have had to ask—as McCormick would certainly have asked—why Iris should be telling her what she presumably would know even better than he:

> Until my last visit with you before closing your mansion built in the 1880's by Nathaniel Jones, member of the Board of Trade, and purchased by you and your ex-husband Harold F. McCormick, the youngest son of Cyrus H. McCormick inventor of the reaper, in 1897, I was unaware that the iron fence surrounding its three sides was one of the attained goals by the previous owner General Joseph T. Torrence, Chicago steel magnate. Nor that on a visit to

> the Columbian Exposition of 1893 the general purchased for
> $50,000 the magnificent iron gates given by Kaiser Wilhelm to the
> German exhibit.

The rest of the letter is peculiar too, as Iris goes on to call the gates and fence a landmark of his childhood. Seemingly unaware of the ironic counterforce to his praise of the "magnificent" gates and the "wonderful" match they made with the fence, he recalls the long shadow they cast on the sidewalk as he went around her mansion to get to Lake Michigan. Perhaps by association (fence suggesting cage), he also recalls her philanthropic generosity in funding the Brookfield Zoo. The irony continues when Iris tells Edith that the gates would make "an imperial sight for the dispossessed of Halsted Street" if installed at Hull-House. He reminds her that he is a poor but honest poet: "I may be short of money but my motives are pure." He blesses her and signs himself as her "devoted friend."

In several of the letters, Iris's falls short in his attempt to establish a matrix of historical fact in which to embed his fiction. Iris's letter to the English poet Rupert Brooke is a case in point. In the letter, Iris thanks Brooke for coming to dinner and says that his mother would have him leave his hotel and stay with them, since he is "too young to be thrown to the wolves or to live in solitary." He arranges to meet him at Eugene Hutchinson's studio in the Fine Arts Building for photographs "and no bill to haunt us." He observes that a "rich, spouting geyser from Lake Forest who rescued Margaret Anderson's *Little Review* out of its financial pinch, thinks she has you on the leash; wants to make a hero-legend of you; but anyone familiar with the growth of such legends knows how a great name attracts to itself in popular report achievements that were really the fruit of scattered lesser men who never made the limelight." He tells him he has just the "girl" to make him a man—a "frolicking nymph up from the country eager for a lover" who will "bring out the potency" in him, he who is afflicted with "the curse of a beauty too feminine for one so masculine." He ends by arranging a Sunday evening dinner at 8:00 p.m. at Mme. Galli's. Brooke's visit to Chicago, between his extended stay in Tahiti and his return to England before his early death in 1915, was factual enough. The primary difficulty, though, is that Iris dated the letter 7 March 1913. Brooke's visit came not in March 1913 but in late April and early May 1914. That is when Brooke had his picture taken by Hutchinson, whose studio in the Fine Arts Building was next door to the Auditorium Hotel, where Brooke stayed. Furthermore, the *Little Review* supposedly saved by the Lake Forest geyser (probably Mary Aldis) was not born until 1914.[12]

A letter to a Mrs. Godfrey Trent, Gordon Square, London, also has a problematic date, 4 April 1907. The letter addresses Trent as someone associated with the Salvation Army, someone who stood at the side of its founder, General William Booth. Iris says that she will therefore like Vachel Lindsay's poem "General William Booth Enters into Heaven," which he says Lindsay wrote out for him on the day he visited him. The trouble is that, as the title of the poem indicates, Lindsay wrote the poem on the occasion of Booth's death. That took place not in the year of the letter or earlier but several years later, on 20 August 1912. Lindsay's poem then appeared in *Poetry* in January 1913. So too, then, must the letter be wrong when it asserts that Yeats "has taken to reading its moving marching lines to aristocrats in lordly mansions along with 'The Return,' by Pound, and one of mine called 'April.'" Iris's "April" first appeared in the *Little Review* in November 1914. Pound's poem was probably written in 1912; Yeats did like the poem and read it aloud after its publication in the *English Review* in June 1912.[13] The letter may have been in part an attempt to authenticate a forged holograph of Lindsay's poem, along with the etching Iris thanks Trent for—a "drypoint of Gen. William Booth, twenty proofs in all, by Francis Dodd, R. A." (Dodd, painter and etcher, did complete an etching of Booth sometime between 1900 and 1912. It is in the collection of the National Portrait Gallery, London.) Iris may have had the same motive in "Shuttlecock" when he wrote that William Onahan gave him "a poem Yeats wrote out for him in Ireland."

In the letters, as in "Shuttlecock," Iris strives to show his unrecognized role behind the scenes in literary history, out of the limelight. Chronology still gives him away, however. Thus, he writes a letter to W. B. Yeats's wife George ("Dear Georgie" to Iris just as she was to W. B.) dated 14 August 1913, about four years before the couple's marriage. At first, it is difficult for Iris himself to say what he is up to in this letter. He begins with a style that might be called High Twaddle:

> Miss Monroe's wholehearted devotion to the divine art of poetry is
> as unassailable as half-hearted service to justice is indefensible.
> Moderation in the pursuit is no virtue. No need to assault a lady in
> a moment without armor. Assaults are made by habitual offenders
> lacking imagination. Should the lady leave us, we would be faced
> with a very unpleasant necrological speculation.

All this from a man who says he hates "meaningless oratory"
and does not "want to be too windy about the matter"—a state-
ment to which he windily adds, "not as windy as an ambassador,
the windiest of all." His point finally emerges from behind the
arras, as it were: he would suggest that Georgie suggest that Yeats
return the prize money awarded him by *Poetry* for his verse play
*The Grey Rock* and that Yeats suggest to Monroe that it be sent to
Ezra Pound instead.

The plot continues in the spurious letter from Yeats, dated 29
November 1914 and thus a year late. This letter pretends to have
enclosed Yeats's two actual letters to Monroe in which he did in
fact ask that the prize money go to Pound. In writing the Yeats
letter, Iris was probably relying on Monroe's autobiography,
which tells of the prize and Yeats's request that Pound receive
the money. Monroe quoted Yeats's letters but was vague about
their date, which was actually 7 November 1913.[14] Another of
Iris's concerns in this letter, though, is authenticating or at least
simply enjoying some praise that he had already made much of
during his career. Here Iris's Yeats says that he sent Pound proofs
(of *Lyrics,* presumably) and that Pound had agreed with him that
Iris's "lyric *April* is one of the best in the English language." See-
ing the poem, he continues, was "like coming upon unexpected
sparkle in an old master after the cleaning away of the grime and
cracked varnish of generations." The poem "is a masterpiece."
This Yeats also says that Sir Walter Raleigh (a professor of English
literature at Oxford from 1904) was "won over" by Iris's letter
saying that "a poet is a man without a country and because this
is so, he establishes a country for all men." Yeats tells Iris that
Raleigh felt impelled to add, "and from an inviolable judgment-
seat he passes sentence on the world." He urges Iris to have a
copy of *Lyrics* sent to him at Oxford by Christmas so he can show
it to Raleigh and give a reading from it, just as he did for the actors
from Hull-House who played at the Abbey Theatre. Meanwhile,

Yeats's sisters are at work on some gifts of their own: "Lolly is knitting a pair of woolen mittens for you; Lily a lace collar and wristlets for your mother for helping to underwrite our Cuala Press."

In a spurious letter dated 10 December 1916, Iris extended his advice and wisdom to William Carlos Williams. The letter also allows him to establish himself as anticommunist and critically prescient. One ostensible occasion for the letter is a request by Williams for assistance "revising or rewriting" a poem sent him by James Oppenheim. Iris refuses the request, urging Williams to return the poem to Oppenheim. The poem, he says, is "communist guff muddled up with totalitarean [*sic*] mischief that cannot yield art." He tells Williams, a poet-physician: "Herod slew the babies, you deliver them. Be his [Oppenheim's] literary midwife if you choose but deliver me from communism's Marxist skin!" Oppenheim was something of a name in 1916 and for a time was championed by anthologist Louis Untermeyer as epitomizing what modern poetry should be—fervent, Whitmanian, socially engaged, prophetic, hopeful, expressive of what Untermeyer termed a "communism of spirit."[15] Iris's dismissal of him in 1916, then would foretell his eventual decline in reputation. So, too, Iris's praise here of Williams foretells his eventual ascendancy. At the time, that is, in 1916, Williams had achieved little recognition. He was still at work on his first notable volume of poetry, *Al Que Quiere,* which would appear (thanks to some self-subvention) in 1918. He was also serving as an editor of the little magazine *Others,* now celebrated for having published Wallace Stevens, Mina Loy, Marianne Moore, and other poetic "radicals" but in 1916 difficult even to give away.[16] Thus, in a letter dated 1916 Iris would have been accurate in using the first-person plural and saying, "There are so few who really care for us that we are indeed lucky if they find us. Let them have the fun of discovery." By the time of the letter's actual composition, of course, Williams had won the National Book Award for Poetry (1950) and the Bollingen Prize (1952) and was increasingly regarded as a central figure in modern American poetry, especially by a new generation of poets looking for a way out from under the shadow of Eliot. The date of forgery may well have been as late as 1963, the year in which Williams died and in which an edition of all five books of Williams's long poem *Paterson* appeared. At least Iris had the poem in mind, since he addressed the letter to Williams in "Patterson," New Jersey, adding an interloping *t* and thus misspelling the name of the city and missing the play on *pater* and *son* that figures in Williams's poem. Iris was not aware that Williams never lived in Paterson; he lived in the nearby town of Rutherford. And in 1916, the date given the forgery, Williams had not begun the poem.

Iris would have this letter stand as evidence that some credit for Williams's success belonged to him, Williams's energetic adviser:

> Quit being a listening Big Brother.
>
> Drop your baby-deliveries in parental laps where they belong and get back to your writing.
>
> Go listen to "the rustling birds of dawn" as Blake heard them and restore your faith in the intelligence and integrity of the reader.
>
> Keep to the act, stay within limits.
>
> And above all, keep away from the intrigues and inanities of literary parties—those standardless, egotistical gossipers pretending to be aesthetes.
>
> Join me in silence and cunning.

The advice, however, contains less wisdom than it does Iris's concern with himself. He plays the foolish Polonius to Williams's Laertes.

The letter also contains what Iris may have considered a cleverly masked confession of his forgery. Having remarked the injustice of performing great work for little reward, Iris tells Williams that he might abandon the writing of poetry. He alludes to William Blake's *The First Book of Urizen* (1794), saying, "I think I'll quit hammering away at the forge like Los creating Urizen's backbone." In Blake's mythic world, Los is the imagination, the poet, represented as a blacksmith who at his forge can give form to reason, represented by Urizen. At the end of the letter, however, Iris-Los admits (mixing his metaphors): "A poem is churning in my head so it's back to the forge again." Actually, in ending the letter, he was leaving the forge, though not for long.

While showing that he could enjoy a bit of salaciousness at times and was not above a bit of gossip, Iris was intent on demonstrating his honesty, proclaiming himself a "sticker [stickler] for sober fact" and taking principled stands in the cause of morality. Consider his 3 August 1964 letter to Pound, the most recent of the letters in the collection. Pound was then 79 and living in Italy, having been released from St. Elizabeths in 1958. Addressed to "Dear Ez," the letter takes as its occasion Iris's purported receipt of an "editorial copy" of John Berryman's *77 Dream Songs,* which Iris refers to as *77 Dream Poems,* in the spring of 1964. Iris is not pleased with the book; indeed, he feels some moral outrage. Even the book's design seems to him suspect. The dust-jacket photograph of Berryman makes him appear to be a "secondhand Jesuit without a Roman collar" and thus part of a commercial deception that "Christianity's founder" would have "frowned upon." From all such enterprises, Iris would distance himself: "Deception boasts a longer tail than a kite but why should I attach myself to that moving target?" Iris also accuses Berryman's publisher, Farrar, Straus and Company, of taking money from the Guggenheim Memorial Foundation and from the Church (figured as a wimpled nun offering a check from her "tax free religious order"), while being inhospitable to poets without such institutional support. Supposing that Pound would ask what all the rumpus was about, Iris goes on to say that, though no Puritan, he objects strongly to the word *fuck* printed there on page 46 in type "proudly supplied by American Book-Straford [i.e., Stratford] Press." (Berryman did use that word in the final stanza of dream song 46.) The word, Iris tells Pound, simply cannot make art, and he imagines with satisfaction Berryman's wife whaling "the hell out of him" for his attempt. Iris them implies that Berryman or his publisher had sought his aid in extracting an endorsement from Pound. Someone, Iris complains, had played "the limping Jesus come to do the lardy-dah, come to angle me to approach you with a little bit of sugar toward an endorsement."

Whatever Iris's conscious intentions were in manufacturing these letters and his largely fictional autobiography, the impression they leave is one of Iris as a pathetic figure, one desperately resorting to fantasy to distance himself from or to remedy all that he found deficient in his life: his lower-class origins, his lack of friendships, his isolation from centers of influence, his lack of both critical and financial success, his absence from the literary histories of his time, and even his reliance on forgery and other deceptive practices—the great number of times he had played the limping Jesus come to do the lardy-dah.

# CHAPTER EIGHT

# LOCAL CELEBRITY, 1960–1967

"The average minor poet is far more minor than he and his friends suppose."—Charles Phillips, San Francisco *Monitor*

While old age brought Iris increased celebrity, it also brought reminders of his mortality. He spent a good part of November 1959 in Cook County Hospital, where at least five faculty members and students from Lewis donated blood on his behalf.[1] Two years later, in October 1961, he again was hospitalized, this time for ten days with a severe case of pneumonia. This second hospitalization allowed Iris himself to bring together the themes of celebrity and mortality in his continuing efforts at self-promotion. His illness coincided with the death of Augustus John, so Iris used the occasion to feed a Joliet newspaper the story of the portrait John made of him and news of his own illness and hospital stay.[2]

In the 1960s Iris continued to pass on to reporters and gossip columnists the "facts" of his life, now sharing with them portions of "Shuttlecock" and his spurious collected letters. Thus, an anonymous reporter for the magazine section of the *Chicago Sunday Sun-Times* for 6 October 1963 presented Iris's fictitious account of helping Harriet Monroe raise money for *Poetry* magazine. Iris intended the account to lend a bit of seemliness to what else he told the reporter. Unable to do anything but write poems, he said, he was "used to begging." Demonstrating the truth of that statement, he in effect begged that someone would publish him again.[3]

Later the same month, Fanny Butcher's column in the *Chicago Tribune* served up Iris's story, developed in "Shuttlecock," about convincing Edith Rockefeller McCormick to support James Joyce. Iris hoped the story might prompt others to support him. Butcher explained that she had gotten the story through "Dr. Vincent Holme," whom she identified as president of Lewis College. Holme, she said, "felt, as others have, that Iris was not enough appreciated." So here was the story. Iris had dedicated his first volume of poetry to Mrs. McCormick for what she had done for opera in Chicago. Admiring the poems, she offered to settle upon him an annuity of $300 a month for life. Although "young and struggling," Iris "had made the dedication from his heart, not for profit, and he refused the boon." That refusal caused Mrs. McCormick to have "complete trust in his integrity," so, when she was approached about aiding Joyce (then at work on *Ulysses*), she cabled Iris from Switzerland. He replied, "Go all out on Joyce." He advised "complete subsidization." Butcher was delighted with her scoop, assuring her readers that it was "a bit of Joyceana" that they would "not find even in Richard Ellman's [*sic*] magnificent Pulitzer prize–winning biography, 'James Joyce.'" She was right, of course: Ellmann had made no mention of Iris in his account of McCormick's patronage of Joyce during 1918–1919. Butcher later repeated the story in her own autobiography.[4]


Iris in effect was already receiving "complete subsidization." Without any official status and without any duties (refusing in fact an offer to teach a course), he continued in residence at Lewis College, where he took his meals first at the college cafeteria and then at the house of the Christian Brothers. He also was receiving public assistance, welfare payments from the state. He needed greater assistance, though, to subsidize publication of a book, and his campaign evidently worked. He raised enough to have Ralph Fletcher Seymour, his publisher back in 1914, bring out another collection of poems, *A Singing*

*Reed.* For the book, he dusted off Robert Morss Lovett's introduction written 18 years earlier for *Bread out of Stone* but not used there. Lovett had died in 1956, so there wouldn't be any complaint from him. Because Lovett had made free use of prompts and material supplied by Iris, there was little need for revision.

The major theme of the two-page "dramatic story" of his life that Iris, as Frederick Vincent, had sent Lovett in 1945 was beauty-born-of-suffering. And Lovett adopted that same theme— and often language very like Iris's along with it. For example, Iris had claimed that "as a little boy" he had "roamed the streets of Chicago begging for bread or foraging through market dumps for half decayed food to ward off starvation." Lovett wrote that "as a little boy, he roamed the dismal West Side, and foraged among the waste in the garbage dumps of that proud city." Iris: "From her window at Hull-House . . . Jane Addams saw the lamp-lighter of Halsted street on his daily round with his poems in a box he had made under his arm followed by his gentle-eyed bitch, Spotty, harassed by the thought that he might lose the poems because his family moved so often." Lovett: "He found a job as a lamp-lighter on Halsted Street, where Hull House was practicing its good neighbor policy. Jane Addams used to see him on his rounds, a box under his arm containing his poems which he was afraid of losing if left at home 'because his family moved so often.'" Most of Lovett's introduction was biographical, with the "facts" having been supplied by Iris. Lovett thus had an explanation for Iris's motives in using pseudonyms in *Poetry* (Iris wanted "to submit his work to the stern test" of Monroe's criticism) and his failure to receive a Guggenheim fellowship ("the Guggenheims apparently did not want to risk their money on a race with death"). Lovett declined to use, though, much that Iris supplied, including comments about Iris's relationships with Æ, Rupert Brooke, Enrico Caruso, Joyce Kilmer, Vaslav Nijinsky, Anna Pavlova, Rabindranath Tagore, and others. Lovett's critical appreciation of the poems consisted of little more than a statement that, of "a singularly uniform excellence," they are characterized by "simplicity and directness, sympathy and pathos."

Iris did cut from Lovett's introduction his statement that the volume had been "blessed by William Butler Yeats and Oliver St. John Gogarty," since that marked the introduction as written for *Bread.* Also, Iris did have to include in the volume three poems from *Bread* that Lovett mentioned by title in his introduction, though he did not include here or in *Bread* one also mentioned,

"Child in Halsted Street." (In the published introduction, that poem is marked with an asterisk, so Iris or the printer may have dropped an explanatory footnote.)

The book appeared in mid-December 1963 as one of Seymour's Alderbrink Press Books, the only book issued that year by the 87-year-old publisher. Physically, the book is not as attractive as *Lyrics of a Lad*. The quality of the paper is poor, and the halftone frontispiece, which is derived from a photograph of the Diego Rivera drawing of Iris, lacks contrast. The book presents sixty-three poems in sixty-four pages. The poems themselves reflect greater variety than is found in any of his other collections. Iris included some poems in which he abandons traditional meters and frees words from their customary work and sends them on holiday, as in these lines from "They Sailed against the Wind":

> Foragers among apples perilous to the core,
> Stiflers in charcoal bags of festive fugues,
> Their torqued cakes harden like stalled aluminum horses.

Many of the poems, though, are distinctly old fashioned in form, language, and theme. That is not surprising: some are reprintings of his earliest poems, such as "Iteration," which had appeared in *Lyrics of a Lad* almost 50 years before. There is still an echo of A. E. Housman (on a bad day) here and there, as in "Of Lads Whom I Was Proud to Know," which may also have a touch of Edwin Arlington Robinson and begins,

> Of lads whom I was proud to know,
>     One had a fiddle and a bow;
> He hit the sky and sped the sun—
>     Our pulses glittered when we were young.

There are also some children's poems, including "Dancer in the Sun," and a group of seven "Christ-centered poems," as well as many other poems on religious themes. The final poem seems to pronounce a farewell. It ends,

> Withered as the lonely who have had their say,
>     A reed by the river I murmur all day:
> I have wooed and won the world and have fallen weary
>     And turn now away.

As a farewell, it would turn out to be quite premature.

The dust jacket of the book, compared to that of *Bread,* is rather modest. The front bears the title and Iris's name, along with Seymour's Alderbrink Book device of Pan on a shield affixed to a tree growing from an open book. The back flap presents a publisher's blurb, probably written by Iris, that likens the volume to "a cool spring in a desert." It then has the almost-accurate quotation from Sandburg and the altogether-spurious quotation from Shaw that appeared on the jacket of *Bread.* To these Iris added the spurious quotation from Sir Walter Raleigh that was contained in the spurious letter from Yeats that Iris had written as part of his collected letters project. It was the quotation about Iris's sitting in "an inviolable judgment seat." Iris also added a quotation attributed to Eleanor Roosevelt: "Scharmel Iris[,] who has persevered and grown in depth, is on the side of the angels."

The book attracted little critical attention. The one genuine review, in the *New York Times Book Review,* lumped it with five other volumes of religious poetry and concluded that it could not "be admired for substantially poetic reasons," since "only in a few poems" is there "an authentic poetic gesture."[5] Locally, the *Joliet Spectator* reported Iris's claim that by the end of January 1964 the book was sold out, and it pictured him signing his book for a local customer and standing with a display of his portraits by De Chirico and John.[6] Next month, in the *Chicago Sun-Times,* Hoke Norris devoted his whole column to Iris. Norris mentioned the publication of the new book, but clearly his focus was not on Iris's poetry but on Iris as a poet, that is, as a curiosity: "Scharmel Iris has been a poet, and nothing but a poet, for more than 50 years, which is another way of saying that for more than 50 years he's had no visible means of support." Like the *Chicago Daily News*'s Van Allen Bradley about ten years earlier, Norris was particularly tickled by Iris as a simultaneously ridiculous and enviable emissary from some noneconomic, aesthetic realm. In fact, Bradley had used that same phrase—"no visible means of support." That repetition and his duplication of information (or misinformation) from Bradley's article suggests that Iris supplied Norris with a clipping of it. Norris also talked with Iris's publisher, for he quoted Seymour as saying he had been surprised when Iris showed up after 50 years with another manuscript, financial sponsorship, plenty of endorsements by

Iris and Eleanor Roosevelt in Joliet, Illinois, in November 1960. Iris used the photograph on the dust jackets of *A Singing Reed*, 1963, and *Spanish Earth*, 1964. Courtesy Lewis University.

great writers, and "a supply of energy and enthusiasm that completely belied his almost 75 years."

> "I don't know how he's lived," Seymour said. "He shows up here every Wednesday, and I always enjoy seeing him. He looks like a tramp you might have dragged out of an alley, but he doesn't care; he's a fine raconteur and a fine poet, a dedicated poet. He came in the other day, a very cold day, and I asked him how he got here from Lockport. . . . He said he'd just gone out to the highway and got a ride. . . . He told me once that he was born in the Everleigh Club. He couldn't have been. He lived out on the West Side."

The skepticism about birth in the Everleigh Club, a notorious Chicago brothel, didn't extend to anything else, even though

Seymour admitted that this "fine poet" was a liar. Norris too flirted with the idea of credibility. He said that Iris was "all-in-all, a man who never met a payroll, and so perhaps not to be trusted in a world of men who have." He quickly added, however, "But making a living, physical appearance, getting and spending—all are irrelevant when you consider the likes of Scharmel Iris." The likes of Iris live in another world, one where credibility is not an issue.[7]

Norris also said that Iris was planning another book of poems. Actually, Iris had on hand several such books, and he was continuing to produce more. It was at about that time that he put together a 90-page typescript of "The Yellow Wind of Cathay," for which he surprisingly wrote his own introduction under his own name.[8] The one-page introduction by Iris claims that in about 1913 he was influenced by Pound's translations of Chinese poems and that he also had then "the good fortune of many meetings and discussions with Arthur Waley, of the British Museum, engaged in a similar venture." As a result, rather than attempt translations himself, he confined himself "to writing poems in the Chinese spirit." Over the previous 50 years that spirit produced these poems. Here is one poem in whole:

### Flown Bird

The bird I fed fallen from the nest
Has taken wing
But not the brushed eyebrows of my love
Of which I sing.

But it was not this book manuscript that was next in line for publication. Iris had approached Regnery, the publisher of *Bread out of Stone,* about taking on *Spanish Earth.* On 7 May 1964, an assistant editor at Regnery, Ray Roberts, wrote Iris that they would like to publish *Spanish Earth* but that, the fall list being complete, they would have to wait until spring 1965. The enthusiastic Roberts figured that they could reissue *Bread,* and he wanted to consider "Shuttlecock" too. Now that he had captured the publisher's interest, Iris turned coy and resorted to a go-between. Rather than perform that role himself under the name Vincent Holme, he used one of the local sponsors who had paid for the publication of

*A Singing Reed,* Herbert M. Johnson, whose letterhead identified him as president of Mid-Continent Life Insurance Company, Chicago. Johnson wrote Roberts on 11 May to inform him that Iris agreed to spring publication, wanted 10 percent royalties, and would forward "Shuttlecock" in the near future.

At the time, Iris thought another publisher might well take on "Shuttlecock." A representative from McGraw-Hill—a college traveler by the name of Lyle Linder—had visited Lewis to meet with faculty members about textbooks they might use in their courses. Iris told him about his manuscripts, including "Shuttlecock." Linder had advised him to send the autobiography to A. L. Hart, Jr., in the trade division of McGraw-Hill.[9] Iris did. As in his dealings with Roberts at Regnery, Iris took on the role of a somewhat difficult author who certainly was not begging for publication. On 4 June 1964, stressing that copying the manuscript had cost $75, Iris wrote Hart that his attorney would be sending it and that the contract should go to Herbert Johnson. Although wanting to be courted by a publisher for a change, Iris also felt the need to boost the autobiography a bit: "The prose is kept rhythmic and bouncingly new, no moss, no Moses-beard. It's myself and I have been put up with for years."

Iris did not long enjoy the sense that two publishers were after him. First, Henry Regnery let Johnson know that his firm would not be reissuing *Bread.* Then McGraw-Hill rejected "Shuttlecock." Finally, Regnery reversed the decision of his assistant editor and rejected *Spanish Earth.* He said that it was not their "sort of book" and that he would not go into all the reasons.[10] On the occasion of the rejection, Iris wrote a poem in which he compared himself to the martyred St. Sebastian:

> Sebastian knew these arrows,
>    The red thrust of dark seas.
> The hurt that has no harbor
>    Can blind the pleiades
> And I in the scarlet whirlwind
> Of trade's grim Babylon
> Struck down upon my knees.[11]

He was not struck down to stay. In fact he rose to new heights of temerity by attempting to place his manuscript "Ascension" with Holt, Rinehart, and Winston.[12] Although Holt was the publisher of Robert Frost, who had died in 1963, Iris included with the manuscript a preface that he had written but had ascribed to Frost, even forging Frost's signature on the last of its three pages. This preface creates some literary history, a conjunction of Frost, Pound, and Iris in London sometime from later 1912 through early 1915. It has Frost saying that he and Iris "met as strangers in the London office of David Nutt" (the publisher of Frost's first two books). Pound, who was then Yeats's secretary, was also there, because when Nutt asked Iris whether he had brought a check (presumably to pay for publication of one of his own volumes), Pound "told the publisher that the immortal Irish poet had pronounced his poem, 'April,' one of the best lyrics in the English language" and that he had been acclaimed by Æ, Brooke, Colum, and so on. "Frost" himself, at the end of the preface, affirms "the greatness of Scharmel Iris." He says that "'April' is as great a poem as 'The Listeners' by Walter de la Mere [*sic*]," and he recalls with approval Pound's calling him, in David Nutt's presence, "merely a bucolic poet." Thus the preface serves to give Iris sufficient praise, to provide authentication for assertions made elsewhere, and to write him into literary history. As the preface suggests, Iris was aware that Frost had brought De la Mare's poetry to Alfred Harcourt's attention and thus got him published by Holt. It would also be like Frost to pun on De la Mare's name by misspelling it into *mere* and thus undo with one hand what he had done with the other. But the misspelling here probably derives from the ignorance of Iris rather than the duplicity of his fictive Frost. There is, however, a more serious problem with the preface. Frost, Iris, and Pound could not have had this session with David Nutt. True enough, Frost's first publisher was David Nutt, but what Iris did not know was that Frost dealt with the publishing company bearing that name, not with David Nutt the person, who had died in 1873, 11 years before Frost's birth.[13]

Iris got more than his facts wrong. In writing the preface, he strove to sound like Frost but finally couldn't manage it. Iris had read Frost's "The Figure a Poem Makes," an essay Frost used to introduce his own *Collected Poems*. In it, Frost compared the composition of a poem to the melting of "a piece of ice on a hot stove."[14] Iris's preface attempted something similar by comparing a poet to a cloud of all the other poets he has ever read. Well, that did seem to describe and excuse Iris. But then, dangerously, Iris extended the metaphor: "First the cloud reaches down toward the water from above and then the water reaches up toward the cloud from below and finally cloud and water join together to roll as one pillar between heaven and earth." Perhaps realizing the difficulty he had gotten into, Iris abruptly abandoned the figure, leaving uncertain the significance of the waterspout. Iris's attempt to mimic Frost went even more awry in the preface's final paragraph, where no one could claim to detect even a hint of Frostian style or sentiment:

> Some of these poems have the joy of a first kiss, others the force of deep commitment; the incandescence of clairvoyance of the God-forsaken brute despair of a raging river. What matter that the poet has not the bread for his butter or butter for the bread if as Yeats remarked, he has made "bread out of stone" to feed the spirit in the same way the Biblical catch of fish and the loaves that grew in number, fed the multitude. An hurrah for Scharmel Iris!

Holt rejected the manuscript. Iris sent it right off to Harcourt Brace, where it got the same treatment.[15]

He then sent both it and *Spanish Earth* to the University of Chicago Press. It was probably for this submission that Iris added to "Ascension" an epilogue that he first concocted in the late 1950s. At that time he had extracted a passage from Cardinal Stritch's 1954 letter expressing sympathy for his failure to find a publisher. He had added a bit to it and produced a one-and-a-half-page epilogue attributed to Stritch and dated 8 February 1958. In this early version, Iris surrounded the authentic passage with the usual references to Yeats and others, and he added some new twists. He decided to have Stritch describe Iris as "a gentleman of heroic courage and dignity on what has come to be the poet's via crucis." Not flamboyant but rather rich in "inner growth," Iris possesses "that joyful virginity open to God." This version also explained Iris's poverty: his mother spent "her and his patrimony" on Jane Addams and Mother Cabrini. Truly, this false Stritch said, Iris has noble blood, being related to princes and cavaliers as well as to Pope Innocent, not to mention Hernando Cortez. For the new version, Iris changed the date to 1 January 1958 (Stritch had died in May 1958), and he made additions that swelled the document to three pages. This version has Stritch saying that Pound "cautioned Frost to stop writing poems like Iris and confine himself to country poems." As a result, it says,

Frost gained fame but considered himself "merely a bucolic poet" and judged Iris "greater than the rest." It explains that Stritch and Iris "met under the fresco fury of Michelangelo's matchless ceiling with its poetic and philosophic profundity," shortly after Iris had fixed Kilmer's "Trees" and secured its publication in Monroe's *Poetry*. The epilogue also speaks of Iris's post–World War II charitable activity (dispensing soap and cash to the poor of France), and it traces Iris's neglect at the hands of critics to his desire to be isolated from a world too profane and corrupt—isolated especially from "sly poets" who band together and "prate of purity" and are proud of "tribal exclusiveness." At this point, the epilogue draws on a little Latin: "Illegitimati non harborundum." Contrary to Iris's intention, though, what this represents is not a cardinal's knowledge of Latin but Iris's ignorance. The phrase is Iris's mishearing of the saying "Illegitimati non carborundum." Worse, that saying is a famous instance of bogus Latin, a humorous invention that plays with the brand name for an abrasive (Carborundum) and pretends to mean "don't let the bastards grind you down."

Iris felt beset by bastards, but his Stritch offered encouragement and reassurance. Oddly for a priest of the Church, he says, "No one has a right to question a poet. A great poet is answerable only to God." Moreover, Iris's "militant vision of human aspiration will strike unrest into the minds of many who will object to his harsh moral imperatives, and to those who fall under the rod of the judgment seat." On 23 November 1964, the University of Chicago Press rejected both "Ascensions" and *Spanish Earth*.[16]


A month before, hoping for good news but planning for bad, Iris had already turned again to Ralph Fletcher Seymour for help with *Spanish Earth*. He told Seymour that he had not been able to raise as much money as he had for the publication of *A Singing Reed*. Instead, he was about to meet with a printer whom the Christian Brothers at Lewis had found to print the volume without charge, "a modern 20th-century miracle only the good Brothers at Lewis could achieve." He wanted Seymour, however, to design the book and oversee its printing. Seymour agreed to take on the job.[17] To call him the publisher of the book, though, is a stretch, and he probably didn't think of himself as such. As he had for *A Singing Reed,* he hand lettered a title page. But he did not name himself publisher there; instead, he indicated a space where the publisher and place of publication should be added, and he did not use his identifying Alderbrink device. Perhaps because his title-page design went to the press late, it was printed up separately from the rest of the book and then pasted onto the page, at the foot of which was already printed Seymour's name as publisher. He evidently did not oversee the printing. Iris or someone else from Lewis took the manuscript to the printer.

Published in December 1964 or early January 1965, *Spanish Earth* contained sixty-four brief lyrics on places (Guernica, Seville, Toledo), musicians (Pablo Casals, Pablo Sarasate, Andrés Segovia), and other Spanish subjects. The poem about Lorca that Campbell had strongly objected to was there. Iris had no keen sense of humor, but he may have exercised what he did have when he placed on the page facing "Lorca" a poem entitled "Boy with Cock." On either side of the poetry were Salvador de Madariaga's preface, revised lightly or not at all by Iris, and Roy Campbell's epilogue, so heavily revised as to be more Iris's than Campbell's. Campbell had died in 1957. Madariaga, three years older than Iris, would not die until 1978, at age 92.[18] Thus, Iris's poems united not only the liberal Madariaga and conservative Campbell but the living and dead, the genuine and spurious.

The book's dust jacket repeats earlier blurbs attributed to Lovett, Raleigh, Roosevelt (with whom Iris is pictured), Sandburg, Santayana, Shaw, and Williams. It quotes from Gogarty's epilogue and "Yeat's" preface to *Bread,* and it adds some new praise supposedly by Pablo Casals ("Magnifique!"). It came from a possibly authentic handwritten note addressed to Holme from the Spanish-born cellist. It is written in French on the hotel-room stationery of the Waldorf-Astoria and dated 6 December 1954. Above the date appears the name of the French town, Prades, where Casals lived at the time. The note thanks Holme for a letter and two poems by Iris, which are "touching and magnificent" ("touchants et magnifiques"). *Spanish Earth* includes what was probably one of the poems, "Pablo Casals." It depicts Casals as standing "against the lie," as his cello "cries out our pain." Even should he die, his "spirit would complain" and his "cello in its case cry out again." The stationery of this note is a bit suspicious, given Iris's fondness for the Waldorf, but the note may be genuine and with it something close to the dust jacket's "Magnifique!"

The jacket also adds a blurb falsely attributed to Eliot:

> I have read *Spanish Earth* with deepest sympathy and satisfaction. May the book find a worthy and widening audience.

Another to Frost:

> I am merely a bucolic poet. Iris is greater than the rest.

To Picasso:

> Only a great poet could have conceived and written *Spanish Earth.*

To Pound:

> Do not underestimate. We have but few great poets and Mr. Iris is one of them.

The blurb attributed to Robert N. Linscott is half his (the last half):

> All should be interested in this book, as it has real power and distinction.

Although the phrase "real power and distinction" is Linscott's, its application here is not. He had used it when referring not to *Spanish Earth* but to "Pardon, Picasso," which he was rejecting on behalf of Random House in 1949.[19] Iris also raided a letter from MacLeish that sympathized with Holme over Iris's plight:

> Poetry not so good as this gets published every year. I think it is a bloody shame *Spanish Earth* is not in print and I've said so to all and sundry. At the very least it should for God's sake be printed.
> His ear and mine hear the same music.

The last sentence lacks MacLeish's crucial negative. MacLeish had said that he and Iris did *not* hear the same music and that he did *not* particularly like Iris's poetry.[20]

Despite the blurbs, the publication of *Spanish Earth* attracted little attention. There was a brief note in the *Chicago Sun-Times* on 17 January 1965. It said that Seymour had published this book "by the delightful and incomparable Scharmel Iris," and it quoted the statement attributed to Picasso but actually written by the poet himself. Several months later, Iris was interviewed by Studs Terkel for WFMT radio in Chicago. Iris read portions of the book for the program.[21]

This quiet reception of the book did not deter Iris. He had more manuscripts and a continuing desire to get them into print. As Vincent Holme, now styling himself as a public relations officer at Lewis College, he persuaded Doubleday and Company to express an interest in seeing "Ascension" and "London Poems" (with the fake introduction by Lord Dunsany), as well as a collection of more recent work, *The Judgment Seat.* He sent them "London Poems," without success.[22] He turned again to Seymour. On Iris's behalf, a Joliet-area physician, Robert J. Becker, asked the publisher for an estimate. Seymour replied, on 15 September 1965, that a thousand copies of a 100-page book of poetry, "designed, printed, and bound properly," would cost between $1,200 and $1,300. The money was collected, and in late 1965 Seymour published Iris's *The Judgment Seat,* the last job he undertook before he was hit by a truck and killed while crossing a highway on New Year's Day 1966. In the book Iris made no effort to hide the patronage that subsidized its publication. He acknowledged twenty-five people without whom the book would not have received "the light of print" and "whose names[,] writ in gold, bear witness to their memorable incandescence." Sir Winston and Lady Churchill join local fans, friends, and charitable souls in the list of patrons. Sir Winston did not live to see publication, having died in January of that year.

The immediate source for the book's title was a statement attributed to Sir Walter Raleigh and reprinted as a note in the book, the one in which Raleigh quotes Iris and then provides an addendum: "Scharmel Iris has said, 'A poet is a man without a country and because this is so, he establishes a country for all men.' I should like to add that from the security of an inviolable judgment-seat, he passes sentence on the world." Used previously on the jackets of *A Singing Reed* and *Spanish Earth,* the statement came from the spurious letter Iris had written to himself from Yeats and dated 29 November 1914.

Iris also dipped into the past for an introduction, coming up with one that he ascribed to Dame Edith Sitwell and dated 4 February 1956. Sitwell, who was two years older than Iris and who died in 1964, may have written something for Iris, since among his papers at Lewis is an envelope (now empty) addressed from her to "The Very Reverend Fr. Manoel Holme" (Iris, of course) and postmarked 7 February 1956. The introduction has her writing from "Castello di Montegulfoni"—the correct spelling is "Montegufoni"—where in fact she was at the time. Further, she had recently converted to Catholicism and thus may have been exercising her charity.[23] There are, however, difficulties in accepting the introduction as Sitwell's. In all likelihood, she did not write it. As he had with letters from Cardinal Stritch and others, though, Iris may well have adopted and revised portions of whatever she sent in that envelope addressed to Holme.

One difficulty with the ascription comes from a later letter, dated 6 May 1957, to Sitwell from Father Manoel Holme. The letter thanks Sitwell for befriending Iris by sending a manuscript of his to "Sir Herbert" (Herbert Read). The letter does not mention the introduction Sitwell supposedly had written the year before. If the introduction were authentic, the writing of it rather than the forwarding of a manuscript would have been the occasion of her befriending Iris. The text of the introduction itself has difficulties too. It quotes Gogarty quoting Yeats praising Iris, in the process deleting a sentence and thus creating a problem of pronoun reference that has critics, not poets, as the only ones attuned to "brave translunary things." Also, an odd echo occurs when the introduction says, "We have a spath [*sic*] of half-poets with prisms of conscious oddity their wonders to perform." The sentence seems indebted to some lines in the version of Marianne Moore's poem "Poetry" that appeared only in an anthology that figured strongly in Iris's life—Monroe's *The New Poetry*, this time in its third edition (1932):

> . . . these phenomena
> are important; but dragged into conscious oddity by
> half poets, the result is not poetry.[24]

Even the misspelling of *spate* as *spath* suggests Iris, who lisped. (On the other hand, a lack of copy editing and sloppy proofreading may be at work, since the book also has *Yeates* for *Yeats*, *putrefication* for *putrefaction*, *asses* for *assess*, *reasses* for *reassess*, *rhymne* for *rhyme*, *symolic* for *symbolic*, *Stradivarious* for *Stradivarius*, and so on.

Seymour's spelling *judgement* appears on the title page, front cover, and jacket front; Iris's *judgment* appears on the acknowledgments page, in Sitwell's introduction, in the running title, and on the jacket back and the front flap.)

The introduction makes use of "knowledge"—some fictional, some not—that Sitwell would not have had unless supplied by Iris: his providing Churchill with the phrase "their finest hour," his dining with Archbishop of Canterbury Fisher, his dancing with Queen Elizabeth II at the postcoronation ball held at the American embassy, his being painted or drawn by Augustus John (in the company of Churchill), De Chirico, Rivera, and Picasso, and his being praised by Eliot and Pound. The introduction has Sitwell confiding that "a London sheet" promised to hand her "a wad of pound notes to keep them posted on Iris's activities." It adds, "They could have had me for a shilling save that they sought a vent for the propagation of canards." The introduction concludes by calling Iris "one of our best poets." Sitwell did not include him when she complied her *Atlantic Book of British and American Verse,* which was published the next year.[25]

The introduction also has Sitwell quoting the blub Iris invented for Eliot and used on the front of the dust jacket of *The Seven Hills of the Dove.* It revises the statement to eliminate reference to that volume and its contents, and it has her quoting the genuine letter Pound sent Iris on 3 May 1957. The introduction quotes Pound this way:

> Our generation flopped from lack of collaboration. Scharmel Iris is setting a fine example to such old frumps as Frost and Sandbag. He does more with the younger generation than a lot of half faded wreathes from buzzards no longer in the height of fashion. Do not underestimate. We have but few great poets and Scharmel Iris is one of them.

Pound had actually written, "Do you [*sic*] more good with the younger generation that [*sic*] a lot of half faded wreathes from buzzards no longer in the height of fashion." And several paragraphs later he had added, "Our generation flopped from lack of collaboration / [*sic*] You are settin fine eggzampl to such old frumps as Frost and Sandbag." The last two sentences quoted in the introduction, those warning us not to underestimate the greatness of Iris, had appeared earlier as a blurb on the jacket of *Spanish Earth.* They did not appear in Pound's letter to Iris.

The purple dust jacket of *Judgment Seat* adds to the usual statements attributed to Frost, Pound, Sandburg, and Yeats another purportedly by Eliot, one that seeks to authenticate the introduction: "I have read THE JUDGMENT-SEAT for which Dame Edith Sitwell wrote the introduction and have found it to be one of the most important contributions to our literature." The blurb on the back of the jacket boosts Iris with an account mingling the significant and insignificant, the invented and actual. It explains that Iris, poet-in-residence at Lewis College, was an early contributor to Monroe's *Poetry* and Anderson's *Little Review* and has been acclaimed by Eliot, Gogarty, Raleigh, Santayana, Shaw, Williams, and Yeats, as well as Eleanor Roosevelt. Further, he has been interviewed by Studs Terkel over WFMT and by Dr. Dalma Brunauer over Television Educational Station Channel 11. "Both interviewers read from his books of poems as well as himself."

As usual, Iris included within the slim volume some poems from earlier in his career. Here we have again, for example, "In This Hour," which had appeared in *Bread* in 1953 and "One Room Apartment," which had been in the "Bread and Hyacinths" manuscript in 1923. Jostling against these, however, are newer poems, in which Iris aspires not to the postwar reticence and formal restraint that had dominated poetry well into the 1950s but to the more thematically unbuttoned and formally open mode of the contemporary beat and confessional poets. Most of the new poems here adopt a somewhat Whitmanian-Sandburgian-Ginsburgian long line for Iris's meditations, judgments, rants, and musings, especially on the subject of art. At one extreme the poems fall into prosaic banality, as in "Eunuchs and Frankfurters," which does not live up to the whimsy of its title. It opens,

> Why do we fear, why do we stumble,
> And our visual arts fall short of the greatest epochs—
> The ages of the Parthenon, the Sistine ceiling, the Chartres Cathedral?

The reason, incidentally, is that "eunuchs run the affairs of State." At the other extreme the poems seem little more than bombast, as in these lines from "The Stylus":

> A stylus-tart of glass bells, stuffed birds and tinsel-winged butterflies,
> The still-lifes of certified stillness, find a home in the portfolios of
> princely cognoscenti.

And this from "A Hinged Gate":

> Naked adolescents, their eyes loaded with precocious sexual receptivity—rubric and decor for the symolic [*sic*] persimmon of the tumescent ego—suffer various beleaguerments.

Both bombast and banality can appear together, for "The Hinged Gate" also has this line that easily could have appeared as one of the sayings he contributed to the San Francisco *Monitor* back in the 1910s:

> A poem, once savored on its own, may well prove one of the day's major consolations.

But there are poems—and even lines within these same poems —that fall between the extremes and could amuse readers or tease them into thought:

> Much that we prize falls to the penney arcade of the temporary soul,
> Goes the way of *La Tour de France*—and the wingless keep feeding the foul.
> The best antidote for an excess of sauce bearnaise is Zwieback. ["The Stylus"]

> If Monet fathered lyrical abstraction, surely Whistler was its mother. ["A Hinged Gate"]

> A handful of young girls is a delight,
> But a whole finishing school can be taxing. ["The Rupture"]

Iris was so pleased with one of his witticisms that he used it here in his poem "Stylus" and in the 1 January 1958 version of the epilogue he was calling Cardinal Stritch's. In both he refers to a cardinal as "a whim of a Pope." Still, though, Iris's modest gift was probably for the brief lyric of tighter form, like "The Ancient Pain":

> Now it is over—as it should be over—
> Nothing remains of the orchard tree
> That Eve and Adam knew, except the memory.

> Yearly the cultured vine
> Bears grapes for wine
> And still the skies range blue
> And green the pine.
>
> Carved by the human hand
> Rock-hewn temples stand—
> Their gods of clay lie buried in the sand.
> Sons of Adam far from wise,
> Try tin haloes on for size.
>
> Bread and bird-song still remain
> And at the heart of joy, the ancient pain.

Although Iris's poems are oddly impersonal, seeming to arise more from exercises in verbal facility than from a thinking, feeling self, a few of the poems in *The Judgment Seat* may nonetheless have lines referring to his career of duplicity. In "On to the Labels, Gentlemen," he takes up the theme of human deception —of the "shell artist" whose "sleight-of-hand convinces the unwary," the forger who "follows the market" and fakes "whatever is in demand," and the journalists who "play little games in Sunday supplements." In contrast to such fakers, he places the poet, presumably himself, who exclaims, "But O, the merciful poplars bleeding light in the blue cathedral of flickering light," and thereby offers an example of the guileless perception of the poet.

Whatever success the book had was purely local. Iris's patrons may have used copies as Christmas gifts, and Iris took to sitting at a Joliet bookstore, offering to sign copies if customers would buy them. One person to whom Iris turned for help at this time, the Reverend Joseph W. Peoples, Jr., rector of Christ Episcopal Church in Joliet, recalled that Iris seemed poverty stricken but bore himself with a kind of personal dignity, combined with a sometimes flamboyant effeminacy. Peoples would take him to his church's rummage store for clothing, doing so, as Iris requested, after the closing hour so that Iris would not be seen getting charity. At the time, Iris grew his now white hair long and would occasionally wear a flowing black cape. On the Lewis campus, he would emerge from his cottage and gather with the hip, long-haired crowd.[26] He also visited students in their dormitories, so much so that the college established a regulation that no student could have visitors in his room after 7:00 p.m. And he was asked that his visits before that hour be brief.[27] This was simply another instance of conflict between Iris and the Brothers administering the college. In fact so much "unnecessary friction, misunderstanding, and poor relations" had been generated over the years that on 12 January 1966 the college told Iris to arrange to move off campus.[28] (Bishop Sheil's retirement to Arizona in 1965 may have made this dismissal easier, Sheil being the one who had arranged for Iris's keep at Lewis.) Iris was given a deadline of 1 May.

Iris began preparations for the move, but first he arranged with the editors of the Lewis yearbook, the *Beacon,* to have his picture taken so that a full-page photograph of him and, on the facing page, a reprinting of his poem "Singer of Cante Jondo" would appear in the 1966 edition. Iris doubtless identified with the poem's flamenco singer whose throat hurtles "spear-notes" that cause the ear to bleed and whose lament and wail "smite as a storm of withering hail."[29] Using the name Fred Leo Scharmell, Iris then contacted the Joliet office of the Social Security Administration, which granted his claim for health insurance.[30]

He found a home at the St. Patrick Retirement Hotel in Joliet, but he could not take the many books he had accumulated over the years. He offered them to Chicago's Newberry Library, saying that they would have to be picked up by 26 April. James W. Wells, the library's associate director, was glad to accept them and arranged for a truck to pick them up from Iris's cottage at Lewis. When the books arrived, Wells was delighted with them. There were about a thousand volumes—mostly art books and poetry, including early work by Frost, Pound, Stevens, and Williams. With the books Wells also found photographs, letters (including the one from Santayana), clippings, and so forth.[31] That Iris did not sell these books suggests that his material needs were in fact being taken care of.

Nonetheless, after he moved to the retirement hotel, Iris continued to peddle the books he had written, since doing so enabled him to enjoy the limelight at Printer's Ink, the Joliet book-store. On 14 May 1966 the store held for Iris a four-hour "author's autograph party" that it announced in a large advertisement in the local paper. The ad featured a photograph of Iris and some 500 words of text. Along with much quoting of luminaries and along with claims that Dali and Picasso had made portraits of Iris—and that Johnny Carson had taken him to dinner—the advertisement listed the 25 people acknowledged in *Judgment Seat* who provided financial assistance for publication. It added that the Churchills had given Iris £50 "when he was in England several years ago."[32]

Iris already had the money for another book. In September 1965 he had received $2,200 from a patron, Juel Delrose, as an "advance," her assumption being that she would be repaid by the proceeds from the sale of the book. In January 1966 he had sent it on to John Pastorelle, one of his enthusiasts who had been a student at Lewis in the 1950s and who now was connected with a bank in New York. Pastorelle was to hold the money in trust. But when no book had appeared after a year, Delrose wanted an explanation, and she finally settled on an agreement that the money be returned to her if the book did not appear before Iris's death.[33] Iris had a sufficient backlog of poems and forged introductions to make several books. His delay in getting a book to press suggests that his primary reward came more from the process than from the product.


Iris was especially pleased to have recruited Father Peoples to work on his behalf, since he in turn agreed to recruit others. As 1966 was coming to a close, he convinced Peoples to impose upon his acquaintanceship with poet W. H. Auden and ask him to provide an introduction to "The Yellow Winds of Cathay," his collection of poetry reflecting Chinese influence. Iris then used Peoples's act of kindness as a piece of news to be fed to the local paper.[34] Not reported later, however, was Auden's letter telling Peoples that he was too busy. Besides, Auden said, "Iris needs no introduction from me." But, perhaps on the suggestion of Archibald MacLeish, Peoples had also written to the critic C. M. Bowra, mentioning his letter to Auden and sending him on 23 January 1967 a manuscript titled "Poems 1964-5-6." He too refused:

> I am afraid I cannot do what you ask. I have neither the experi-
> ence nor the authority to say anything on this matter. Mr. Iris is
> plainly a serious writer and it would be impertinent of me to intro-
> duce him. What is more, nobody would pay attention to what I
> say. I am sure that you should get a proper man of letters like Mr.
> Auden, who would be exactly what you need.[35]

Undaunted, Peoples then wrote MacLeish. Or he signed a let-
ter at least partly written by Iris, or Iris wrote and signed the let-
ter with People's name. Iris's part in the authorship is suggested
by its repetition of a bit of cleverness Iris had used in a letter
from Holme to Pound back in 1958. There he had written, "He
[Iris] will soon be seventy, has given upward of fifty years to liter-
ature and its creation, and his wages are about as dire as the
wages of sin in these United States." Here, in the People's letter,
appeared a similar bit: "Scharmel Iris has given 50 years to cre-
ation and the reward has been as dire as the wages of sin."[36]
Whoever wrote the letter enclosed Bowra's letter and the poetry
manuscript and asked for MacLeish's intervention with Auden.
He supposed that Auden might now be less busy and more will-
ing to help a fellow poet who has suffered the world's neglect.
MacLeish wrote his reply across People's letter. It would be "pre-
sumptuous" to tell Auden "what his duty was." Also, no intro-
duction should be needed for "a man of Mr. Iris's age and pro-
ductivity." He suggested that Peoples could aid Iris by making a
small selection of his best work and submitting it to a university
press, such as Wesleyan.

While Iris had Peoples soliciting an introduction, he encour-
aged John Pastorelle's brother Francis, also a Lewis alumnus, to
try to arrange a television appearance. Francis, an insurance
agent in the Joliet area, having failed in his attempt to get Iris on
the Johnny Carson show, decided to give Merv Griffin a try. He
recommended Iris as someone with "a fine wit and wonderful
sense of humor even at age 70 plus." He added that Iris wanted
nothing for himself but did have a few manuscripts ready for
publication. He imagined that "exposure on the show might do
the trick."[37] Another of the Pastorelle brothers, Peter, who made
documentary films for the United Nations, also tried Merv Grif-
fin. He was sure that Iris, a "personal friend of Picasso, Dali,
Yeats, Frost, etc.," would be a good guest, what with his "anec-
dotes of world famous characters and his witticisms which have

a freshness unmatched by professional entertainers."[38] Iris now, not his work, had become the attraction, the entertainment to be presented to the great audience. The Pastorelles' plan failed.

But really Iris had always been the main attraction for his primary audience, himself. The fact was that, as MacLeish had said, Iris did not need introductions, forged or real. His last four volumes would have appeared regardless. Further, Iris's linking of his unusual name to the names of Eliot, Frost, Kipling, Pound, Ruskin, Sitwell, Swinburne, Yeats, and many others never made much practical difference. It did attract some notice, and the preface attributed to Yeats may have helped Iris secure Regnery as the publisher of *Bread out of Stone,* but the dropping of names and the attaching of prefaces, introductions, and epilogues to manuscripts probably raised the suspicions of other publishers— and even of potential reviewers, who may have chosen silence as preferable to voicing those suspicions. The names certainly gained him no other publishers, all of whom aside from Regnery insisted on subsidy or subscription. Here, late in life, he may have understood that the satisfaction—or the need—all along had been developing and sustaining his fantasy. His lying and forging, like his writing of poetry, sprang more from inner compulsion than from pursuit of external reward. They were primarily for his own consumption. The letters, blurbs, prefaces, autobiography, and so on—along with the visual portraits Iris was so fond of—constituted for him a narcissian pool in which to gaze upon his own reflected fantasy. Iris never succeeded in forging fame in the sense of using forgery to achieve fame, yet he did forge fame in the sense of faking fame, that is, of creating a spurious fame, one that was the product of his fantasy and a great deal of time at his typewriter.

Throughout his life Iris had been exhibiting the strange symptom sometimes called pseudologia fantastica—an extreme form of pathological lying in which the liar, the pseudologue, weaves together a life of fact and fiction, creating a grandiose identity to counter low self-esteem or a sense of nonidentity. The symptom may accompany narcissistic personality disorder, Munchausen syndrome, and other psychiatric diagnoses, but those exhibiting it are not psychotically delusional. If confronted and pressed, they will acknowledge that they are lying or at least will alter their story. In effect they have chosen to live in their daydreams. That also means that their created selves are fragile and require constant maintenance and repair.[39] It was pretty much a full-time job for Iris. Like others exhibiting the symptom, Iris used other people to help create and maintain his sense of identity. He may have gotten some satisfaction, some sense of power, out of duping them and using them to dupe others, but telling lies to others served even more to help him lie to himself. The outrageousness or incredibility of many of Iris's deceptions does not necessarily suggest a desire to be discovered. It may stem instead from the same source as the rhetorical ineptitude of Iris's letters, the pratfalls that his poems sometimes took, the stylistic excesses he fell into, and even the plagiarism to which he resorted. All of these could be related to a common accompaniment of pseudologia fantastica: a brain dysfunction in which verbal skills exceed other aspects of intelligence and in which the logical and critical portions of the brain do not adequately monitor what a person says or writes.

Iris's fantasy was not entirely his creation. When Federico Scaramella set out to make a name for himself, he stepped out of Little Italy and into an available role, that of American poet. It not only satisfied the call for cultural fortification and ethnic assimilation but also encouraged him in his sense of grandiosity and victimhood. Early in the twentieth century, its residual Romanticism favored imagination over observation, the idealized over the real, not what happened but the story as it should be. It was a role in which credibility did not much matter and Iris's extension of fantasy from his poetry to his life would receive little scrutiny, in part because of the association of the literary with the spurious and in part because poetry itself did not command much attention from the public.[40] He also received a surprising amount of cooperation. His earliest editors, Charles Phillips and the O'Malleys, displayed an eager gullibility and a penchant for outrageously inflated praise. Harriet Monroe accepted his pseudonymous poems as much on the basis of improbable tales of woe as on the merit of the poetry. Padraic Colum recognized the Yeats preface as spurious but agreed to write his own preface anyway. Paul Engle and Archibald MacLeish did not admire Iris's poetry but agreed to help get it published. Columnists relished the opportunity to present him as a poet, that is, as someone for whom normal standards of credibility do not apply. Reviewers gave no serious look at the suspicious blurbs and introductions accompanying his books. No one voiced much concern about the contradictory accounts of his life of genius or about the improbable claims of contacts with the famous and celebrated, from John Ruskin to Johnny Carson.

Iris died on 6 July 1967, at age 78, at the retirement hotel in Joliet. Without his own hand to supply the usual blend of fact and fiction, the obituary in the *Joliet Herald News* was brief. It identified him, incorrectly, as a native of Chicago, author of five books of verse (the correct number is six), and former poet in residence at Lewis College for 14 years. The requiem mass was held at the Lewis College chapel and the burial at Resurrection Cemetery. The obituary listed no relatives, surviving or otherwise.[41] There were no quotations from the famous.

# NOTES

## 1—YOUTH OF GENIUS, 1889–1913

1. This "elite-sponsored upward movement" is described in Donald L. Miller, *City of the Century: The Epic of Chicago and the Making of America* (New York: Simon & Schuster, 1996), 421. See also Bernard Duffey, *The Chicago Renaissance in American Letters: A Critical History* (East Lansing: Michigan State College P, 1954), 27–28 and passim.

2. I here have perilously based my account of Iris's early years on articles about Iris for which he supplied information, much of it a mix of fact and fantasy. See, for example, Charles Phillips, "Scharmel Iris: A Florentine American," *Monitor* (San Francisco) 10 April 1909: 4; Van Allen Bradley, "Chicago Genius," *Chicago Daily News* 22 Aug. 1953: 26; "Poet Gets Recognition Due Him after Waiting 39 Years," *Garfieldian* 10 Sept. 1953: 1; Gerald DiPego, "America's Christian Poet Resides at Lewis College," *Spectator* (Joliet, IL) 12 Dec. 1963: 4. I also accept as probably true a few details from Iris's manuscript "Father," and I have seen his Italian birth certificate.

3. Charles J. O'Malley, "The Literary Brink," *New World* 26 June 1904: 9.

4. O'Malley, "Catholic Literators of Chicago," *New World* 26 Aug. 1905: 17. Iris had poems in the issues of 22 and 29 July, 12 and 26 Aug., 9 and 16 Sept., and 21 Oct. 1905.

5. Charles Shanabruch, *Chicago's Catholics: The Evolution of an American Identity* (Notre Dame, IN: U of Notre Dame P, 1981), 147.

6. O'Malley, "Little Light on Yeats," *New World* 11 June 1904: 12. The previous week, in "Some Recent Irish Poetry," *New World* 8 June 1904: 14, O'Malley had faulted Yeats for his paganism and "evil influence on the young poets of Ireland."

7. "Family Sitting Room," *New World* 16 Jan. 1909: 7; 6 March 1909: 7.

8. O'Malley, "Evidences of Non-Christianity," *New World* 2 May 1908: 31.

9. See, for example, O'Malley, "Under the Library Lamp," *New World* 20 June 1908: 7, which looks for evidence to refute "the statement sometimes made that becoming a Catholic blights the intellect." See also the first page of the 22 July 1911 *Monitor*, which runs a long article under the headline "Not Opposed to Science" and subhead "Many People Regard Catholics as a Lot of Brainless Sentimentalists When It Comes to Religion."

10. "Chief of Our Authors Dies," *Monitor* 2 April 1910: 1; Henry Coyle, "Charles J. O'Malley: An Appreciation," 9 April 1910: 3; Charles Phillips, "Some Catholic Writers of Today," *Monitor* 20 May 1911: 7.

11. Phillips, "Our Catholic Reading Public," *Monitor* 12 Oct. 1912: 12.

12. The *New World* periodically published lists of the subscribers. See, for example, "Would Publish Chas. J. O'Malley's Poems," *New World* 14 Dec. 1912: 7; and the list published 22 Feb. 1913: 7

13. The sonnet appeared also in *New World* 14 Jan. 1911: 4 under the title "Dante in Ravenna." This revised version, very close to that later used in Iris's *Lyrics of a Lad* (Chicago: Ralph Fletcher Seymour, 1914), has the full 14 lines expected of an Italian sonnet. Iris or the *Monitor* may have inadvertently dropped what is line 10 in the *New World* version: "My eyes have seen the woe, the suffering."

14. Phillips, editorial comment, *Monitor* 28 Dec. 1907: 4.

15. See also Phillips, "Some Catholic Writers of Today," *Monitor* 20 May 1911: 6–7, which refers to Iris as "a young Florentine American who has the divine fire of the poet" (7).

16. S. M. O'Malley, "Under the Library Lamp," *Monitor* 15 July 1911: 7.

17. S. M. O'Malley, "Under the Library Lamp," *Monitor* 25 Dec. 1911: 7.

18. The 1920 census lists at the address the nine-member Vincenzo family and gives the name and age of each. None of the sons or daughters is listed as married. All but Frank and Rosie, whose parents were also Italian, could read and write English. All but Rosie, Fred (Iris), and Tony were employed—a city water pipe worker, canning factory clerk, bricklayer, mail order clerk, railroad cook, and another mail order clerk. Fourteenth Census of the United States, Cook County, Illinois, 1920, 13th ward, enumeration district 765.

19. Addams to Iris, 12 Dec. 1911; Addams to Monroe, 15 Dec. 1911. The second letter is also available in *The Jane Addams Papers*, ed. Mary Lynn McCree Bryan (Ann Arbor: UMI, 1984), reel 6.

20. Harriet Monroe, *A Poet's Life: Seventy Years in a Changing World* (New York: Macmillan, 1938), 240.

21. Monroe, *Poet's Life*, 123–44.

22. Quoted in Ellen Williams, *Harriet Monroe and the Poetry Renaissance: The First Ten Years of* Poetry, *1912–22* (Urbana: U of Illinois P, 1977), 15.

23. Alice Corbin Henderson to Monroe, 28 Aug. 1922.

24. Louise Imogen Guiney to Addams, 4 Jan. 1913. The letter is annotated in Monroe's hand, "Ans'd ltr at Miss Addams' request." She evidently made no copy of her response.

25. Robert Hewison, "Ruskin, John (1819–1900)," *Oxford Dictionary of National Biography*, ed. H. C. G. Matthew and Brian Harrison (Oxford: Oxford UP, 2004), online ed., ed. Lawrence Goldman, May 2006, 15 Nov. 2006 <http://www.oxforddnb.com/view/article/24291>.

26. On poetry's marginalized status and loss of readership, see Christopher Clausen, *The Place of Poetry: Two Centuries of an Art in Crisis* (Lexington: UP of Kentucky, 1981), which begins with a statement of its thesis and scope: "Since the end of the eighteenth century, poetry in England (and subsequently in America) has been an art in continual crisis. As its cultural status declined, as its place as a bearer of truth was more and more

taken by the sciences, its practitioners made an endless series of revolutions in poetic doctrine while seeking unsuccessfully to make society once again listen to them" (1).

## 2—NEW POET, 1913–1922

1. Harriet Monroe, *A Poet's Life: Seventy Years in a Changing World* (New York: Macmillan, 1938), 318–19, 324. Unlike Sherwood Anderson, Maxwell Bodenheim, Ben Hecht, Edgar Lee Masters, Carl Sandburg, and other Chicago writers, Iris evidently did not participate in the bohemian gatherings associated with Schlogl's restaurant and Jack Jones Dill Pickle Club on Chicago's Near North Side during the 1910s and 1920s.

2. See S. M. O'Malley, "Under the Library Lamp," *Monitor* 13 Jan. 1912: 7, which welcomes the news that Monroe "is projecting" the magazine.

3. S. M. O'Malley, "Under the Library Lamp," *Monitor* 3 May 1913: 7.

4. Williams, *Harriet Monroe and the Poetry Renaissance* 45; Monroe, *Poet's Life* 303–6, 310–11.

5. The banquet and Yeats's speech were reported in "Chicago Poets Tether Pegasus," *Chicago Daily Tribune* 2 March 1914: 1, and in Monroe's *Poet's Life* 332–39. Neither mentions Iris specifically, but his name was on Monroe's invitation list.

6. Editorial, *New York Times Book Review* 22 Nov. 1914: 514. Anderson does not mention Iris in her autobiography *My Thirty Years' War* (New York: Covici-Friede, 1930).

7. Ralph Fletcher Seymour does not mention Iris in his autobiography *Some Went This Way: A Forty Year Pilgrimmage among Artists, Bookmen, and Printers* (Chicago: Ralph Fletcher Seymour, 1945). For Seymour's work as a publisher, see also Kathryn Mary Camp, "Ralph Fletcher Seymour and His Alderbrink Press (Chicago, 1898–1965): A History and Checklist of His Publications," M.A. thesis, U of Chicago, 1979.

8. Monroe, *Dance of the Seasons,* 1911; Alice Corbin [Henderson], *The Spinning Woman of the Sky,* 1912.

9. The publication date appears on the Certificate of Copyright issued by the Library of Congress. The book is not listed in among Seymour's Alderbrink Press books in the incomplete checklist provided by Will Ransom's *Private Presses and Their Books* (New York Bowker, 1929; rptd. New York: Philip C. Duschnes, 1963), 195–98. Contrary to what is suggested by the listing in Camp's thesis (56), there were not two editions of 1,000 copies each but rather one edition of perhaps 1,000 copies. Within this edition there was a first issue, the title page of which has the imprint of Ralph Fletcher Seymour Co. Then there was a second issue, bound in light brown paper over boards and with light brown cloth around the spine. It has a cancel title page bearing the imprint of Seymour Daughaday & Co., reflecting the brief partnership of Fletcher and Carlos Colton Daughaday in 1915.

10. Iris's claim may be found in Van Allen Bradley, "Chicago Genius," *Chicago Daily News* 22 Aug. 1953: 26, which prints Brooke's and Iris's photographs. Christopher Hassall, *Rupert Brooke: A Biography* (London: Faber, 1964), gives an account of Brooke's Chicago visit (see esp. p. 441), with no

mention of Iris. Nor is Iris mentioned in Maurice Browne's "Recollections of Rupert Brooke" (1927), reprinted in *Rupert Brooke* (Port Washington, NY: Kennikat Press, 1968), 1–68.

11. Hutchinson is quoted in Browne 441. Monroe recalls the portrait in *Poet's Life,* 340.

12. Iris is not mentioned in Egan's *Recollections of a Happy Life* (New York: Doran, 1924), but the two probably had met, and they would have seen one another's poetry in the *Monitor* and *New World.* I have not found the original manuscript of Egan's preface.

13. *All Our Years: The Autobiography of Robert Morss Lovett* (New York: Viking, 1948), 128. For other biographical information on Edith Rockefeller McCormick, see Clarice Stasz, *The Rockefeller Women: Dynasty of Piety, Privacy, and Service* (New York: St. Martin's, 1995).

14. Laurence Hope [Adela Nicolson], *India's Love Lyrics* (New York: John Lane; London: Heinemann, 1902), 145–46; F. L. Bickley, "Nicolson, Adela Florence (1865–1904)," rev. Sayoni Basu, *Oxford Dictionary of National Biography* (Oxford: Oxford UP, 2004), online ed., 20 Nov. 2006 <http://www.oxforddnb.com/view/article/35237>.

15. Milo Winter, "Scharmel Iris: Italian Poet," rev. of *Lyrics of a Lad, Little Review* Dec. 1914: 25–27. "Chicago Youth Publishes a Book of Verse," *New World* 26 Dec. 1914: 1, 4.

16. "'Newsie' Becomes a Poet," *Chicago Daily News* 1 Dec 1914.

17. Ethel M. Colson, rev. of *Lyrics of a Lad, Chicago Herald* 12 Jan. 1915.

18. S. M. O'Malley, rev. of *Lyrics of a Lad,* "Under the Library Lamp," *Monitor* 16 Jan. 1915.

19. Ella W. Peattie, rev. of *Lyrics of a Lad, Chicago Daily Tribune* 6 Feb. 1915.

20. Monroe, rev. of *Lyrics of a Lad, Poetry* May 1915: 97–98. Monroe too did not see Iris's plagiarism. Later, in a letter to Henry Allen Moe, 8 Jan. 1926 (misdated 1925), Monroe said that the *Chicago Examiner* had revealed Iris's plagiarism of a poem by Hope. I have not found the *Examiner* article but assume that the poem in question is "The Heart Cry of the Celtic Maid."

21. Monroe and Henderson, ed., *The New Poetry: An Anthology* (New York: Macmillan, 1917). For a history of the anthology, see Craig Abbott, "Publishing the New Poetry: Harriet Monroe's Anthology," *Journal of Modern Literature* 11 (1984): 89–108. In this period Iris had poems in two additional anthologies: three poems from *Lyrics*—"April," "Presage," and "After the Martyrdom"—appeared in *The Chicago Anthology: A Collection of Verse from the Work of Chicago Poets,* ed. Charles G. Blanden and Minna Mathison (Chicago: Roadside Press, 1916), 54, 98–99, 145; and his poem "The Friar of Genoa," also from *Lyrics,* appeared in *Dreams and Images: An Anthology of Catholic Poetry,* ed. Joyce Kilmer (New York: Boni and Liveright, 1917), 102–3.

22. F. Scott Fitzgerald, *This Side of Paradise* (New York: Scribner's, 1920), 218.


## 3—APPARITIONAL SCHEMER, 1923–1939

1. In "Lyric in the Culture of Capitalism," *American Literary History* 1 (1989): 63–88, Frank Lentricchia contrasts Pound as a representative of "emerging high modernist art," which was finding its honor precisely in

economic unviability," and Frost, who sought "to make it economically as America's poet," reaching a mass audience while also pleasing "those accustomed to Pound's aesthetic caviare."

2. This portion of my account is based on Monroe's 24 Nov. 1923 letter to her friend and attorney Charles H. Hamill and on Amberg's 19 Oct. letter of apology to Monroe.

3. See Cary Wolfe, "Ezra Pound and the Politics of Patronage," *American Literature* 63 (1991): 26–42.

4. Lawrence Rainey, *Institutions of Modernism: Literary Elites and Public Culture* (New Haven, CT: Yale UP, 1998), 91. For Rainey's full treatment of the publication of *The Waste Land,* see 77–106.

5. Carl Sandburg later used the definitions as a sort of preface to his *Good Morning, America* (1928). See his *Complete Poems* (New York: Harcourt, 1950), 317–19.

6. Harry Hansen, *Midwest Portraits: A Book of Memories and Friendships* (New York: Harcourt, 1923), 22–23

7. Maurice Francis Egan, *Recollections of a Happy Life* (New York: Doran, 1924), 373; *New York Times* 19 Sept. 1923: 7; 23 Sept. 1923: 7; 24 Sept. 1923: 4; 26 Sept. 1923: 4; 1 Oct. 1923: 3; 7 Oct. 1923: S6; 26 Oct. 1923: 17.

8. Alfred Kreymborg, rev. of *The New Poetry, Poetry* July 1918: 223.

9. Ellen Williams, *Harriet Monroe and the Poetry Renaissance: The First Ten Years of* Poetry, *1912–22* (Urbana: U of Illinois P, 1977), 224.

10. Monroe, "Looking Backward," *Poetry* Oct. 1928: 32–38.

11. T. S. Eliot, *For Lancelot Andrewes: Essays on Style and Order* (Garden City, NY: Doubleday, 1929), vii.

12. Jane Addams on Hull House letterhead to Selection Committee, John Simon Guggenheim Memorial Foundation, 21 Dec. 1925. The letter is stamped at bottom with Guggenheim receipt date 26 Dec. 1925 and a note: "This document sent by the applicant himself." The foundation at some point must have returned the letter to Iris, because it was found among his papers at Lewis University.

13. In the papers at Lewis is Iris's typed copy, 20 Feb. 1926.

14. Monroe to Moe, 8 Jan. 1926 [misdated 1925]. The plagiarism was probably that of Hope's "Love Lightly."

15. The phrase, quoted by Ellen Williams (234), was Edgar Jepson's, from his "Recent United States Poetry," *English Review* May 1918; the article was reprinted in the *Little Review* Sept. 1918.

16. Monroe, "Coming of Age," *Poetry* Oct. 1930: 35.

17. I have seen only Iris's typed copy of the column. I have found no evidence that Iris was the subject of portraits by John Singer Sargent (1856–1925) or Giovanni Boldini (1845–1931). Boldini did complete a portrait of opera star Lina Cavalieri (1874–1944) in 1901. The Chinese acting troupe that included Mei Lan-Fang opened in New York in February, played Chicago in April, and then moved on to the West Coast. The group's performances of classical Chinese drama, in which Mei played the parts of women, were immensely popular. See *Mei Lan-Fang in America: Reviews and Criticism,* ed. P. C. Chang (Np: np, 1935).

18. Quoted here is the note on James printed in *Poetry* Aug. 1931: 294; I have not found the letter on which the note is based.

19. Wesley Ames to Monroe, 18 Jan. and 28 Feb. 1931; John Creagh to Monroe, 11 and 24 April, 6 and 22 Dec. 1933; Everett Owens to Monroe, 10 Dec. 1933 and 22 Feb. 1934; and Stanley Blackpool to Monroe, 11 Dec. 1933.

20. Monroe to Blackpool, 2 Jan. 1934.

21. Monroe, "Mephistopheles and the Poet," *Poetry* July 1926: 210–15.

22. "Announcement of Awards," *Poetry* Nov. 1931: 103–4.

## 4—NONPUBLISHING POET, 1940–1949

1. Pound to Monroe, 27 Mar. 1931, *Dear Editor: A History of* Poetry *in Letters, The First Fifty Years, 1912–1962,* ed. Joseph Parisi and Stephen Young (New York: Norton, 2002), 294.

2. Monty Noam Penkower, *The Federal Writers' Project: A Study in Government Patronage of the Arts* (Urbana: U of Illinois P, 1977).

3. Milton S. Mayer, "Chicago's First Citizen," *Reader's Digest* Feb. 1940: 25–28; rptd. from *Independent Woman* Feb. 1940: 47–48.

4. Ann Richtmyer, secretary to Louise de Koven Bowen, to Iris, 28 Oct. 1940.

5. Quoted from Iris's typescript copy of Sobol's column. The "immortal Duse" was Eleonora Duse, a great Italian actress who had died in her mid-sixties in 1924. I will examine the claims regarding Yeats, Bernhardt, and Rodin shortly.

6. Referred to is the coverage in the Mexico City newspapers *Excelsior* 25 Feb. 1943 and *Novedades* 4 April 1943 and in the Mexican magazine *Tiempo* 9 April 1943. I have seen these only as Iris's transcriptions. Iris also makes his trip the subject of one section of his so-called autobiography, "Shuttlecock," which remains unpublished.

7. Edward R. Kantowicz, *Corporation Sole: Cardinal Mundelein and Chicago Catholicism* (Notre Dame, IN: U of Notre Dame P, 1983), 153.

8. Steven M. Avella, *This Confident Church: Catholic Leadership and Life in Chicago, 1940–1965* (Notre Dame, IN: U of Notre Dame P, 1992), 122–23.

9. The whereabouts of the painting and sketch are unknown, though the sketch was reproduced as the frontispiece of Iris's *Bread out of Stone* (Chicago: Regnery, 1953).

10. Memorandum, Acting Captain, 25th District, to Commissioner of Police, 31 May 1944. Iris's sister's married name may have been Bockman rather than Beckman. The *Chicago Daily Tribune* 29 Oct. 1944 has an article on a Jeanne Bockman, Josephine's daughter perhaps, living at the same address. She had joined the Women's Air Corps.

11. Olive M. Wakeman, Conrad Hilton's executive secretary, to Frederick Vincent, 10 Dec. 1944, summarizes the request and says that she is referring it to Joseph Binns, vice president of Hilton Hotels Corp. and the person responsible for the company's New York hotels.

12. Geraldine Udell, business manager of *Poetry,* to Iris, 25 Aug. 1943.

13. Robert Buchanan, *The Complete Poetical Works,* 2 vols. (London: Chatto, 1901), 1: 2.

14. John L. Tancock, *The Sculpture of Auguste Rodin* (Philadelphia: David R. Godine and the Philadelphia Museum of Modern Art, 1976), 141–47.

15. Yeats to Monroe, undated but stamped as received on 29 Jan. 1916. Among Iris's papers is his typed copy of the letter.

16. For information on Field, including his friendship with Sheil, see Stephen Becker, *Marshall Field III: A Biography* (New York: Simon & Schuster, 1964).

17. Elizabeth Bullock to A. C. Spectorsky, 25 June 1945.

18. *All Our Years: The Autobiography of Robert Morss Lovett* (New York: Viking, 1948), however, does not mention Iris.

19. Jean G. Parker, Ann Watkins Agency, to Iris, 23 Jan. 1947.

20. Treasurer, William Wrigley Jr. Co., to Dr. Frederick Vincent, 28 Dec. 1945.

21. Nick Forte to Fr. Lawrence Quigley, 27 Feb 1946.

22. "Widow Killed in Fall," *Chicago Tribune* 28 Oct. 1946: 13.


## 5—RESURRECTED GENIUS, 1950–1953

1. On the title page of the typescript for "Twelve Pins for Fairyland" Iris typed "Macmillan."

2. Iris submitted "A Singer in the Sun" to Dodd, Mead on 19 June 1951.

3. Edward R. Kantowicz, *Corporation Sole: Cardinal Mundelein and Chicago Catholicism* (Notre Dame, IN: U of Notre Dame P, 1983), 46.

4. The poems appeared in the *Chicago Tribune*'s "Line o' Type or Two" column, edited by Charles Collins, on 24 Feb., 17 March, 24 March, 1 April, 7 April, 20 April, 27 April, 13 May, 26 May, 27 May, 26 June, 7 July, 15 July, 7 Aug., 5 Oct. 1950.

5. Vincent Holme [Iris], "Nijinski's Elegy," *Chicago Tribune* 27 April 1950: 22.

6. It may be that the original manuscript of *Bread* was in fact long and that only after the shortening achieved by Colum did Iris add the final paragraph of "Yeats's" preface to explain the slimness of the volume. In an envelope postmarked 31 May 1951, Colum returned to Holme a manuscript of about a hundred poems he had deemed "non-acceptable verses."

7. Canfield to Holme 6 July 1951.

8. Santayana to Holme, 3 Nov. 1951. This letter is quoted at length by John McCormick, *George Santayana: A Biography* (New York: Knopf, 1987), 498. McCormick says that Santayana's letter, especially in its statement about the "revulsion from ordinary life," explains Santayana at least as much as it does Spain (498).

9. Miguel de Unamuno, *Tragic Sense of Life* (1912), trans. J. E. Crawford Flitch (New York: Macmillan, 1921), 330, 51.

10. *Poetry* Oct.–Nov. 1913; Harriet Monroe, *A Poet's Life: Seventy Years in a Changing World* (New York: Macmillan, 1938), 329–31.

11. I have not seen a manuscript of Madariaga's preface, nor a letter from Madariaga forwarding it to Iris. But from Oxford, on 8 June 1965, after publication of *Spanish Earth,* Madariaga sent Iris a brief autograph letter saying that the book was handsome and had stayed on his desk "to be picked up at random." He offered "very many thanks." The published preface, then, may be genuine or only mildly touched up by Iris. It is dated 29 July 1952.

12. Roy Campbell's heavily corrected, four-page draft of the epilogue is in one of his notebooks at the Harry Ransom Humanities Research Center at the University of Texas at Austin. I have seen neither the final draft Campbell sent Iris nor Iris's manuscript in which he revises what Campbell sent.

13. A draft of the letter to Eliot, 15 May 1952, is at Lewis College but is so adorned with interlineations, marginal revisions, crossings-out, and the like that it is largely unintelligible.

14. The speech appears in Winston Churchill, *His Complete Speeches,* ed. Robert Rhodes James, vol. 6: 1935–1942 (New York: Chelsea, 1974), 6231–38. The phrase appears as the title of Churchill's *Their Finest Hour,* vol. 2 of *The Second World War* (Boston: Houghton, 1949).

15. Arthur Quiller-Couch, *Poetry* (New York: Dutton, 1914), 60. Fond of Tasso's saying, which he got by way of Shelley, Quiller-Couch also used it—in sentences of slightly different wording—in "Poets on Their Own Art" (1895), in *Adventures in Criticism* (Cambridge: Cambridge UP, 1926), 134, and in "Milton (1)," *Studies in Literature, Second Series* (Cambridge: Cambridge UP, 1923), 99.

16. Quiller-Couch, *Poetry* 59, 1.

17. Holme to Cass Canfield, 12 June 1952; Canfield to Holme, 23 June 1952.

18. Holme to Canfield, 15 Sept. 1952.

19. George Santayana, *The Sense of Beauty: Being the Outlines of Aesthetic Theory* (1896), ed. William G. Holzberger and Herman J. Saatkamp, Jr. (Cambridge, MA: MIT P, 1998), 30, 33, 141, 164, 165, 167.

20. Benedetto Croce, *Aesthetic as Science of Expression and General Linguistic,* trans. Douglas Ainslie (London: Macmillan, 1909), 6.

21. Sen. Paul H. Douglas to Marshall Field, 6 Dec. 1954; I have seen only a copy Iris made of the letter but believe it represents a genuine letter. Typed on the same page is a copy of a letter from Douglas to Holme, 7 Dec. 1954, saying that he "was much touched" by his letter and is enclosing a copy of a letter to Field, the original having gone to Field. About a year earlier, Iris (as Holme) had written Illinois Governor Adlai E. Stevenson, who replied on 24 Dec. 1953, thanking him for his letter about Iris and looking forward to receiving and reading a copy of *Bread.*

22. Stephen Elwell, "Henry Regnery Company," *American Literary Publishing Houses, 1900–1980: Trade and Paperback,* ed. Peter Dzwonkoski, vol. 46 of *The Dictionary of Literary Biography* (Detroit: Gale, 1986), 313.

23. Henry Regnery to William H. O'Donnell, Pennsylvania State U, 18 July 1983. O'Donnell sent me a copy of the letter.

24. See the advertisement for Regnery books in the *Chicago Tribune* 20 Sept. 1953: B13.

25. "Books Published Today," *New York Times* 16 Sept. 1953: 31.

26. Frederic Babcock, "Among the Authors," *Chicago Daily Tribune* 23 Aug. 1953: B6.

27. James Hall and Martin Steinmann, eds., *The Permanence of Yeats: Selected Criticism* (New York: Macmillan, 1950), reissued as a Collier Book in 1961.

28. Russell MacFall, "Sundae Reading," *Chicago Sunday Tribune* 27 Sept. 1953: 16.

29. Gerald D. McDonald, rev. of *Bread, Library Journal* 15 Sept. 1953: 1541.

30. Bernard Theall, "Some Good Poems and Some Others," *Books on Trial* 12 (Dec. 1953): 119–20.

31. Carl Sandburg to Iris, 24 April 1953.

32. Iris, "Dancer in the Sun," *Best Loved Poems*, ed. Marjorie Barrows, Children's Hour series (Chicago: Spencer, 1953), 257. Quoted is the first of the poem's two stanzas. Barrows also included two poems by Iris ("Flowering Night" and "April") in another of her anthologies: *The Quintessence of Beauty and Romance* (Chicago: Spencer, 1955), 69, 281.

33. The *New York Times* published poems by Iris on 25 May and 14 Aug. 1953; 28 April, 8 July, 20 Sept., and 26 Nov. 1954; and 22 Feb. 1955.


## 6—INTERNATIONAL POET IN RESIDENCE, 1954–1959

1. Archibald MacLeish to Holme, 8 June [1954].

2. Edward M. Burke to Iris, 9 Aug. 1951.

3. Samuel Cardinal Stritch, in a letter to Iris, 27 Sept. 1952, arranged to see him.

4. Augustus John to Holme ("Dear Sir"), 30 Oct. 1952.

5. Iris to Stritch, 12 Nov. 1954.

6. Lord, Day & Lord to Iris, 25 Feb. 1955.

7. Marion Edey, *Do Not Awake Me and Other Poems* (New York: Macmillan, 1951), 5.

8. *The Memoirs of Giorgio de Chirico*, trans. Margaret Crosland (London: Owen, 1971), 130, 187. The original in Italian, *Memorie della mia vita*, was published in 1962. Iris is not mentioned.

9. Margaret Crosland, *The Enigma of Giorgio de Chirico* (London: Owen, 1999), 121–23.

10. Iris to Stritch, 31 July 1955.

11. Assistant Director, St. Anne's House [signature illegible] to John, 23 June 1955.

12. Michael Holroyd, *Augustus John: A Biography* (New York: Holt, 1975), 589–90, 578–79.

13. Holroyd 590.

14. David Cecil, "John as Portraitist," *Fifty-Two Drawings*, by Augustus John (Greenwich, Conn.: New York Graphic Society; London: Rainbird, 1957), 15. Iris's portrait is drawing 44, dated 1955

15. John Lehmann to Iris, 20 July 1955.

16. He completed a form entitled Receipt and Promise to Repay Funds Advanced as Financial Assistance Loans for Repatriation on 3 Aug. 1955. The form was stamped as paid on 5 Oct. 1955.

17. "Julio de Diego, 79, Artist Who Was Also an Actor" [obituary], *New York Times* 24 Aug. 1979: D15.

18. Draft letter, Iris to Sheil, Aug., 1955; whether Iris completed and sent the letter is unknown.

19. T. S. Eliot, introd., *Selected Poems*, by Marianne Moore (New York: Macmillan, 1935), xiv.

20. Louis Untermeyer to Max Schuster, 2 May 1945.

21. Harvey Breit, "In and Out of Books," *New York Times Book Review* 18 Nov. 1956: 8.

22. Iris to Pound, 27 March 1957. Earlier, on 8 Oct. 1952, as Holme, Iris had written Winfred Overholser, M.D., Superintendent of Saint Elizabeths Hospital, asking for a preface from Pound. Overholser's reply to Holme, 14 Oct. 52, acknowledged his letter and told him to write directly to Pound. Whether Iris did at the time is not known. For an account of Pound's circumstances and activity at St. Elizabeths, I rely on Humphrey Carpenter, *A Serious Character: The Life of Ezra Pound* (Boston: Houghton, 1988), 716–845.

23. Iris, "Before the Cathedral," "Vincent," and "How Shall I Sing Again," *Poetry* Nov. 1957: 101–2.

24. John H. Pastorelle to Boston Better Business Bureau, 7 Jan. 1958.

25. Boston Better Business Bureau *Bulletin* 16 April 1952. It was enclosed with a reply from Edward Gallagher to Pastorelle, 13 Jan. 1958.

26. Clifford J. Laube, "A Pilgrimage Record," *Spirit* (Seton Hall U), 26 (May 1959): 58.

27. Dom Wulstan Phillipson, rev. of *The Seven Hills of the Dove, Downside Review* (Downside Abbey, Bath, England), 78 (Winter 1960): 77.

28. Jeanne Boyd's published scores of Iris's poems include *Adoration* (New York: Galaxy Music, 1943), *In Italy* (Chicago: Gamble Hinged Music, 1915), *Invitation* (New York: Schirmer, 1918), and *Invocation* (New York: Schirmer, 1918), *Lewis College Song* (Lewis College, 1953).


## 7—AUTOBIOGRAPHER, 1950S AND 1960S

1. Kenna and Coughlin, in the early decades of the twentieth century, created a political machine based on graft and protection money from brothels, saloons, and gambling houses in Chicago's notorious Levee district. See Douglas Knox, "The Era of 'Hinky Dink' and 'Bathhouse John,'" *The Encyclopedia of Chicago,* ed. James R. Grossman, Ann Durkin Keating, and Janice L. Reiff (Chicago: U of Chicago P, 2004), 500.

2. Maurice Francis Egan, *Recollections of a Happy Life* (New York: Doran, 1924), 211. Egan's earlier account, which appeared as "Theodore Roosevelt in Retrospect," *Atlantic* May 1919: 676–85, differed substantially from that in *Recollections*. It also, though, does not mention Iris. Nor does Yeats in a letter that refers to the luncheon; see *The Collected Letters of W. B. Yeats,* vol.3: *1901–1904,* ed. John Kelley and Ronald Schuchard (Oxford: Clarendon, 1994), 500. In *W. B. Yeats: A Life,* vol. 1: *The Apprentice Mage, 1865–1914* (Oxford: Oxford UP, 1997), R. F. Foster notes that the lunch had been arranged by John Quinn. He does not mention Iris. He does say, though, that "a fellow-guest's assertion that WBY astounded his host by discoursing on 'the little people' is probably *ben trovato*," that is, an appropriate story even if untrue (308).

3. Harriet Monroe, *A Poet's Life: Seventy Years in a Changing World* (New York: Macmillan, 1938), 386.

4. Louis Untermeyer, ed., *A Treasury of Great Poems, English and American* (New York: Simon & Schuster, 1942), li.

5. Untermeyer, ed., *Modern American Poetry,* 1st–6th eds. (New York: Harcourt, 1919, 1921, 1925, 1930, 1936, 1942).

6. Cleanth Brooks and Robert Penn Warren, *Understanding Poetry: An Anthology for College Students* (New York: Holt, 1938), 387–89.

7. James Hart, "Alfred Joyce Kilmer," *American Poets, 1880–1945,* 1st series, vol. 45 of *Dictionary of Literary Biography* (Detroit: Gale, 1986), 225.

8. The font of the typewriter used for the first part differs from his, and the typist uses a *1* rather than the *I* Iris uses for the numeral one.

9. In *Harriet Monroe and the Poetry Renaissance: The First Ten Years of* Poetry, *1912-22* (Urbana: U of Illinois P, 1977), Ellen Williams sees the years 1914–1915 as the height of *Poetry* and 1916 as the beginning of its decline. Joseph Parisi agrees, in *Dear Editor: A History of Poetry in Letters, The First Fifty Years, 1912-1962,* ed. Parisi and Stephen Young (New York: Norton, 2002), 168–69, 185–88.

10. In submitting the manuscript, he used as a go-between Herbert M. Johnson, who was president of Mid-Continent Life Insurance Co. and presumably a friend of Iris's. See Johnson to Ray Roberts, at Regnery, 11 May 1964, and Roberts to Holme, 7 May 1964; also A. L. Hart, Jr., at McGraw-Hill, to Johnson, 29 July 1964.

11. Clarice Staz, *The Rockefeller Women: Dynasty of Piety, Privacy, and Service* (New York: St. Martin's, 1995), 137, 223, 278–81.

12. For Brooke's Chicago visit, see Christopher Hassall, *Rupert Brooke: A Biography* (London: Faber, 1964), 440–43; also Maurice Browne, *Recollections of Rupert Brooke* (1927; rptd. Port Washington, NY: Kennikat, 1968), 11–18; Monroe, *Poet's Life* 340. None of these mentions Iris in connection with Brooke.

13. Humphrey Carpenter, *A Serious Character: The Life of Ezra Pound* (Boston: Houghton, 1988), 173–74.

14. Monroe printed Yeats's letters in *Poetry* (Jan. 1914) and again in her autobiography, *Poet's Life* 330–31. See also *The Letters of William Butler Yeats,* ed. Allen Wade (New York: Macmillan, 1954). The text of Yeats's letters, dated 7 Nov. 1913, may also be found in Parisi and Young, eds., *Dear Editor* 81–82.

15. Louis Untermeyer, *American Poetry since 1900* (New York: Holt, 1923), 267.

16. Paul Mariani, *William Carlos Williams: A New World Naked* (New York: McGraw-Hill, 1981), 136.


## 8—LOCAL CELEBRITY, 1960–1967

1. In Iris's papers at Lewis University are blood donors' cards, dated 16 Nov. 1959, from Cook County Hospital.

2. "Augustus John, Painter, Dies," a clipping from a Joliet newspaper, ca. 31 Oct. 1961 (the date of John's death). The clipping claims that Picasso too completed a portrait of Iris.

3. "He Lives by Poetry Alone," *Midwest Magazine, Chicago Sunday Sun-Times,* 6 Oct. 1963: 14.

4. Fanny Butcher, "The Mountains Where Literary Giants Roamed," *Chicago Tribune Magazine of Books* 27 Oct. 1963: 4; Butcher *Many Lives—One Love* (New York: Harper, 1972). For Richard Ellmann's account, see his *James Joyce* (New York: Oxford UP, 1959), 434–35, 480–82.

5. Francis Sweeney, "Poets Speak of Religion," *New York Times Book Review* 18 Oct. 1964: 51.

6. "Poet's Book a Sell-Out," *Joliet Spectator* 30 Jan. 1964: 3.

7. Hoke Norris, "Critic At-Large: Scharmel Sings," *Chicago Sun Times* 9 Feb. 1964; Van Allen Bradley, "The Fantastic Story of a Lost and Now Found Genius," *Chicago Daily News* 22 Aug. 1953.

8. Some of the poems for "The Yellow Winds of Cathay" were typed on the back of National Library Week flier from April 1964.

9. Lyle Linder to Iris, 26 May 1964.

10. Henry Regnery to Herbert M. Johnson, 15 July 1964; A. L. Hart, Jr., to Johnson, 29 July 1964; Regnery to Iris, 9 Oct. 1964.

11. On the typescript of the untitled poem, Iris noted that it was written on the occasion of a rejection by Regnery.

12. It was sent by Lawrence J. Zeeb, director, development and public relations, Lewis College, to editor-in-chief Arthur Cohen, Holt, 8 Oct. 1964.

13. Lawrance Thompson, *Robert Frost: The Early Years, 1874–1915* (New York: Holt, 1966), 400–401. The person with whom Frost dealt was M. L. Nutt, the widow of David Nutt's son Alfred.

14. Robert Frost, *Collected Poems* (New York: Holt, 1942), vi.

15. Holme to Julian P. Muller, Harcourt, 2 Nov. 1964.

16. Maurice English, U of Chicago P, to Iris, 23 Nov. 1964.

17. Iris to Ralph Fletcher Seymour, 14 Oct. 1964; Seymour to Iris, 20 Oct. 1964.

18. Contacted by Iris, Madariaga wrote on 3 Feb. 1965 to ask that the book be sent to his Oxford address.

19. Robert N. Linscott to Frederick Vincent, 4 Aug. 1949.

20. Archibald MacLeish to Holme, 8 June [1954?].

21. The WFMT interview by Terkel was broadcast on 21 July 1965; Terkel had also interviewed Iris sometime in 1964.

22. The expression of interest came from Ken McCormick, Doubleday & Company, Inc., to Holme, 1 Feb. 1965; the rejection was in McCormick to Holme, 10 March 1965.

23. John Pearson, *Façades: Edith, Osbert, and Sacheverell Sitwell* (London: Macmillan, 1978), 447. There is no mention of Iris in the biography.

24. Marianne Moore, "Poetry," *The New Poetry: An Anthology of Twentieth-Century Verse in English,* new ed., ed. Harriet Monroe and Alice Corbin Henderson (New York: Macmillan, 1932), 414–15.

25. Edith Sitwell, ed., *Atlantic Book of British and American Verse* (Boston: Little, 1958).

26. These impressions came from the Very Reverend Joseph W. Peoples, Jr., whom I interviewed on 18 Nov. 1980.

27. Brother H. Philip, faculty prefect, Lewis College, to Iris, 29 Sept. 1965.

28. Brother L. Paul to Iris, 12 Jan. 1966.

29. *Beacon 1966* (Lewis College), 24–25.

30. Social Security Administration, Joliet, to Fred Leo Scharmell, 4 April 1966.

31. Iris's offer was made in a letter to the Newberry Library, 14 April 1966; Wells responded to Iris on 25 April and acknowledged receipt of the books on 29 April.

32. "Author's Autograph Party," advertisement, *Joliet Herald-News* 13 May 1966.

33. Iris to John Pastorelle, First Westchester National Bank, New Rochelle, NY, 10 Jan. 1966; Francis A. Dunn of Dunn, Stefanich, McGarry & Kennedy, attorneys, Joliet, to Iris, 10 Nov. 1966; W. W. Stefanich of Dunn, Stefanich, McGarry & Kennedy to H. John Pastorelle, White Plains, NY, n.d.

34. Iris to Peoples, 19 Dec. 1966; "Iris Wins Many Honors," *Joliet Herald News* 8 Jan. 1967: B7.

35. C. M. Bowra to Peoples, 29 March 1967.

36. Peoples [Iris?] to Archibald MacLeish, 5 May 1967. The earlier letter, Holme to Pound, was undated but evidently written to accompany Iris's 20 Oct. 1958 letter to Pound.

37. Francis X. Pastorelle to Jean Meegan, Merv Griffin Show, 5 May 1967.

38. Peter J. Pastorelle to Merv Griffin, 2 May 1967.

39. Charles V. Ford, *Lies! Lies!! Lies!!! The Psychology of Deceit* (Washington, DC: American Psychiatric Press, 1996), 31–32, 61–63, 133–37.

40. K. K. Ruthven, in *Faking Literature* (Cambridge: Cambridge UP, 2001), questions the binary opposition "between literarity and spuriosity." For him, "literary forgery is not so much the disreputable Other of 'genuine' literature as its demystified and disreputable Self" (3).

41. "Funeral Monday for Lewis Poet," *Joliet Herald News* 9 July 1967.


## A NOTE ON THE SOURCES

Most of the correspondence, unpublished works, and other manuscript materials, as well as newspaper clippings and photographs, referred to in this study may be found in Scharmel Iris's papers in the archives of Lewis University, Romeoville, Illinois. Iris's correspondence relating to his submissions to *Poetry* magazine, under whatever name, are in the *Poetry* archives at the Special Collection Research Center at the University of Chicago. There, too, are Harriet Monroe's personal papers, the source of correspondence relating to Iris's forgery over Monroe's name and his attempt to extract money from William Wrigley, and his solicitation of praise from Louise Imogen Guiney. The Newberry Library, Chicago, has Iris's letters to or from Augustus John, George Santayana, M. Lincoln Schuster, Adlai Stevenson, and James W. Wells, as well as a letter Iris wrote under the name Ellen Van Doren-Wells. In the chancery correspondence files of the Archdiocese of Chicago's Joseph Cardinal Bernadin Archives and Records Center are Iris's correspondence with Bishop Bernard Sheil and Samuel Cardinal Stritch. The Harry Ransom Humanities Research Center, University of Texas at Austin, has Iris's correspondence with Edgar Lee Masters and Edith Sitwell and his correspondence related to submissions of manuscripts to Harper, along with Roy Campbell's draft epilogue to *Spanish Earth*. The Yale Collection of American Literature at the Beinecke Rare Book and Manuscript Library, Yale University, has Iris's correspondence with Ezra Pound. Iris's typescript of "Bread and Hyacinths," including its preface attributed to Woodrow Wilson and accompanying letter attributed to Maurice Francis Egan, is in the Adelman Collection, Bryn Mawr College Library.

# INDEX